MESOPOTAMIA

THE WORLD'S EARLIEST CIVILIZATION

THE BRITANNICA GUIDE TO ANCIENT CIVILIZATIONS

MESOPOTAMIA

THE WORLD'S EARLIEST CIVILIZATION

EDITED BY KATHLEEN KUIPER, MANAGER, ARTS AND CULTURE

Britannica
Educational Publishing

IN ASSOCIATION WITH

ROSEN
EDUCATIONAL SERVICES

Published in 2011 by Britannica Educational Publishing
(a trademark of Encyclopædia Britannica, Inc.)
in association with Rosen Educational Services, LLC
29 East 21st Street, New York, NY 10010.

Distributed exclusively by Rosen Educational Services.
For a listing of additional Britannica Educational Publishing titles, call toll free (800) 237-9932.

First Edition

Britannica Educational Publishing
Michael I. Levy: Executive Editor
J.E. Luebering: Senior Manager
Marilyn L. Barton: Senior Coordinator, Production Control
Steven Bosco: Director, Editorial Technologies
Lisa S. Braucher: Senior Producer and Data Editor
Yvette Charboneau: Senior Copy Editor
Kathy Nakamura: Manager, Media Acquisition
Kathleen Kuiper: Manager, Arts and Culture

Rosen Educational Services
Jeanne Nagle: Senior Editor
Nelson Sá: Art Director
Cindy Reiman: Photography Manager
Matthew Cauli: Designer, Cover Design
Introduction by Dan Faust

Library of Congress Cataloging-in-Publication Data

Mesopotamia : the world's earliest civilization / edited by Kathleen Kuiper.—1st ed.
    p. cm.—(The Britannica guide to ancient civilizations)
"In association with Britannica Educational Publishing, Rosen Educational Services."
Includes bibliographical references and index.
ISBN 978-1-61530-112-6 (library binding)
1. Iraq—Civilization—To 634. I. Kuiper, Kathleen.
DS71.M55 2010
935—dc22

                                                                    2009053644

Manufactured in the United States of America

On the cover: *The reconstructed Ishtar Gate, an enormous burnt-brick entryway located over the main thoroughfare in the ancient city of Babylon. Ishtar is the goddess of war and sexual love in the Sumerian tradition.* Nico Tondini/Robert Harding World Imagery/ Getty Images

Pp. 17, 40, 66, 78, 115, 133, 150: *Panel from a bronze door showing the storming of the Syrian city of Hazazu.* DEA/G. Dagli Orti/Getty Images

CONTENTS

23

41

55

116

141

145

167

171

INTRODUCTION

Fantastic and massive human-headed, winged bulls and a curious wedge-shaped writing system are the best-known legacies of the place known as Mesopotamia. Although these objects give some sense of the grandeur and mystery of an ancient culture, the influence of the region and its people extends far beyond them. Long described as the "cradle of civilization," Mesopotamia is clearly one of the earliest civilizations in the world. Its many contributions include the development of written language, as well as several advances in science, economics, law, and religion. Mesopotamian astronomers, for example, devised a 12-month lunar calendar and divided the year into two seasons. Mesopotamian mathematics is a sexagesimal, or base 60, system, which survives to this day in 60-minute hours and 24-hour days. The Sumerian calendar was divided into seven-day weeks. Many of these remarkable contributions are discussed in the pages of this volume.

When contemporary historians use the term *Mesopotamia*, they typically mean the region in southwest Asia that includes modern-day Iraq, as well as portions of Turkey, Iran, and Syria. Originally, however, the Hellenistic Greeks used the name *Meso-potamos*, "the land between the rivers," to refer specifically to the region between the Tigris and Euphrates rivers. These rivers provided the fertile soil and water needed to support a sedentary, agrarian way of life, allowing humankind to abandon a nomadic hunter-gatherer lifestyle. Largely because of this feature, Mesopotamia was one of several regions in which agriculture was born.

For nearly 2,000 years, information about Mesopotamia was limited. The Hebrew Bible provided some insight into the history and culture of the region. The Greek historian Herodotus first reported on the region in the 5th century BC. Some 100 years later, the Greek mercenary, historian, and philosopher Xenophon wrote in *Anabasis* ("Upcountry March") about his experiences as part of an expedition that crossed Anatolia and traveled along both the Tigris and the Euphrates. Although extant in fragments only, the writings of Berosus—a Chaldean priest of Bel who immigrated to Greece—provide some of the most thorough and reliable accounts of the region.

Writing at the beginning of the 3rd century BC, while living on the island of Cos, Berosus produced the *Babyloniaka*, which consisted of three books. The first of these described the land of Babylonia and the Babylonian creation myth. It also described and a half man–half fish known as Oannes, who taught early humans about things such as law, the arts, and agriculture, thus bringing civilization from the sea. The second and third books contained the chronology and history of

Artist's depiction of the biblical Tower of Babel. The story of the tower may have been inspired by the Babylonian tower temple Bab-ilu ("Gate of God"), or in Hebrew Babel or Bavel, located north of the Marduk temple. Hulton Archive/Getty Images

Babylonia and of later Assyria, from prehistory to King Nabonassar (Nabu-nasir; 747–734 BC) down to Berosus's own time.

Urban areas of considerable size began to emerge in ancient Mesopotamia during the early sixth millennium BC. The region supported important settlements such as Uruk, Nineveh, and Babylon. These centres of social and cultural life possessed one or more shrines to major deities as well as extensive granaries that served as a focal point for smaller settlements.

The central structure in any ancient Mesopotamian city was the ziggurat, or temple complex. These massive step pyramids, as the name suggests, had receding tiers and were each topped with a shrine. Each shrine was dedicated to a single god or goddess, and each city had its own patron deity. So close was the link between city and god that wars between cities were frequently considered to reflect wars between the gods and goddesses.

The other principal structure in a Mesopotamian city was the ruler's palace, a large compound containing private residences, sanctuaries, courtyards, and storehouses. Both the ziggurat and the palace were adorned with bas-reliefs and inscriptions that depicted cultic practices and civic and military accomplishments. Gates and important passageways were flanked by massive sculptures of mythological guardian figures, usually possessing a human head on the body of a winged bull or lion.

The region's geography was such that Mesopotamian cities were separated from one another by vast stretches of desert or swamp. This circumstance led to the development of city-states, autonomous entities whose territory consisted of a single city and the surrounding area. Tensions often developed between neighbouring city-states, leading to armed conflicts over land and dominion. The first successful forced unification of city-states came in 2331 BC, when Sumer was conquered by what would become known as the Akkadian empire—which would, itself, be conquered several generations later by the Babylonian empire. As such, there is no unified Mesopotamian culture, but rather, a patchwork of cultures formed as conquering civilizations either adopted, co-opted, or superseded the traditions and beliefs of vanquished city-states.

With each successive conquest, Mesopotamia's political centre moved from one city-state to another. This can best be illustrated in the Sumerian King List, an ancient document that provides a record of the kings of Sumer, wherein each dynasty is listed according to the location of the "official" seat of power. The veracity of some claims in the King List has been called into question, notably where the regnal periods of individual monarchs have spanned hundreds, even thousands, of years. Still, when understood as being part official record and part embellishment, the list provides an interesting and useful window into Mesopotamian history. Beyond a simple chronology of rulers, it gives an intriguing glimpse into the nature of war, justice, and religion as practiced by the people of the various city-states.

The King List survives by means of logograms, which are pictures or symbols intended to represent a whole word. By refining logograms and adding phonetic signs, the Sumerians created cuneiform, one of the earliest forms of written language. Their scribes used blunt reeds to imprint the wedge-shaped symbols of cuneiform script on wet clay tablets. Tablets unearthed by archaeological excavation make it clear that cuneiform spread quickly from Sumer throughout the region and that the language evolved as it moved. The arrival of the Akkadians, a Semitic tribe that entered Mesopotamia in the third millennium BC, further expanded the Sumerian pictorial and phonetic "vocabulary." Several variants of Old Akkadian cuneiform have been discovered in Babylon and northern Mesopotamia.

A written language allowed the civilizations of Mesopotamia to document the receipt of commodities imported and exported through trade and laws. These commercial documents were catalogued and housed primarily—but not always—within temples. One noteworthy exception to the general rule was a treasure trove of cuneiform writings that were discovered at Nineveh in the library of the palace built by the Babylonian ruler Ashurbanipal.

Cuneiform also provided an early example of transformation of the oral tradition to the literary. Also discovered in the Nineveh palace library were an incomplete set of tablets containing *The Epic of Gilgamesh*, an ancient odyssey story and one of the earliest known works of literature.

In addition to cuneiform, Mesopotamian art and architecture reveal much about the region's history. The excavation and examination of ruins over the decades has led experts to postulate that the temples of this time were characterized by buttresses and recessed walls with interior mosaics. Temples were built either at ground level or on a raised platform, with the latter being the more popular and common mode. Secular buildings were of simpler design and construction—chiefly flat roofs upheld by the trunks of palm trees or columns of brick made from dried riverbank clay.

Artwork consisted primarily of wood carvings, metal sculpture, and decorative clay pottery. Cylinder seals, which acted like identifying stamps, moved beyond their utilitarian purpose to become some of the greatest examples of art to come out of the region. Rather than being adorned with the visages of gods and goddess, the remains of temple sculptures more commonly depict supplicants, revealing the physical characteristics of a given city-states' inhabitants; bearded men and women with upswept hair.

Stone was difficult to come by in Mesopotamia, and was considered an extravagance for building. Yet examples of ornate stone decoration and sculptures abound among the ruins of temples. This speaks directly to the importance places of worship within the region. Religion was a central aspect of life in Mesopotamia. The focus of Mesopotamian worship was a pantheon of gods, around which were built elaborate myths to explain natural occurrences (such as floods and drought) and the creation of universe itself. Religion and politics frequently meshed. Kings were crowned during sacred festivals, and they oversaw the administration of temples within their domain.

Many achievements in the realms of economics, law, and government also are attributed to Mesopotamian civilizations. The earliest known system of economics was developed by the Babylonians. Early laws created by the ancient Mesopotamians included the Code of Ur-Nammu, the Laws of Eshnunna, and, perhaps best known of all, the Code of Hammurabi. As the first king of the Babylonian empire (c. 1728-1686 BC), Hammurabi composed more

Statuettes found at Tall al-Asmar, Early Dynastic II (c. 2775–c. 2650 BC). Courtesy of the Oriental Institute, the University of Chicago

than 200 laws that cover a wide variety of subjects, including family, commercial, and criminal law. Many of the Code's criminal laws follow the familiar "an eye for an eye" approach; however, its commercial laws are something else entirely. The Code of Hammurabi firmly codified the newly created economic system with a series of commercial laws. The Code addressed things such as property rights, inheritance laws, fair trade, taxation, statutory wages, and debt management.

Despite the region's cultural significance, very little was known about it before the first excavations in the mid-19th century. Over the centuries, between the decline of the Roman Empire and the European Renaissance, Europeans made occasional forays into the region. Among these visitors was the Spanish rabbi Benjamin of Tudela, who traveled in the Middle East between 1160 and 1173 AD. It was the Italian Pietro della Valle, however, who in the early part of the 17th century rediscovered the ruins of Babylon in Iraq (roughly 60 miles south of present-day Baghdad). Della Valle was responsible for bringing the very first specimens of cuneiform writing back to Europe. From that point on, European interest in Mesopotamia grew, and its visitors included the German traveler Carsten Niebuhr (1733–1815), the British business agent and proto-archaeologist Claudius James Rich (1787–1820), and the English painter and traveler Sir Robert Ker Porter (1777–1842).

The era of modern archaeological research in Mesopotamia began with the French excavations at Nineveh (1842) and Dur-Sharrukin (modern Khorsabad; 1843–55), as well as English expeditions to Nineveh (1846–55) and Calah (modern Nimrud; 1845). Excavations of other important cities, among them Babylon, Ashur, Erech (Uruk), and Ur, soon followed. A second phase of research focusing on "provinces" and outlying areas, as well as capital cities, began in 1925 when American archaeologists began excavations at Nuzu (modern Yorgan Tepe; about 140 miles north of Baghdad).

Each of these excavations contributed to what we now know about the ancient Mesopotamian civilizations.

CHAPTER 1

THE ORIGINS OF MESOPOTAMIAN HISTORY

M esopotamia is the region in southwestern Asia where the world's earliest civilization developed. The name "Mesopotamia" comes from a Greek word meaning "between rivers," referring to the land between the Tigris and Euphrates rivers, but the region can be broadly defined to include the area that is now eastern Syria, southeastern Turkey, and most of Iraq. This region was the centre of a culture whose influence extended throughout the Middle East and as far as the Indus Valley in the Indian subcontinent, Egypt, and the Mediterranean. This book covers the history of Mesopotamia from the prehistoric period up to the Arab conquest in the seventh century AD.

BACKGROUND INFORMATION

In the narrow sense, Mesopotamia is the area between the Euphrates and Tigris rivers, north or northwest of the bottleneck at Baghdad, in modern Iraq; it is Al-Jazīrah ("The Island") of the Arabs. South of this lies Babylonia, named after the city of Babylon. However, in the broader sense, the name "Mesopotamia" has come to be used for the area bounded on the northeast by the Zagros Mountains and on the southwest by the edge of the Arabian Plateau and stretching from the Persian Gulf in the southeast to the spurs of the

Anti-Taurus Mountains in the northwest. Only from the latitude of Baghdad do the Euphrates and Tigris truly become twin rivers, the *rāfidān* of the Arabs, which have constantly changed their courses over the millennia. The low-lying plain of the Kārūn River in Persia has always been closely related to Mesopotamia, but it is not considered part of Mesopotamia as it forms its own river system.

Mesopotamia, south of Al-Ramādī (about 70 miles, or 110 kilometres, west of Baghdad) on the Euphrates and the bend of the Tigris below Sāmarrā' (about 70 miles north-northwest of Baghdad), is flat alluvial land. Between Baghdad and the mouth of the Shaṭṭ al-'Arab (the confluence of the Tigris and Euphrates, where it empties into the Persian Gulf) there is a difference in height of only about 100 feet (30 metres). As a result of the slow flow of the water, there are heavy deposits of silt, and the riverbeds are raised. Consequently, the rivers often overflow their banks (and may even change their course) when they are not protected by high dikes. In recent times they have been regulated above Baghdad by the use of escape channels with overflow reservoirs. The extreme south is a region of extensive marshes and reed swamps, *hawrs*, which, probably since early times, have served as an area of refuge for oppressed and displaced peoples.

The supply of water in the area is not regular. As a result of the high average temperatures and a very low annual rainfall, the ground of the plain of latitude 35° N is hard and dry and unsuitable for plant cultivation for at least eight months in the year. Consequently, agriculture without risk of crop failure, which seems to have begun in the higher rainfall zones and in the hilly borders of Mesopotamia in the 10th millennium BC, began in Mesopotamia itself, the real heart of the civilization, only after artificial irrigation had been invented, bringing water to large stretches of territory through a widely branching network of canals. Since the ground is extremely fertile and, with irrigation and the necessary drainage, will produce in abundance, southern Mesopotamia became a land of plenty that could support a considerable population. The cultural superiority of north Mesopotamia, which may have lasted until about 4000 BC, was finally overtaken by the south when the people there had responded to the challenge of their situation.

The present climatic conditions are fairly similar to those of 8,000 years ago. An English survey of ruined settlements in the area 30 miles (48 km) around ancient Hatra (180 miles [290 km] northwest of Baghdad) has shown that the southern limits of the zone in which agriculture is possible without artificial irrigation has remained unchanged since the first settlement of Al-Jazīrah.

The availability of raw materials is a historical factor of great importance, as is the dependence on those materials that had to be imported. In Mesopotamia, agricultural products and those from

TIGRIS-EUPHRATES RIVER SYSTEM

The great river system of Southwest Asia comprises the Tigris and Euphrates rivers, which have their sources within 50 miles (80 km) of each other in eastern Turkey. They travel southeast through northern Syria and Iraq to the head of the Persian Gulf. They are the rivers that define the region and provide the name for Mesopotamia, one of the cradles of civilization. The total length of the Euphrates (called in Sumerian: Buranun; Akkadian: Purattu; biblical: Perath; Arabic: Al-Furāt; Turkish: Fırat) is about 1,740 miles (2,800 km). The Tigris (Sumerian: Idigna; Akkadian: Idiklat; biblical: Hiddekel; Arabic: Dijlah; Turkish: Dicle) has a length of about 1,180 miles (1,900 km).

Having risen in close proximity, the Tigris and Euphrates diverge sharply in their upper courses, to a maximum distance of some 250 miles (400 km) apart near the Turkish-Syrian border. Their middle courses gradually approach each other, bounding a triangle of mainly barren limestone desert known as Al-Jazīrah (Arabic: "The Island"). There the rivers have cut deep and permanent beds in the rock, so their courses have undergone only minor changes since prehistoric times. Along the northeastern edge of Al-Jazīrah, the Tigris drains the rain-fed heart of ancient Assyria, while along the southwestern limit the Euphrates crosses true desert.

On the alluvial plain, south of Sāmarrā' and Al-Ramādī, both rivers have undergone major shifts throughout the millennia, some as a consequence of human intervention. The 7,000 years of irrigation farming on the alluvium have created a complex landscape of natural levees, fossil meanders, abandoned canal systems, and thousands of ancient settlement sites. The location of tells, or raised mounds—under which are found the ruins of towns and cities of ancient Babylonia and Sumeria—often bears no relation to modern watercourses. In the vicinity of Al-Fallūjah and the Iraqi capital, Baghdad, the distance separating the rivers is some 30 miles (48 km), so small that, prior to its damming, floodwaters from the Euphrates often reached the capital on the Tigris. During the Sāsānian period (third century AD), an elaborate feat of engineering linked the two rivers along this narrow neck by five navigable canals (the Īsā, Ṣarṣar, Malik, Kūthā, and Shaṭṭ al-Nīl canals), allowing Euphrates water to empty into the Tigris.

South of Baghdad the rivers exhibit strongly contrasting characteristics. The Tigris, especially after its confluence with the silt-laden Diyālā, carries a greater volume than the Euphrates; cuts into the alluvium; forms tortuous meanders; and, even in modern times, has been subject to great floods and consequent natural levee building. Only below Al-Kūt does the Tigris ride high enough over the plain to permit tapping for flow irrigation. The Euphrates, by contrast, builds its bed at a level considerably above the alluvial plain and has been used throughout history as the main source of Mesopotamian irrigation.

The Gharrāf River, now a branch of the Tigris but in ancient times the main bed of that river, joins the Euphrates below Al-Nāṣiriyyah. In the southern alluvial plain, both rivers flow through marshes, and the Euphrates flows through Lake Al-Ḥammār, an open stretch of water. Finally, the Euphrates and Tigris join and flow as the Shaṭṭ al-'Arab to the Persian Gulf.

stock breeding, fisheries, date palm cultivation, and reed industries—in short, grain, vegetables, meat, leather, wool, horn, fish, dates, and reed and plant-fibre products—were available in plenty and could easily be produced in excess of home requirements to be exported. There are bitumen springs at Hīt (90 miles [145 km] northwest of Baghdad) on the Euphrates (the Is of Herodotus). On the other hand, wood, stone, and metal were rare or even entirely absent. The date palm—virtually the national tree of Iraq—yields a wood suitable only for rough beams and not for finer work. Stone is mostly lacking in southern Mesopotamia, although limestone is quarried in the desert about 35 miles (56 km) to the west and "Mosul marble" is found not far from the Tigris in its middle reaches. Metal can only be obtained in the mountains, and the same is true of precious and semiprecious stones. Consequently, southern Mesopotamia in particular was destined to be a land of trade from the start. Only rarely could "empires" extending over a wider area guarantee themselves imports by plundering or by subjecting neighbouring regions.

The raw material that epitomizes Mesopotamian civilization is clay: in the almost exclusively mud-brick architecture and in the number and variety of clay figurines and pottery artifacts, Mesopotamia bears the stamp of clay as does no other civilization, and nowhere in the world but in Mesopotamia and the regions over which its influence was diffused was clay used as the vehicle for writing. Such phrases as cuneiform civilization, cuneiform literature, and cuneiform law can apply only where people had had the idea of using soft clay not only for bricks and jars and for the jar stoppers on which a seal could be impressed as a mark of ownership but also as the vehicle for impressed signs to which established meanings were assigned—an intellectual achievement that amounted to nothing less than the invention of writing.

THE CHARACTER AND INFLUENCE OF ANCIENT MESOPOTAMIA

Questions as to what ancient Mesopotamian civilization did and did not accomplish, how it influenced its neighbours and successors, and what its legacy has transmitted are posed from the standpoint of 20th-century civilization and are in part coloured by ethical overtones, so that the answers can only be relative. Modern scholars assume the ability to assess the sum total of an "ancient Mesopotamian civilization"; but, since the publication of an article by the Assyriologist Benno Landsberger on "Die Eigenbegrifflichkeit der babylonischen Welt" (1926; "The Distinctive Conceptuality of the Babylonian World"), it has become almost a commonplace to call attention to the necessity of viewing ancient Mesopotamia and its civilization as an independent entity.

Ancient Mesopotamia had many languages and cultures, and its history is broken up into many periods and eras.

CUNEIFORM

The system of writing used in the ancient Middle East is called cuneiform. The name, a coinage from Latin and Middle French roots meaning "wedge-shaped," has been the modern designation from the early 18th century onward. Cuneiform was the most widespread and historically significant writing system in the ancient Middle East. Its overall significance as an international graphic medium of civilization is second only to that of the Phoenician-Greek-Latin alphabet.

The origins of cuneiform may be traced back approximately to the end of the fourth millennium BC. At that time the Sumerians, a people of unknown ethnic and linguistic affinities, inhabited southern Mesopotamia and the region west of the mouth of the Euphrates known as Chaldea. It is to them that the first attested traces of cuneiform writing are conclusively assigned. The earliest written records in the Sumerian language are pictographic tablets from Erech (Uruk), evidently lists or ledgers of commodities identified by drawings of the objects and accompanied by numerals and personal names.

The Sumerian writing system was adopted by the Akkadians, Semitic invaders who established themselves in Mesopotamia about the middle of the third millennium. In adapting the script to their wholly different language, the Akkadians retained the Sumerian format for more complex notions, but pronounced them as the corresponding Akkadian words. They also kept the phonetic values, but extended them far beyond the original Sumerian inventory of simple types.

The expansion of cuneiform writing outside Mesopotamia began in the third millennium, when the country of Elam in southwestern Iran was in contact with Mesopotamian culture and adopted the system of writing. In the second millennium the Akkadian of Babylonia became a lingua franca in the entire Middle East, and cuneiform writing thus became a universal medium of written communication. Even after the fall of the Assyrian and Babylonian kingdoms in the seventh and sixth centuries BC, when Aramaic had become the general popular language, varieties of Late Babylonian and Assyrian survived as written languages in cuneiform almost down to the time of Christ.

The area had no real geographic unity and, above all, no permanent capital city, so that by its very variety it stands out from other civilizations with greater uniformity, particularly that of Egypt. The script and the religious pantheon constitute the unifying factors, but in these also Mesopotamia shows its predilection for multiplicity and variety. Written documents were turned out in quantities, and there are often many copies of a single text. The pantheon consisted of more than 1,000 deities, even though many divine names may apply to different manifestations of a single god.

During Mesopotamia's 3,000 years of existence, each century brought a rebirth to the area. Thus classical Sumerian civilization influenced that of the Akkadians, and the Ur III empire, which itself represented a Sumero-Akkadian synthesis, exercised its influence on the first quarter of the second millennium BC. With the Hittites, large areas of Anatolia were infused with the culture of Mesopotamia from 1700 BC onward. Contacts, via Mari, with Ebla in Syria, some 30 miles (48 km) south of Aleppo, go back to the 24th century BC, so that links between Syrian and Palestinian scribal schools and Babylonian civilization during the Amarna period (14th century BC) may have had much older predecessors. At any rate, the similarity of certain themes in cuneiform literature and the Hebrew Bible, such as the story of the Flood or the motif of the righteous sufferer, is due to such early contacts and not to direct borrowing.

ACHIEVEMENTS

The world of mathematics and astronomy owes much to the Babylonians—for instance, the sexagesimal system for the calculation of time and angles, which is still practical because of the multiple divisibility of the number 60; the Greek day of 12 "double-hours"; and the zodiac and its signs. In many cases, however, the origins and routes of borrowings are obscure, as in the problem of the survival of ancient Mesopotamian legal theory.

The achievement of the civilization itself may be expressed in terms of its best points—moral, aesthetic, scientific, and, not least, literary. Legal theory flourished and was sophisticated early on, being expressed in several collections of legal decisions, the so-called codes, of which the best-known is the Code of Hammurabi. Throughout these codes recurs the concern of the ruler for the weak, the widow, and the orphan—even if, sometimes, the phrases were regrettably only literary clichés.

The aesthetics of art are too much governed by subjective values to be assessed in absolute terms, yet certain peaks stand out above the rest, notably the art of Uruk IV, the seal engraving of the Akkad period, and the relief sculpture of Ashurbanipal. Nonetheless, there is nothing in Mesopotamia to match the sophistication of Egyptian art.

Science the Mesopotamians had, of a kind, though not in the sense of Greek science. From its beginnings in Sumer before the middle of the third millennium BC, Mesopotamian science was characterized by endless, meticulous enumeration and ordering into columns and series, with the ultimate ideal of including all things in the world, but without the wish or ability to synthesize and reduce the material to a system. Not a single general scientific law has been found, and only rarely has the use of analogy been found. Nevertheless, it remains a highly commendable achievement that Pythagoras's law (that the sum of the squares on the two shorter sides of a right-angled triangle equals the square on the longest side), even though it was never formulated, was being applied as early as the 18th century BC.

Northeastern facade (the ascents partly restored) of the ziggurat at Ur, southern Iraq. Hirmer Fotoarchiv, Munich

Technical accomplishments were perfected in the building of the ziggurats (temple towers resembling pyramids), with their huge bulk, and in irrigation, both in practical execution and in theoretical calculations. At the beginning of the third millennium BC, an artificial stone often regarded as a forerunner of concrete was in use at Erech (Uruk; 160 miles [257 km] south-southeast of modern Baghdad), but the secret of its manufacture apparently was lost in subsequent years.

Writing pervaded all aspects of life and gave rise to a highly developed bureaucracy—one of the most tenacious legacies of the ancient Middle East.

Remarkable organizing ability was required to administer huge estates, in which, under the third dynasty of Ur, for example, it was not unusual to prepare accounts for thousands of cattle or tens of thousands of bundles of reeds. Similar figures are attested at Ebla, three centuries earlier.

Above all, the literature of Mesopotamia is one of its finest cultural achievements. Though there are many modern anthologies and chrestomathies (compilations of useful learning), with translations and paraphrases of Mesopotamian literature, as well as attempts to write its history, it cannot

LAW CODES

Written statements of laws—law (or legal) codes—were compiled by the most ancient peoples. The oldest extant evidence for a code is tablets from the ancient archives of the city of Ebla (now at Tell Mardikh, Syria), which date to about 2400 BC. The best known ancient code is the Babylonian Code of Hammurabi. The Romans began keeping legal records, such as the Law of the Twelve Tables (451–450 BC), but there was no major codification of Roman law until the Code of Justinian (AD 529–565), which was compiled long after the dissolution of the Western Empire. The peoples who overran the Western Empire also made codes of law, such as the Salic Law of the Salian Franks. During the later Middle Ages in Europe, various collections of maritime customs, drawn up for the use of merchants and lawyers, acquired great authority throughout the continent.

From the 15th through the 18th century, movements in various European countries to organize and compile their numerous laws and customs resulted in local and provincial compilations rather than national ones. The first national codes appeared in the Scandinavian countries in the 17th and 18th centuries.

truly be said that "cuneiform literature" has been resurrected to the extent that it deserves. There are partly material reasons for this. Many clay tablets survive only in a fragmentary condition, and duplicates that would restore the texts have not yet been discovered, so there are still large gaps. A further reason is the inadequate knowledge of the languages: insufficient acquaintance with the vocabulary and, in Sumerian, major difficulties with the grammar. Consequently, another generation of Assyriologists will pass before the great myths, epics, lamentations, hymns, "law codes," wisdom literature, and pedagogical treatises can be presented to the reader in such a way that he can fully appreciate the high level of literary creativity of those times.

CLASSICAL, MEDIEVAL, AND MODERN VIEWS OF MESOPOTAMIA

Before the first excavations in Mesopotamia, about 1840, nearly 2,000 years had passed during which knowledge of the ancient Middle East was derived from three sources only: the Bible, Greek and Roman authors, and the excerpts from the writings of Berosus, a Babylonian who wrote in Greek. In 1800 very little more was known than in AD 800, although these sources had served to stir the imagination of poets and artists, down to *Sardanapalus* (1821) by the 19th-century English poet Lord Byron.

Apart from the building of the Tower of Babel, the Hebrew Bible mentions Mesopotamia only in those historical contexts in which the kings of Assyria and Babylonia affected the course of events in Israel and Judah; in particular Tiglath-pileser III, Shalmaneser V, and Sennacherib, with their policy of deportation, and the Babylonian Exile introduced by Nebuchadrezzar II. Of the Greeks, Herodotus of Halicarnassus (fifth century BC, a contemporary of Xerxes I and Artaxerxes I) was the first to report on "Babylon and the rest of Assyria." At that date the Assyrian empire had been overthrown for more than 100 years. The Athenian Xenophon took part in an expedition (during 401–399 BC of Greek mercenaries who crossed Anatolia, made their way down the Euphrates as far as the vicinity of Baghdad, and returned up the Tigris after the famous Battle of Cunaxa.) In his *Cyropaedia*, Xenophon describes the final struggle between Cyrus II and the neo-Babylonian empire.

Later, the Greeks adopted all kinds of fabulous tales about King Ninus, Queen Semiramis, and King Sardanapalus. These stories are described mainly in the historical work of Diodorus Siculus (first century BC), who based them on the reports of a Greek physician, Ctesias (405–359 BC). Herodotus saw Babylon with his own eyes, and Xenophon gave an account of travels and battles. All later historians, however, wrote at second or third hand, with one exception, Berosus (b. *c.* 340 BC), who emigrated at an advanced age to the Aegean island of Cos, where he is said to have composed the three books of the *Babylōniaka.*

Unfortunately, only extracts from them survive, prepared by one Alexander Polyhistor (first century BC), who, in his turn, served as a source for the Church Father Eusebius (d. AD 342). Berosus derided the "Greek historians" who had so distorted the history of his country. He knew, for example, that it was not Semiramis who founded the city of Babylon, but he was himself the prisoner of his own environment and cannot have known more about the history of his land than was known in Babylonia itself in the fourth century BC.

Berosus' first book dealt with the beginnings of the world and with a myth of a composite being, Oannes, half fish, half man, who came ashore in Babylonia at a time when men still lived like the wild beasts. Oannes taught them the essentials of civilization: writing, the arts, law, agriculture, surveying, and architecture. The name "Oannes" must have been derived from the cuneiform U'anna (Sumerian) or Umanna (Akkadian), a second name of the mythical figure Adapa, the bringer of civilization. The second book of Berosus contained the Babylonian king list from the beginning to King Nabonassar (Nabu-naṣir, 747–734 BC), a contemporary of Tiglath-pileser III. Berosus's tradition, beginning with a list of primeval kings before the Flood, is reliable. It agrees with the tradition of the Sumerian king list, and even individual names can be traced back exactly to their Sumerian originals. Even the immensely long reigns of the primeval kings, which lasted as long as "18 sars" (= 18 × 3,600 = 64,800) of years, are found in Berosus. Furthermore, he was acquainted with the story of the Flood, with Cronus as its instigator and Xisuthros (or Ziusudra) as its hero, and with the building of an ark. The third book is presumed to have dealt with the history of Babylonia from Nabonassar to the time of Berosus himself.

Diodorus made the mistake of locating Nineveh on the Euphrates, and Xenophon gave an account of two cities, Larissa (probably modern Nimrūd [ancient Kalakh], 20 miles [32 km] southeast of modern Mosul) and Mespila (ancient Nineveh, just north of Mosul). The name "Mespila" probably was nothing more than the word of the local Aramaeans for ruins; there can be no clearer instance of the rift that had opened between the ancient Middle East and the classical West. In sharp contrast, the East had a tradition that the ruins opposite Mosul (in north Iraq) concealed ancient Nineveh. When a Spanish rabbi from Navarre, Benjamin of Tudela, was traveling in the Middle East between 1160 and 1173, Jews and Muslims alike knew the position of the grave of the prophet Jonah.

The credit for the rediscovery of the ruins of Babylon goes to an Italian, Pietro della Valle, who correctly identified the vast ruins north of modern Al-Ḥillah, Iraq (60 miles [96 km] south of Baghdad); he must have seen there the large rectangular tower that represented the ancient ziggurat. Previously, other travelers had sought the Tower of Babel in two

other monumental ruins, Birs Nimrūd, the massive brick structure of the ziggurat of ancient Borsippa (modern Birs, near Al-Ḥillah), vitrified by lightning, and the ziggurat of the Kassite capital, Dur-Kurigalzu, at Burj 'Aqarqūf, 22 miles (35 km) west of Baghdad. Pietro della Valle brought back to Europe the first specimens of cuneiform writing, stamped brick, of which highly impressionistic reproductions were made. Thereafter, European travelers visited Mesopotamia with increasing frequency, among them Carsten Niebuhr (an 18th-century German traveler), Claudius James Rich (a 19th-century Orientalist and traveler), and Sir Robert Ker Porter (a 19th-century traveler).

In modern times a third Middle Eastern ruin drew visitors from Europe—Persepolis, in the land of Persia east of Susiana, near modern Shīrāz, Iran. In 1602, reports had filtered back to Europe of inscriptions that were not in Hebrew, Arabic, Aramaic, Georgian, or Greek. In 1700 an Englishman, Thomas Hyde, coined the term "cuneiform" for these inscriptions, and by the middle of the 18th century it was known that the Persepolis inscriptions were related to those of Babylon. Niebuhr distinguished three separate alphabets (Babylonian, Elamite, and Old Persian cuneiform). The first promising attempt at decipherment was made by the German philologist Georg Friedrich Grotefend in 1802, by use of the kings' names in the Old Persian versions of the trilingual inscriptions, although his later efforts led him up a blind alley. Thereafter, the efforts to decipher cuneiform gradually developed in the second half of the 19th century into a discipline of ancient Oriental philology, which was based on results established through the pioneering work of Èmile Burnouf, Edward Hincks, Sir Henry Rawlinson, and many others.

Today this subject is still known as Assyriology, because at the end of the 19th century the great majority of cunei-form texts came from the Assyrian city of Nineveh, in particular from the library of King Ashurbanipal in the mound of Kuyunjik at Nineveh.

MODERN ARCHAEOLOGICAL EXCAVATIONS

More than 150 years separate the first excavations in Mesopotamia—adventurous expeditions involving great personal risks, far from the protection of helpful authorities—from those of the present day with their specialist staffs, modern technical equipment, and objectives wider than the mere search for valuable antiquities. The progress of six generations of excavators has led to a situation in which less is recovered more accurately; in other words, the finds are observed, measured, and photographed as precisely as possible.

At first digging was unsystematic, with the consequence that, although huge quantities of clay tablets and large and small antiquities were brought to light, the locations of the finds were rarely described with any accuracy. Not until the beginning of the 20th century did excavators learn to isolate the individual bricks in the walls that had previously been erroneously thought to be nothing more than packed clay. The result was that various characteristic brick types could be distinguished and successive architectural levels established. Increased care in excavation does, of course, carry with it the risk that the pace of discovery will slow down. Moreover, the eyes of the local inhabitants are now sharpened and their appetite for finds is whetted, so that clandestine diggers have established themselves as the unwelcome colleagues of the archaeologists.

A result of the technique of building with mud brick (mass production of baked bricks was impossible because of the shortage of fuel) was that the buildings were highly vulnerable to the weather and needed constant renewal. Layers of settlement rapidly built up, creating a tell (Arabic: *tall*), a mound of occupation debris that is the characteristic ruin form of Mesopotamia. The word itself appears among the most original vocabulary of the Semitic languages and is attested as early as the end of the third millennium BC. Excavation is made more difficult by this mound formation, since both horizontal and vertical axes have to be taken into account. Moreover, the depth of each level is not necessarily constant, and foundation trenches may be dug down into earlier levels. A further problem is that finds may have been removed from their original context in antiquity. Short-lived settlements that did not develop into mounds mostly escape observation, but aerial photography can now pick out ground discolorations that betray the existence of settlements. Districts with a high water level today, such as the reed marshes (hawrs), or ruins that are covered by modern settlements, such as Irbīl (ancient Arbela), some 200 miles (322 km) north of Baghdad, or sites that are surmounted by shrines and tombs of holy men are closed to archaeological research.

Excavations in Mesopotamia have mostly been national undertakings (France, England, the United States, Germany, Iraq, Denmark, Belgium, Italy, Japan, and the former Soviet Union), but joint expeditions like the one sent to Ur (190 miles [306 km] south-southeast of Baghdad) in the 1920s have become more frequent since the 1970s. The history of archaeological research in Mesopotamia falls into four categories, represented by phases of differing lengths. The first, and by far the longest, begins with the French expedition to Nineveh (1842) and Khorsabad (the ancient Dur-Sharrukin, 20 miles [32 km] northeast of modern Mosul; 1843–55) and that of the English to Nineveh (1846–55) and Nimrūd (ancient Kalakh, biblical Calah; 1845, with interruptions until 1880). This marked the beginning of the "classic" excavations in the important ancient capitals, where spectacular finds might be anticipated. The principal gains were the Assyrian bull colossi and wall reliefs and the library of Ashurbanipal from Nineveh, although

Female figure made of gypsum, with a gold mask, which stood at a temple altar in Nippur, c. 2700 BC; in the Iraq Museum, Baghdad. Courtesy of the Iraq Museum, Baghdad; photograph, David Lees

the ground plans of temples and palaces were quite as valuable.

While these undertakings had restored the remains of the neo-Assyrian empire of the first millennium BC, from 1877 onward new French initiatives in Telloh (Arabic: Tall Lōhā, 155 miles [249 km] southeast of Baghdad) reached almost 2,000 years further back into the past. There they rediscovered a people whose language had already been encountered in bilingual texts from Nineveh—the Sumerians. Telloh (ancient Girsu) yielded not only inscribed material that, quite apart from its historical interest, was critical for the establishment of the chronology of the second half of the third millennium BC, but also many artistic masterpieces. Thereafter excavations in important cities spread to form a network including Susa, 150 miles (241 km) west of Eṣfahān in Iran (France; 1884 onward); Nippur, 90 miles (145 km) southeast of Baghdad (the United States; 1889 onward); Babylon, 55 miles (89 km) south of Baghdad (Germany; 1899–1917 and again from 1957 onward); Ashur, modern Al-Sharqāṭ, 55 miles (89 km) south of Mosul (Germany; 1903–14); Erech, or Uruk (Germany; 1912–13 and from 1928 onward); and Ur (England and the United States; 1918–34). Mention also should be made of the German excavations at Boğazköy in central Turkey, the ancient Hattusa, capital of the Hittite empire, which have been carried on, with interruptions, since 1906.

The second phase began in 1925 with the commencement of American excavations at Yorghan Tepe (ancient Nuzu),

140 miles (225 km) north of Baghdad, a provincial centre with Old Akkadian, Old Assyrian, and Middle Assyrian/Hurrian levels. There followed, among others, French excavations at Arslan Tash (ancient Hadatu; 1928), at Tall al-Aḥmar (ancient Til Barsip; 1929–31) and, above all, Tall Ḥarīrī (ancient Mari; 1933 onward), and American excavations in the Diyālā region (east of Baghdad), Tall al-Asmar (ancient Eshnunna), Khafājī, and other sites. Thus, excavation in Mesopotamia had moved away from the capital cities to include the "provinces." Simultaneously, it expanded beyond the limits of Mesopotamia and Susiana and revealed outliers of "cuneiform civilization" on the Syrian coast at Ras Shamra (ancient Ugarit; France, 1929 onward) and the Orontes of northern Syria at Al-'Aṭshānah (ancient Alalakh; England, 1937–39 and 1947–49). Since 1954, Danish excavations on the islands of Bahrain and Faylakah, off the Tigris-Euphrates delta, have disclosed staging posts between Mesopotamia and the Indus Valley civilization. Short-lived salvage operations have been undertaken at the site of the Assad Dam on the middle Euphrates (e.g., German excavations at Ḥabūba al-Kabīra, 1971–76). Italian excavations at Tall Mardīkh (ancient Ebla; 1967 onward) have yielded spectacular results, including several thousand cuneiform tablets dating from the 24th century BC.

In its third phase, archaeological research in Mesopotamia and its neighbouring lands has probed back into prehistory and protohistory. The objective of these investigations, initiated by American archaeologists, was to trace as closely as possible the successive chronological stages in the progress of man from hunter-gatherer to settled farmer and, finally, to city dweller. These excavations are strongly influenced by the methods of the prehistorian, and the principal objective is no longer the search for texts and monuments. Apart from the American investigations, Iraq itself has taken part in this phase of the history of investigation, as has Japan since 1956 and the former Soviet Union from 1969 until the early 1990s.

Finally, the fourth category, which runs parallel with the first three phases, is represented by "surveys," which do not concentrate on individual sites but attempt to define the relations between single settlements, their positioning along canals or rivers, or the distribution of central settlements and their satellites. Since shortages of time, money, and an adequate task force preclude the thorough investigation of large numbers of individual sites, the method employed is that of observing and collecting finds from the surface. Of these finds, the latest in date will give a rough termination date for the duration of the settlement, but, since objects from earlier, if not the earliest, levels work their way to the surface with a predictable degree of certainty or are exposed in rain gullies, an intensive search of the surface of the mound allows conclusions as to the total period of occupation with some degree of probability. If the individual periods of settlement are marked on superimposed maps, a very clear picture is obtained of the fluctuations in settlement patterns, of the changing proportions between large and small settlements, and of the equally changeable systems of riverbeds and irrigation canals—for, when points on the map lie in line, it is a legitimate assumption that they were once connected by watercourses.

During the four phases outlined, the objectives and methods of excavation have broadened and shifted. At first the chief aim was the recovery of valuable finds suitable for museums, but at the same time there was, from early on, considerable interest in the architecture of Mesopotamia, which has won for it the place it deserves in architectural history. Alongside philology, art history has also made great strides, building up a chronological framework by the combination of evidence from stratigraphic and stylistic criteria, particularly in pottery and cylinder seals.

The discovery of graves and a variety of burial customs has thrown new light on the history of religion, stimulated by the interest of Bible studies. While pottery was previously collected for purely aesthetic motives or from the point of view of art history, attention has come to be paid increasingly to everyday wares, and greater insight into social and economic history is based on knowledge of the distribution and frequency of shapes and materials. The observation and investigation of animal bones and plant remains (pollen and seed analysis) have

NUZU

The ancient Mesopotamian city of Nuzu (modern Yorghan Tepe) is located southwest of what is now Kirkūk, Iraq. Excavations undertaken there by American archaeologists in 1925–31 revealed material extending from the prehistoric period to Roman, Parthian, and Sāsānian periods. In Akkadian times (2334–2154 BC) the site was called Gasur; but early in the second millennium BC the Hurrians, of northern Mesopotamia, occupied the city, changed its name to Nuzu, and during the 16th and 15th centuries built there a prosperous community and an important administrative centre.

Excavations uncovered excellent material for a study of Hurrian ceramics and glyptic art (carving on gems and hard stones). An especially outstanding type of pottery, called Nuzu ware (or Mitanni ware) because of its original discovery there, was characterized by one primary shape—a tall, slender, small-footed goblet—and an intricate black and white painted decoration. In addition to these extraordinary ceramic artifacts, more than 4,000 cuneiform tablets were discovered at the site. Although written mostly in Akkadian, the majority of the personal names are Hurrian, and the Akkadian used often shows strong Hurrian influence. The Nuzu material also made possible an insight into specific Hurrian family law and societal institutions and clarified many difficult passages in the contemporary patriarchal narratives of the biblical Book of Genesis.

supplied invaluable information on the process of domestication, the conditions of animal husbandry, and the advances in agriculture. Such studies demand the cooperation of both zoologists and paleobotanists. In addition, microscopic analysis of the floors of excavated buildings may help to identify the functions of individual rooms.

THE EMERGENCE OF MESOPOTAMIAN CIVILIZATION

Between about 10,000 BC and the genesis of large permanent settlements, the following stages of development are distinguishable, some of which run parallel:

(1) the change to sedentary life, or the transition from continual or seasonal change of abode, characteristic of hunter-gatherers and the earliest cattle breeders, to life in one place over a period of several years or even permanently, (2) the transition from experimental plant cultivation to the deliberate and calculated farming of grains and leguminous plants, (3) the erection of houses and the associated "settlement" of the gods in temples, (4) the burial of the dead in cemeteries, (5) the invention of clay vessels, made at first by hand, then turned on the wheel and fired to ever greater degrees of hardness, at the same time receiving almost invariably decoration of incised designs or

painted patterns, (6) the development of specialized crafts and the distribution of labour, and (7) metal production (the first use of metal—copper—marks the transition from the Late Neolithic to the Chalcolithic period).

These stages of development can only rarely be dated on the basis of a sequence of levels at one site alone. Instead, an important role is played by the comparison of different sites, starting with the assumption that what is simpler and technically less accomplished is older. In addition to this type of dating, which can be only relative, the radiocarbon, or carbon-14, method has proved to be an increasingly valuable tool since the 1950s. By this method the known rate of decay of the radioactive carbon isotope (carbon-14) in wood, horn, plant fibre, and bone allows the time that has elapsed since the "death" of the material under examination to be calculated. Although a plus/minus discrepancy of up to 200 years has to be allowed for, this is not such a great disadvantage in the case of material 6,000 to 10,000 years old. Even when skepticism is necessary because of the use of an inadequate sample, carbon-14 dates are still very welcome as confirmation of dates arrived at by other means. Moreover, radiocarbon ages can be converted to more precise dates through comparisons with data obtained by dendrochronology, a method of absolute age determination based on the analysis of the annual rings of trees.

THE BEGINNINGS OF AGRICULTURE

The first agriculture, the domestication of animals, and the transition to sedentary life took place in regions in which animals that were easily domesticated, such as sheep, goats, cattle, and pigs, and the wild prototypes of grains and leguminous plants, such as wheat, barley, bitter vetch, pea, and lentil, were present. Such centres of dispersion may have been the valleys and grassy border regions of the mountains of Iran, Iraq, Anatolia, Syria, and Palestine, but they also could have been, say, the northern slopes of the Hindu Kush. As settled life, which caused a drop in infant mortality, led to the increase of the population, settlement spread out from these centres into the plains—although it must be remembered that this process, described as the Neolithic Revolution, in fact took thousands of years.

Representative of the first settlements on the borders of Mesopotamia are the adjacent sites of Zawi Chemi Shanidar and Shanidar itself, which lie northwest of Rawāndūz. They date from the transition from the 10th to the ninth millennium BC and are classified as prepottery. The finds included querns (primitive mills) for grinding grain (whether wild or cultivated is not known), the remains of huts about 13 feet (4 metres) in diameter, and a cemetery with grave goods. The presence of copper beads is evidence of acquaintance with metal, though not necessarily with the technique of working it into tools, and the presence of obsidian (volcanic glass) is indicative of the acquisition of nonindigenous raw materials by means of trade. The bones found testify that sheep were already domesticated at Zawi Chemi Shanidar.

At Karīm Shahir, a site that cannot be accurately tied chronologically to Shanidar, clear proof was obtained both of the knowledge of grain cultivation, in the form of sickle blades showing sheen from use, and of the baking of clay, in the form of lightly fired clay figurines. Still in the hilly borders of Mesopotamia, a sequence of about 3,000 years can be followed at the site of Qal'at Jarmo, east of Kirkūk, some 150 miles (241 km) north of Baghdad. The beginning of this settlement can be dated to about 6750 BC; excavations uncovered 12 archaeological levels of a regular village, consisting of about 20 to 25 houses built of packed clay, sometimes with stone foundations, and divided into several rooms. The finds included types of wheat (emmer and einkorn) and two-row barley, the bones of domesticated goats, sheep, and pigs, and obsidian tools, stone vessels, and, in the upper third of the levels, clay vessels with rough painted decorations, providing the first certain evidence for the manufacture of pottery. Jarmo must be roughly contemporary with the sites of Jericho (13 miles [21 km] east of Jerusalem) and of Çatalhüyük in Anatolia (central Turkey). Those sites, with their walled settlements, seem to have achieved a much higher level of civilization, but too much weight must not be placed on the comparison because no other sites in and around Mesopotamia confirm the picture deduced from Jarmo alone. Views on the earliest Neolithic in Iraq have undergone radical revisions in the light of discoveries made since the 1970s at Qermez Dere, Nemrik, and Maghzaliyah.

About 1,000 years later are two villages that are the earliest so far discovered in the plain of Mesopotamia: Ḥassūna, near Mosul, and Tall Ṣawwān, near Sāmarrā'. At Ḥassūna the pottery is more advanced, with incised and painted designs, but the decoration is still unsophisticated. One of the buildings found may be a shrine, judging from its unusual ground plan. Apart from emmer there occurs, as the result of mutation, six-row barley, which was later to become the chief grain crop of southern Mesopotamia. In the case of Tall Ṣawwān, it is significant that the settlement lay south of the boundary of rainfall agriculture; thus it must have been dependent on some form of artificial irrigation, even if this was no more than the drawing of water from the Tigris. This, therefore, gives a date after which the settlement of parts of southern Mesopotamia would have been feasible.

THE EMERGENCE OF CULTURES

For the next millennium, the fifth, it is customary to speak in terms of various "cultures" or "horizons," distinguished in general by the pottery, which may be classed by its colour, shape, hardness, and, above all, by its decoration. The name of each horizon is derived either from the type site or from the place where the pottery was first found: Sāmarrā' on the Tigris, Tall Ḥalaf in the central Jazīrah, Ḥassūna Level V, Al-'Ubayd near Ur, and Ḥājj Muḥammad on the Euphrates, not far from Al-Samāwah (some 150 miles [241 km] south-southeast of Baghdad). Along with the improvement of tools, the first evidence for water transport (a model boat from the prehistoric cemetery at Eridu, in the extreme south of Mesopotamia, *c.* 4000 BC), and the development of terracottas, the most impressive sign of progress is the constantly accelerating advance in architecture. This can best be followed in the city of Eridu, which in historical times was the centre of the cult of the Sumerian god Enki.

Originally a small, single-roomed shrine, the temple in the Ubaid period consisted of a rectangular building, measuring 80 by 40 feet (24 by 12 metres), that stood on an artificial terrace. It had an "offering table" and an "altar" against the short walls, aisles down each side, and a facade decorated with niches. This temple, standing on a terrace probably originally designed to protect the building from flooding, is usually considered the prototype of the characteristic religious structure of later Babylonia, the ziggurat. The temple at Eridu is in the very same place as that on which the Enki ziggurat stood in the time of the third dynasty of Ur (*c.* 2112–*c.* 2004 BC), so the cult tradition must have existed on the same spot for at least 1,500 to 2,000 years before Ur III itself. Remarkable as this is, however, it is not justifiable to assume a continuous ethnic tradition. The flowering of architecture reached its peak with the great temples (or assembly halls?) of Erech (Uruk), built around the turn of the fourth to third millennium BC (Uruk Levels VI to IV).

In extracting information as to the expression of mind and spirit during the six millennia preceding the invention of writing, it is necessary to take account of four major sources: decoration on pottery, the care of the dead, sculpture, and the designs on seals. There is, of course, no justification in assuming any association with ethnic groups.

The most varied of these means of expression is undoubtedly the decoration of pottery. It is hardly coincidental that, in regions in which writing had developed, high-quality painted pottery was no longer made. The motifs in decoration are either abstract and geometric or figured, although there is also a strong tendency to geometric stylization. An important question is the extent to which the presence of symbols, such as the bucranium (a sculptured ornament representing an ox skull), can be considered as expressions of specific religious ideas, such as a bull cult, and, indeed, how much the decoration was intended to convey meaning at all.

It is not known how ancient is the custom of burying the dead in graves nor whether its intention was to maintain communication (by the cult of the dead) or to guard against the demonic power of the unburied dead left free to wander. A cemetery, or collection of burials associated with grave goods, is first attested at Zawi Chemi Shanidar. The presence of pots in the grave indicates that the bodily needs of the dead person were provided for, and the discovery of the skeleton of a dog and of a model boat in the cemetery at Eridu suggests that it was believed that the activities of life could be pursued in the afterlife.

The earliest sculpture takes the form of very crudely worked terra-cotta representations of women; the Ubaid Horizon, however, has figurines of both women and men, with very slender bodies, protruding features, arms akimbo, and the genitals accurately indicated, and also of women suckling children. It is uncertain whether it is correct to describe these statuettes as idols, whether the figures were cult objects, such as votive offerings, or whether they had a magical significance, such as fertility charms, or, indeed, what purpose they did fulfill.

Seals are first attested in the form of stamp seals at Tepe Gawra, north of Mosul. Geometric designs are found earlier than scenes with figures, such as men, animals, conflict between animals, copulation, or dance. Here again it is uncertain whether the scenes are intended to convey a deeper meaning. Nevertheless, unlike pottery, a seal has a direct relationship to a particular individual or group, for the seal identifies what it is used to seal (a vessel, sack, or other container) as the property or responsibility of a specific person. To that extent, seals represent the earliest pictorial representations of persons. The area of distribution of the stamp seal was northern Mesopotamia, Anatolia, and Iran. Southern Mesopotamia, on the other hand, was the home of the cylinder seal, which was either an independent invention or was derived from stamp seals engraved on two faces. The cylinder seal, with its greater surface area and more practical application, remained in use into the first millennium BC. Because of the continuous changes in the style of the seal designs, cylinder seals are among the most valuable of chronological indicators for archaeologists.

In general, the prehistory of Mesopotamia can only be described by listing and comparing human achievements, not by recounting the interaction of individuals or peoples. There is no basis for reconstructing the movements and migrations of peoples unless one is prepared to equate the spread of particular archaeological types with the extent of a particular population, the change of types with a change of population, or the appearance of new types with an immigration.

The only certain evidence for the movement of peoples beyond their own territorial limits is provided at first by material finds that are not indigenous. The discovery of obsidian and lapis lazuli at sites in Mesopotamia or in its

CYLINDER SEALS

Cylinder seals are small stone cylinders engraved in intaglio that leave a distinctive impression when rolled on wet clay. They are characteristic artifacts of ancient Mesopotamian civilization and are considered some of its finest artistic achievements. The seals first appear during the Protoliterate period (c. 3400–2900 BC), and, although the earliest examples used primarily geometric, magical, or animal patterns, later seals incorporated the owner's name and depicted a variety of motifs. Sometimes the elements were arranged in symmetrical, decorative patterns; often, however, an action was represented.

Cylinder seals were employed in marking personal property and in making documents legally binding. Their fashioning and use were adopted by surrounding civilizations, such as those of Egypt and the Indus Valley.

Horned animals engraved in the brocade style, seal impression from Tall al-Asmar, Iraq, first Early Dynastic period (c. 2900–c. 2750 BC). In the Oriental Institute, the University of Chicago. Courtesy of the Oriental Institute, the University of Chicago

neighbouring lands is evidence for the existence of trade, whether consisting of direct caravan trade or of a succession of intermediate stages.

Just as no ethnic identity is recognizable, so nothing is known of the social organization of prehistoric settlements. It is not possible to deduce anything of the "government" in a village nor of any supraregional connections that may have existed under the domination of one centre. Constructions that could only have been accomplished by the organization of workers in large numbers are first found in Uruk Levels VI to IV: the dimensions of these buildings suggest that they were intended for gatherings of hundreds of people. As for artificial irrigation, which was indispensable for agriculture in south Mesopotamia, the earliest form was probably not the irrigation canal. It is assumed that at first floodwater was dammed up to collect in basins, near which the fields were located. Canals, which led the water farther from the river, would have become necessary when the land in the vicinity of the river could no longer supply the needs of the population.

MESOPOTAMIAN PROTOHISTORY

Attempts have been made by philologists to reach conclusions about the origin of the flowering of civilization in southern Mesopotamia by the analysis of Sumerian words. It has been thought possible to isolate an earlier, non-Sumerian substratum from the Sumerian vocabulary by assigning certain words on the basis of their endings to either a Neolithic or a Chalcolithic language stratum. These attempts are based on the phonetic character of Sumerian at the beginning of the second millennium BC, which is at least 1,000 years later than the invention of writing. Quite apart, therefore, from the fact that the structure of Sumerian words themselves is far from adequately investigated, the enormous gap in time casts grave doubt on the criteria used to distinguish between Sumerian and "pre-Sumerian" vocabulary.

The earliest peoples of Mesopotamia who can be identified from inscribed monuments and written tradition—people in the sense of speakers of a common language—are, apart from the Sumerians, Semitic peoples (Akkadians or pre-Akkadians) and Subarians (identical with, or near relatives of, the Hurrians, who appear in northern Mesopotamia around the end of the third millennium BC). Their presence is known, but no definite statements about their past or possible routes of immigration are possible.

At the turn of the fourth to third millennium BC, the long span of prehistory is over, and the threshold of the historical era is gained, captured by the existence of writing. Names, speech, and actions are fixed in a system that is composed of signs representing complete words or syllables. The signs may consist of realistic pictures, abbreviated representations, and perhaps symbols selected at random. Since clay is not well suited to the drawing of curved lines, a tendency to use straight lines rapidly gained ground. When the writer pressed the reed in harder at the beginning of a stroke, it made a triangular "head," and thus "wedges" were impressed into the clay. It is the Sumerians who are usually given the credit for the invention of this, the first system of writing in the Middle East. As far as they can be assigned to any language, the inscribed documents from before the dynasty of Akkad (c. 2334–c. 2154 BC) are almost exclusively in Sumerian. Moreover, the extension of the writing system to include the creation of syllabograms by the use of the sound of a logogram (sign representing a word), such as *gi*, "a reed stem," used to render the verb *gi*, "to return," can only be explained in terms of the Sumerian language. It is most probable, however, that Mesopotamia in the fourth millennium BC, just as in later times, was composed of many races. This makes it likely that, apart from the Sumerians, the interests and even initiatives of other language groups may have played their part in the formation of the writing system. Many scholars believe that certain clay objects or tokens that are found in prehistoric strata may have been used for some kind of primitive accounting. These tokens, some of which are incised and which have various forms, may thus be three-dimensional predecessors of writing.

Sumerian is an agglutinative language: prefixes and suffixes, which express various grammatical functions and relationships, are attached to a noun or verb root in a "chain." Attempts to identify Sumerian more closely by comparative methods have as yet been unsuccessful and will very probably remain so, as languages of a comparable type are known only from AD 500 (Georgian) or 1000 (Basque)—that is, 3,000 years later. Over so long a time, the rate of change in a language, particularly one that is not fixed in a written norm, is so great that one can no longer determine whether apparent similarity

between words goes back to an original relationship or is merely fortuitous. Consequently, it is impossible to obtain any more accurate information as to the language group to which Sumerian may once have belonged.

The most important development in the course of the fourth millennium BC was the birth of the city. There were precursors, such as the unwalled prepottery settlement at Jericho of about 7000 BC, but the beginning of cities with a more permanent character came only later. There is no generally accepted definition of a city. In this context, it means a settlement that serves as a centre for smaller settlements, one that possesses one or more shrines of one or more major deities, has extensive granaries, and, finally, displays an advanced stage of specialization in the crafts.

The earliest cities of southern Mesopotamia, as far as their names are known, are Eridu, Erech (Uruk), Bad-tibira, Nippur, and Kish (35 miles [56 km] south-southeast of Baghdad). The surveys of the American archaeologist Robert McCormick Adams and the German archaeologist Hans Nissen have shown how the relative size and number of the settlements gradually shifted: the number of small or very small settlements was reduced overall, whereas the number of larger places grew. The clearest sign of urbanization can be seen at Erech (Uruk), with the almost explosive increase in the size of the buildings. Uruk Levels VI to IV had rectangular buildings covering areas as large as 275 by 175 feet (84 by 53 metres) These buildings are described as temples, since the ground plans are comparable to those of later buildings whose sacred character is beyond doubt, but other functions, such as assembly halls for noncultic purposes, cannot be excluded.

The major accomplishments of the period Uruk VI to IV, apart from the first inscribed tablets (Level IV B), are masterpieces of sculpture and of seal engraving and also of the form of wall decoration known as cone mosaics. Together with the everyday pottery of gray or red burnished ware, there is a very coarse type known as the beveled-rim bowl. These are vessels of standard size whose shape served as the original for the sign *sila*, meaning "litre." It is not too rash to deduce from the mass production of such standard vessels that they served for the issue of rations. This would have been the earliest instance of a system that remained typical of the southern Mesopotamian city for centuries: the maintenance of part of the population by allocations of food from the state.

Historians usually date the beginning of history, as opposed to prehistory and protohistory, from the first appearance of usable written sources. If this is taken to be the transition from the fourth to the third millennium BC, it must be remembered that this applies only to part of Mesopotamia: the south, the Diyālā region, Susiana (with a later script of its own invented locally), and the district of the middle Euphrates, as well as Iran.

CHAPTER 2

SUMERIAN CIVILIZATION

The earliest known civilization was that of Sumer, located in the southernmost part of Mesopotamia between the Tigris and the Euphrates rivers, in the area that later became Babylonia and is now southern Iraq covering the region roughly from Baghdad to the Persian Gulf.

Sumer was first settled between 4500 and 4000 BC by a non-Semitic people who did not speak the Sumerian language. These people now are called proto-Euphrateans or Ubaidians, for the village Al-'Ubayd, where their remains were first discovered. The Ubaidians were the first civilizing force in Sumer, draining the marshes for agriculture, developing trade, and establishing industries, including weaving, leatherwork, metalwork, masonry, and pottery. After the Ubaidian immigration to Mesopotamia, various Semitic peoples infiltrated their territory, adding their cultures to the Ubaidian culture, and creating a high pre-Sumerian civilization.

The people called Sumerians, whose language became the prevailing language of the territory, probably came from around Anatolia, arriving in Sumer about 3300 BC. By the third millennium BC the country was the site of at least 12 separate city-states: Kish, Erech (Uruk), Ur, Sippar, Akshak, Larak, Nippur, Adab, Umma, Lagash, Bad-tibira, and Larsa. Each of these states was comprised of a walled city and its surrounding villages and land, and each worshiped its own deity, whose temple was the central structure of the city.

Columns decorated by the Sumerians in a mosaic-like technique with polychrome terra-cotta cones, from Uruk, Mesopotamia, early 3rd millennium BC; in the National Museums of Berlin. Courtesy of Staatliche Museen zu Berlin

Political power originally belonged to the citizens, but, as rivalry between the various city-states increased, each adopted the institution of kingship. An extant document, *The Sumerian King List,* records that eight kings reigned before the great Flood.

After the Flood, various city-states and their dynasties of kings temporarily gained power over the others. The first king to unite the separate city-states was Etana, ruler of Kish (c. 2800 BC). Thereafter, Kish, Erech, Ur, and Lagash vied for ascendancy for hundreds of years, rendering Sumer vulnerable to external conquerors, first the Elamites (c. 2530–2450 BC) and later the Akkadians, led by their king Sargon (reigned 2334–2279 BC). Although Sargon's dynasty lasted only about 100 years, it united the city-states and created a model of government that influenced all of Middle Eastern civilization.

After Sargon's dynasty ended and Sumer recovered from a devastating invasion by the semibarbaric Gutians, the city-states once again became independent. The high point of this final era of Sumerian civilization was the reign of the third dynasty of Ur, whose first king, Ur-Nammu, published the earliest law code yet discovered in Mesopotamia.

After 1900 BC, when the Amorites conquered all of Mesopotamia, the Sumerians lost their separate identity, but they bequeathed their culture to their Semitic successors, and they left the world a number of technological and cultural contributions, including the first wheeled vehicles and potter's wheels; the first system of writing, cuneiform; the first codes of law; and the first city-states.

SUMERIAN LANGUAGE

The Sumerian language is the oldest written language in existence. First attested about 3100 BC in southern Mesopotamia, it flourished during the third millennium BC. About 2000 BC, Sumerian was replaced as a spoken language by Semitic Akkadian (Assyro-Babylonian) but continued in written usage almost to the end of the life of the Akkadian language, lasting to about the beginning of the Christian era. Sumerian never extended much beyond its original boundaries in southern Mesopotamia; the small number of its native speakers was entirely out of proportion to the tremendous importance and influence Sumerian exercised on the development of the Mesopotamian and other ancient civilizations in all their stages.

Four periods of Sumerian can be distinguished: Archaic Sumerian, Old or Classical Sumerian, New Sumerian, and Post-Sumerian. Archaic Sumerian covered a period from approximately 3100 BC, when the first Sumerian records make their appearance, down to about 2500 BC. The earliest Sumerian writing is almost exclusively represented by texts of business and administrative character. There are also school texts in the form of simple exercises in writing signs and words. The Archaic Sumerian language is still very poorly understood, partly because of the difficulties surrounding the reading and interpretation of early Sumerian writing and partly because of the meagreness of sources.

The Old, or Classical, period of Sumerian lasted from about 2500 to 2300 BC and is represented mainly by records of the early rulers of Lagash. The records are business, legal, and administrative texts, as well as royal and private inscriptions, mostly of votive character; letters, both private and official; and incantations. These sources are much more numerous than those of the preceding period, and the writing is explicit enough to make possible an adequate reconstruction of Sumerian grammar and vocabulary.

During the period of the Sargonic dynasty, the Semitic Akkadians took over the political hegemony of Babylonia, marking a definite setback in the progress of the Sumerian language. At this time the Akkadian language was used extensively throughout the entire area of the Akkadian empire, while the use of Sumerian gradually was limited to a small area in Sumer proper. After a brief revival during the third dynasty of Ur, the New Sumerian period came to an end about 2000 BC, when new inroads of the Semitic peoples from the desert succeeded in destroying the third dynasty of Ur and in establishing the Semitic dynasties of Isin, Larsa, and Babylon.

The period of the dynasties of Isin, Larsa, and Babylon is called the Old Babylonian period, after Babylon, which became the capital and the most important city in the country. During this time the Sumerians lost their political identity, and Sumerian gradually disappeared as a spoken language. It did, however, continue to be written to the very end of the use of cuneiform writing. This is the last stage of the Sumerian language, called Post-Sumerian.

In the early stages of the Post-Sumerian period the use of written Sumerian is extensively attested in legal and administrative texts, as well as in royal inscriptions, which are often bilingual, in Sumerian and Babylonian. Many Sumerian literary compositions, which came down from the older Sumerian periods by way of oral tradition, were recorded in writing for the first time in the Old Babylonian period. Many more were copied by industrious scribes from originals now lost. The rich Sumerian literature is represented by texts of varied nature, such as myths and epics, hymns and lamentations, rituals and incantations, and proverbs and the so-called wisdom compositions. For many centuries after the Old Babylonian period, the study of Sumerian continued in the Babylonian schools. As late as the seventh century BC, Ashurbanipal, one of the last rulers of Assyria, boasted of being able to read the difficult Sumerian language, and from an even later period, in Hellenistic times, there are some cuneiform tablets that show Sumerian words transcribed in Greek letters.

Around the time of Christ, all knowledge of the Sumerian language disappeared along with that of cuneiform writing, and in the succeeding centuries even the name Sumer vanished from memory. Unlike Assyria, Babylonia, and Egypt, whose histories and traditions are amply documented in biblical and classical sources, there was nothing to be found in non-Mesopotamian sources to make one even suspect the existence of the Sumerians in antiquity, let alone fully appreciate their important role in the history of early civilizations.

When the decipherment of cuneiform writing was achieved in the early decades of the 19th century, three languages written in cuneiform were discovered: Semitic Babylonian, Indo-European Persian, and Elamite, of unknown linguistic affiliation. Only after the texts written in Babylonian had become better understood did scholars become aware of the existence of texts written in a language different from Babylonian. When the new language was discovered it was variously designated as Scythian, or even Akkadian (that is, by the very name now given to the Semitic language spoken in Babylonia and Assyria). It was only after knowledge of the new language had grown that it was given the correct name of Sumerian.

SUMERIAN CITY LIFE

In Erech (Uruk) and probably also in other cities of comparable size, the Sumerians led a city life that can be more or less reconstructed as follows: temples and residential districts; intensive agriculture, stock breeding, fishing, and date palm cultivation forming the four mainstays of the economy; and highly specialized industries carried on by sculptors, seal engravers, smiths, carpenters, shipbuilders, potters, and workers of reeds and textiles. Part of the population was supported with rations from a central point of distribution, which relieved people of the necessity of providing their basic food themselves, in return for their work all day and every day, at least for most of the year. The cities kept up active trade with foreign lands.

That organized city life existed is demonstrated chiefly by the existence of inscribed tablets. The earliest tablets contain figures with the items they enumerate and measures with the items they measure, as well as personal names and, occasionally, probably professions. This shows the purely practical origins of writing in Mesopotamia: it began not as a means of magic or as a way for the ruler to record his achievements, for example, but as an aid to memory for an administration that was ever expanding its area of operations. The earliest examples of writing are very difficult to penetrate because of their extremely laconic formulation, which presupposes a knowledge of the context, and because of the still very imperfect rendering of the spoken word. Moreover, many of the archaic signs were pruned away after a short period of use and cannot be traced in the paleography of later periods, so that they cannot be identified.

One of the most important questions that has to be met when dealing with "organization" and "city life" is that of social structure and the form of government; however, it can be answered only with difficulty, and the use of evidence from later periods carries with it the danger of anachronisms. The Sumerian word for ruler par excellence is *lugal*, which etymologically means "big person." The first occurrence comes from Kish about 2700 BC, since an earlier instance from Erech (Uruk) is uncertain because it could simply be intended as a personal name: "Monsieur Legrand." In Erech the ruler's special title was *en*. In later periods this word (etymology unknown), which is also found in divine names such as Enlil and Enki, has a predominantly religious connotation that is translated, for want of a better designation, as "en-priest, en-priestess." *En*, as the ruler's title, is encountered in the traditional epics of the Sumerians (Gilgamesh is the "*en* of Kullab," a district of Erech) and particularly in personal names, such as "The-*en*-has-abundance," "The-*en*-occupies-the-throne," and many others.

It has often been asked if the ruler of Erech is to be recognized in artistic representations. A man feeding sheep with flowering branches, a prominent personality in seal designs, might thus represent the ruler or a priest in his capacity as administrator and protector of flocks. The same question may be posed in the case of a man who is depicted on a stela aiming an arrow at a lion. These questions are purely speculative, however: even if the "protector of flocks" were identical with the *en*, there is no ground for seeing in the ruler a person with a predominantly religious function.

LITERARY AND OTHER HISTORICAL SOURCES

The picture offered by the literary tradition of Mesopotamia is clearer but not necessarily historically relevant. The Sumerian king list has long been the greatest focus of interest. This is a literary composition, dating from Old Babylonian times, that describes kingship (*nam-lugal* in Sumerian) in Mesopotamia from primeval times to the end of the first dynasty of Isin. According to the theory—or rather the ideology—of this work, there was officially only one kingship in Mesopotamia, which was vested in one particular city at any one time; hence the change in dynasties brought with it the change of the seat of kingship:

Kish-Erech-Ur-Awan-Kish-Hamazi-Erech-Ur-Adab-Mari-Kish-Akshak-Kish-Erech-Akkad-Erech-Gutians-Erech-Ur-Isin.

The king list gives as coming in succession several dynasties that now are known to have ruled simultaneously. It is a welcome aid to chronology and history, but, so far as the regnal years are concerned, it loses its value for the time before the dynasty of Akkad, for here the lengths of reign of single rulers are given as more than 100 and sometimes even several hundred years. One group of versions of the king list has adopted the tradition of the Sumerian Flood story, according to which Kish was the first seat of kingship after the Flood, whereas five dynasties of primeval kings ruled before the Flood in Eridu, Bad-tibira, Larak, Sippar, and Shuruppak. These kings all allegedly ruled for multiples of 3,600 years (the maximum being 64,800 or, according to one variant, 72,000 years). The tradition of the Sumerian king list is still echoed in Berosus.

It is also instructive to observe what the Sumerian king list does not mention. The list lacks all mention of a dynasty as important as the first dynasty of Lagash (from King Ur-Nanshe to UruKAgina) and appears to retain no memory of the archaic florescence of Erech at the beginning of the third millennium BC.

Besides the peaceful pursuits reflected in art and writing, the art also provides the first information about violent contacts: cylinder seals of the Uruk Level IV depict fettered men lying or squatting on the ground, being beaten with sticks or otherwise maltreated by standing figures. They may represent the execution of prisoners of war. It is not known from where these captives came or what form "war" would have taken or how early organized battles were fought. Nevertheless, this does give the first, albeit indirect, evidence for the wars that are henceforth one of the most characteristic phenomena in the history of Mesopotamia.

Just as with the rule of man over man, with the rule of higher powers over man it is difficult to make any statements about the earliest attested forms of religion or about the deities and their names without running the risk of anachronism. Excluding prehistoric figurines, which provide no evidence for determining whether men or anthropomorphic gods are represented, the earliest testimony is supplied by certain symbols that later became the cuneiform signs for gods' names: the "gatepost with streamers" for Inanna, goddess of love and war, and the "ringed post" for the moon god Nanna. A scene on a cylinder seal—a shrine with an Inanna symbol and a "man" in a boat—could be an abbreviated illustration of a procession of gods or of a cultic journey by ship. The constant association of the "gatepost with streamers" with sheep and of the "ringed post" with cattle may possibly reflect the area of responsibility of each deity. The Sumerologist Thorkild Jacobsen sees in the pantheon a reflex of the various economies and modes of life in ancient Mesopotamia: fishermen and marsh dwellers, date palm cultivators, cowherds, shepherds, and farmers all have their special groups of gods.

Both Sumerian and non-Sumerian languages can be detected in the divine names and place-names. Since the pronunciation of the names is known only from 2000 BC or later, conclusions about their linguistic affinity are not without problems. Several names, for example, have been reinterpreted in Sumerian by popular etymology. It would be particularly important to isolate the Subarian components (related to Hurrian), whose significance was probably greater than has hitherto been assumed. For the south Mesopotamian city HA.A (the noncommittal transliteration of the signs) there is a pronunciation gloss "shubari," and non-Sumerian incantations are known in the language of HA.A that have turned out to be "Subarian."

There have always been in Mesopotamia speakers of Semitic languages (which belong to the Afro-Asiatic group and also include ancient Egyptian, Berber, and various African languages). This element is easier to detect in ancient Mesopotamia, but whether people began to participate in city civilization in the fourth millennium BC or only during the third is unknown. Over the last 4,000 years, Semites (Amorites, Canaanites, Aramaeans, and Arabs) have been partly nomadic, ranging the Arabian fringes of the Fertile Crescent, and partly settled;

CHRONOLOGY AND KING LISTS

Despite the Sumerians' leading role, the historical role of other races should not be underestimated. While with prehistory only approximate dates can be offered, historical periods require a firm chronological framework, which, unfortunately, has not yet been established for the first half of the third millennium BC. The basis for the chronology after about 1450 BC is provided by the data in the Assyrian and Babylonian king lists, which can often be checked by dated tablets and the Assyrian lists of eponyms (annual officials whose names served to identify each year). It is, however, still uncertain how much time separated the middle of the 15th century BC from the end of the first dynasty of Babylon, which is therefore variously dated to 1594 BC ("middle"), 1530 BC ("short"), or 1730 BC ("long" chronology). As a compromise, the middle chronology is used here.

From 1594 BC several chronologically overlapping dynasties reach back to the beginning of the third dynasty of Ur, about 2112 BC. From this point to the beginning of the dynasty of Akkad (c. 2334 BC) the interval can only be calculated to within 40 to 50 years, via the ruling houses of Lagash and the rather uncertain traditions regarding the succession of Gutian viceroys. With Ur-Nanshe (c. 2520 BC), the first king of the first dynasty of Lagash, there is a possible variation of 70 to 80 years, and earlier dates are a matter of mere guesswork: they depend upon factors of only limited relevance, such as the computation of occupation or destruction levels, the degree of development in the script (paleography), the character of the sculpture, pottery, and cylinder seals, and their correlation at different sites. In short, the chronology of the first half of the third millennium is largely a matter for the intuition of the individual author. Carbon-14 dates are at present too few and far between to be given undue weight. Consequently, the turn of the fourth to third millennium is to be accepted, with due caution and reservations, as the date of the flourishing of the archaic civilization of Erech and of the invention of writing.

and the transition to settled life can be observed in a constant, though uneven, rhythm. There are, therefore, good grounds for assuming that the Akkadians (and other pre-Akkadian Semitic tribes not known by name) also originally led a nomadic life to a greater or lesser degree. Nevertheless, they can only have been herders of domesticated sheep and goats, which require changes of pasturage according to the time of year and can never stray more than a day's march from the watering places. The traditional nomadic life of the Bedouin makes its appearance only with the domestication of the camel at the turn of the second to first millennium BC.

The question arises as to how quickly writing spread and by whom it was adopted in about 3000 BC or shortly thereafter. At Kish, in northern Babylonia, almost 120 miles northwest of Erech, a stone tablet has been found with the same repertoire of archaic signs as those found at Erech itself. This fact demonstrates that intellectual contacts existed between northern and southern Babylonia. The dispersion of writing in an unaltered form presupposes the existence of schools in various cities that worked according to the same principles and adhered to one and the same canonical repertoire of signs. It would be wrong to assume that Sumerian was spoken throughout the area in which writing had been adopted. Moreover, the use of cuneiform for a non-Sumerian language can be demonstrated with certainty from the 27th century BC.

FIRST HISTORICAL PERSONALITIES

The specifically political events in Mesopotamia after the flourishing of the archaic culture of Erech (Uruk) cannot be pinpointed. Not until about 2700 BC does the first historical personality appear—historical because his name, Enmebaragesi (Me-baragesi), was preserved in later tradition. It has been assumed, although the exact circumstances cannot be reconstructed, that there was a rather abrupt end to the high culture of Uruk Level IV. The reason for the assumption is a marked break in both artistic and architectural traditions: entirely new styles of cylinder seals were introduced; the great temples (if in fact they were temples) were abandoned, flouting the rule of a continuous tradition on religious sites; and on a new site a shrine was built on a terrace, which was to constitute the lowest stage of the later Eanna ziggurat. On the other hand, since the writing system developed organically and was continually refined by innovations and progressive reforms, it would be overhasty to assume a revolutionary change in the population.

In the quarter or third of a millennium between Uruk Level IV and Enmebaragesi, southern Mesopotamia became studded with a complex pattern of cities, many of which were the centres of small independent city-states, to judge from the situation in about the middle of the millennium. In these cities, the central point was the temple, sometimes encircled by an oval boundary wall (hence the term "temple oval"); but non-religious buildings, such as palaces serving as the residences of the rulers, could also function as centres.

Enmebaragesi, king of Kish, is the oldest Mesopotamian ruler from whom there are authentic inscriptions. These are vase fragments, one of them found in the temple oval of Khafajah (Khafājī). In the Sumerian king list, Enmebaragesi is listed as the penultimate king of the first dynasty of Kish; a Sumerian poem, "Gilgamesh and Agga of Kish," describes the siege of Erech by Agga, son of Enmebaragesi. The discovery of the original vase inscriptions was of great significance because it enabled scholars to ask with somewhat more justification whether Gilgamesh, the heroic figure of Mesopotamia who has entered world literature, was actually a historical personage. The indirect synchronism notwithstanding, the possibility exists that even remote antiquity knew its

"Ninus" and its "Semiramis," figures onto which a rapidly fading historical memory projected all manner of deeds and adventures. Thus, though the historical tradition of the early second millennium believes Gilgamesh to have been the builder of the oldest city wall of Erech, such may not have been the case. The palace archives of Shuruppak (modern Tall Fa'rah, 125 miles [201 km] southeast of Baghdad), dating presumably from shortly after 2600, contain a long list of divinities, including Gilgamesh and his father Lugalbanda. More recent tradition, on the other hand, knows Gilgamesh as judge of the netherworld. However that may be, an armed conflict between two Mesopotamian cities such as Erech and Kish would hardly have been unusual in a country whose energies were consumed, almost without interruption from 2500 to 1500 BC, by clashes between various separatist forces. The great "empires," after all, formed the exception, not the rule.

EMERGENT CITY-STATES

Kish must have played a major role almost from the beginning. After 2500, southern Babylonian rulers, such as Mesannepada of Ur and Eannatum of Lagash, frequently called themselves king of Kish when laying claim to sovereignty over northern Babylonia. This does not agree with some recent histories in which Kish is represented as an archaic "empire." It is more likely to have figured as representative of the north,

calling forth perhaps the same geographic connotation later evoked by "the land of Akkad."

Although the corpus of inscriptions grows richer both in geographic distribution and in point of chronology in the 27th and increasingly so in the 26th century, it is still impossible to find the key to a plausible historical account, and history cannot be written solely on the basis of archaeological findings. Unless clarified by written documents, such findings contain as many riddles as they seem to offer solutions. This applies even to as spectacular a discovery as that of the royal tombs of Ur with their hecatombs (large-scale sacrifices) of retainers who followed their king and queen to the grave, not to mention the elaborate funerary appointments with their inventory of tombs. It is only from about 2520 to the beginnings of the dynasty of Akkad that history can be written within a framework, with the aid of reports about the city-state of Lagash and its capital of Girsu and its relations with its neighbour and rival, Umma.

Sources for this are, on the one hand, an extensive corpus of inscriptions relating to nine rulers, telling of the buildings they constructed, of their institutions and wars, and, in the case of UruKAgina, of their "social" measures. On the other hand, there is the archive of some 1,200 tablets—insofar as these have been published—from the temple of Baba, the city goddess of Girsu, from the period of Lugalanda and UruKAgina (first half of the 24th century). For generations,

Lagash and Umma contested the possession and agricultural usufruct of the fertile region of Gu'edena. To begin with, some two generations before Ur-Nanshe, Mesilim (another "king of Kish") had intervened as arbiter and possibly overlord in dictating to both states the course of the boundary between them, but this was not effective for long. After a prolonged struggle, Eannatum forced the ruler of Umma, by having him take an involved oath to six divinities, to desist from crossing the old border, a dike.

The text that relates this event, with considerable literary elaboration, is found on the Stele of Vultures. These battles, favouring now one side, now the other, continued under Eannatum's successors, in particular Entemena, until, under UruKAgina, great damage was done to the land of Lagash and to its holy places. The enemy, Lugalzagesi, was vanquished in turn by Sargon of Akkad. The rivalry between Lagash and Umma, however, must not be considered in isolation. Other cities, too, are occasionally named as enemies, and the whole situation resembles the pattern of changing coalitions and short-lived alliances between cities of more recent times. Kish, Umma, and distant Mari on the middle Euphrates are listed together on one occasion as early as the time of Eannatum. For the most part, these battles were fought by infantry, although mention is also made of war chariots drawn by onagers (wild asses).

The lords of Lagash rarely fail to call themselves by the title of ensi, of as yet undetermined derivation; "city ruler," or "prince," are only approximate translations. Only seldom do they call themselves lugal, or "king," the title given the rulers of Umma in their own inscriptions. In all likelihood, these were local titles that were eventually converted, beginning perhaps with the kings of Akkad, into a hierarchy in which the lugal took precedence over the ensi.

TERRITORIAL STATES

More difficult than describing its external relations is the task of shedding light on the internal structure of a state like Lagash. For the first time, a state consisting of more than a city with its surrounding territory came into being, because aggressively minded rulers had managed to extend that territory until it comprised not only Girsu, the capital, and the cities of Lagash and Nina (Zurghul) but also many smaller localities and even a seaport, Guabba. Yet it is not clear to what extent the conquered regions were also integrated administratively. On one occasion UruKAgina used the formula "from the limits of Ningirsu [that is, the city god of Girsu] to the sea," having in mind a distance of up to 125 miles. It would be unwise to harbour any exaggerated notion of well-organized states exceeding that size.

For many years, scholarly views were conditioned by the concept of the Sumerian temple city, which was used to convey the idea of an organism whose ruler, as representative of his god,

LUGALZAGESI

Lugalzagesi (Lugalzaggisi), who reigned c. 2375–50 BC, was the ensi ("sacred king") of the southern Mesopotamian city of Umma. He conquered the major cities of Lagash (c. 2375 BC) and Kish, then overcame the Sumerian cities of Ur and Erech (Uruk); he alone represents the third dynasty of Erech. After uniting all of Sumer, he extended his dominion to the Mediterranean coast; but, after a reign of 25 years, he lost his empire to the ascendant dynasty of Sargon, the powerful Semitic ruler of Akkad.

theoretically owned all land, privately held agricultural land being a rare exception. The concept of the temple city had its origin partly in the overinterpretation of a passage in the so-called reform texts of UruKAgina, that states "on the field of the *ensi* [or his wife and the crown prince], the city god Ningirsu [or the city goddess Baba and the divine couple's son]" had been "reinstated as owners." On the other hand, the statements in the archives of the temple of Baba in Girsu, dating from Lugalanda and UruKAgina, were held to be altogether representative. Here is a system of administration, directed by the *ensi*'s spouse or by a *sangu* (head steward of a temple), in which every economic process, including commerce, stands in a direct relationship to the temple: agriculture, vegetable gardening, tree farming, cattle raising and the processing of animal products, fishing, and the payment in merchandise of workers and employees.

The conclusion from this analogy proved to be dangerous because the archives of the temple of Baba provide information about only a portion of the total temple administration and that portion, furthermore, is limited in time. Understandably enough, the private sector, which of course was not controlled by the temple, is scarcely mentioned at all in these archives. The existence of such a sector is nevertheless documented by bills of sale for land purchases of the pre-Sargonic period and from various localities. Written in Sumerian as well as in Akkadian, they prove the existence of private land ownership or, in the opinion of some scholars, of lands predominantly held as undivided family property. Although a substantial part of the population was forced to work for the temple and drew its pay and board from it, it is not yet known whether it was year-round work.

It is probable, if unfortunate, that there will never exist a detailed and numerically accurate picture of the demographic structure of a Sumerian city. It is assumed that in the oldest cities the government was in a position to summon sections of the populace for the performance of public works. The construction of monumental buildings or the excavation of long and deep canals could be carried out only by means of such a levy.

The large-scale employment of indentured persons and of slaves is of no concern in this context. Evidence of male slavery is fairly rare before Ur III, and even in Ur III and in the Old Babylonian period slave labour was never an economically relevant factor. It was different with female slaves. According to one document, the temple of Baba employed 188 such women. The temple of the goddess Nanshe employed 180, chiefly in grinding flour and in the textile industry, and this continued to be the case in later times. For accuracy's sake it should be added that the terms "male slave" and "female slave" are used here in the significance they possessed about 2,000 and later, designating persons in bondage who were bought and sold and who could not acquire personal property through their labour. A distinction is made between captured slaves (prisoners of war and kidnapped persons) and others who had been sold.

In one inscription, Entemena of Lagash boasts of having "allowed the sons of Erech, Larsa, and Bad-tibira to return to their mothers" and of having "restored them into the hands" of the respective city god or goddess. Read in the light of similar but more explicit statements of later date, this laconic formula represents the oldest known evidence of the fact that the ruler occasionally endeavoured to mitigate social injustices by means of a decree. Such decrees might refer to the suspension or complete cancellation of debts or to exemption from public works. Whereas a set of inscriptions of the last ruler from the first dynasty of Lagash, UruKAgina, has long been considered a prime document of social reform in the third millennium, the designation "reform texts" is only partly justified. Reading between the lines, it is possible to discern that tensions had arisen between the "palace"—the ruler's residence with its annex, administrative staff, and landed properties—and the "clergy"—that is, the stewards and priests of the temples. In seeming defiance of his own interests, UruKAgina, who in contrast to practically all of his predecessors lists no genealogy and has therefore been suspected of having been a usurper, defends the clergy, whose plight he describes somewhat tearfully.

If the foregoing passage about restoring the *ensi*'s fields to the divinity is interpreted carefully, it would follow that the situation of the temple was ameliorated and that palace lands were assigned to the priests. Along with these measures, which resemble the policies of a newcomer forced to lean on a specific party, are found others that do merit the designation of "measures taken toward the alleviation of social injustices"—for instance, the granting of delays in the payment of debts or their outright cancellation and the setting up of prohibitions to keep the economically or socially more powerful from forcing his inferior to sell his house, his ass's foal, and the like. Besides this, there were tariff regulations, such as newly established fees for weddings and burials, as well as the precise regulation of the food rations of garden workers.

Ur-Nanshe, king of Lagash, detail of a limestone relief, c. 2500 BC; in the Louvre, Paris. © Photos.com/Jupiterimage

These conditions, described on the basis of source materials from Girsu, may well have been paralleled elsewhere, but it is equally possible that other archives, yet to be found in other cities of pre-Sargonic southern Mesopotamia, may furnish entirely new historical aspects. At any rate, it is wiser to proceed cautiously, keeping to analysis and evaluation of the available material rather than making generalizations.

This, then, is the horizon of Mesopotamia shortly before the rise of the Akkadian empire. In Mari, writing was introduced at the latest about the mid-26th century BC, and from that time this city, situated on the middle Euphrates, forms an important centre of cuneiform civilization, especially in regard to its Semitic component. Ebla (and probably many other sites in ancient Syria) profited from the influence of Mari scribal schools. Reaching out across the Diyālā region and the Persian Gulf, Mesopotamian influences extended to Iran, where Susa is mentioned along with Elam and other, not yet localized, towns. In the west the Amanus Mountains were known, and under Lugalzagesi the "upper sea"—in other words, the Mediterranean—is mentioned for the first time. To the east the inscriptions of Ur-Nanshe of Lagash name the isle of Dilmun (modern Bahrain), which may have been even then a transshipment point for trade with the Oman coast and the Indus region, the Magan and Meluhha of more recent texts. Trade with Anatolia and Afghanistan was nothing new in the third millennium, even if these regions are not yet listed by their names. It was the task of the Akkadian dynasty to unite within these boundaries a territory that transcended the dimensions of a state of the type represented by Lagash.

SARGON'S REIGN

According to the Sumerian king list, the first five rulers of Akkad (Sargon, Rimush, Manishtusu, Naram-Sin, and Shar-kali-sharri) ruled for a total of 142 years; Sargon alone ruled for 56. Although these figures cannot be checked, they are probably trustworthy, because the king list for Ur III, even if 250 years later, did transmit dates that proved to be accurate.

As stated in an annotation to his name in the king list, Sargon started out as a cupbearer to King Ur-Zababa of Kish. There is an Akkadian legend about Sargon, describing how he was exposed after birth, brought up by a gardener, and later beloved by the goddess Ishtar. Nevertheless, no historical data about his career exist. Yet it is feasible to assume that in his case a high court office served as springboard for a dynasty of his own. The original inscriptions of the kings of Akkad that have come down to posterity are brief, and their geographic distribution generally is more informative than is their content.

The main sources for Sargon's reign, with its high points and catastrophes, are copies made by Old Babylonian scribes in Nippur from the very extensive

Stone relief depicting Sargon (c. 2334–c. 2279 BC) standing before a tree of life; in the Louvre, Paris. © Photos.com/Jupiterimages

originals that presumably had been kept there. They are in part Akkadian, in part bilingual Sumerian-Akkadian texts. According to these texts, Sargon fought against the Sumerian cities of southern Babylonia, threw down city walls, took prisoner 50 *ensis*, and "cleansed his weapons in the sea." He is also said to have captured Lugalzagesi of Erech, the former ruler of Umma, who had vigorously attacked UruKAgina in Lagash, forcing his neck under a yoke and leading him thus to the gate of the god Enlil at Nippur. "Citizens of Akkad" filled the offices of *ensi* from the "nether sea" (the Persian Gulf) upward, which was perhaps a device used by Sargon to further his dynastic aims.

Aside from the 34 battles fought in the south, Sargon also tells of conquests in northern Mesopotamia: Mari, Tuttul on the Balīkh, where he venerated the god Dagan (Dagon), Ebla (Tall Mardīkh in Syria), the "cedar forest" (Amanus or Lebanon), and the "silver mountains"; battles in Elam and the foothills of the Zagros are mentioned. Sargon also relates that ships from Meluhha (Indus region), Magan (possibly the coast of Oman), and Dilmun (Bahrain) made fast in the port of Akkad.

Impressive as they are at first sight, these reports have only a limited value because they cannot be arranged chronologically, and it is not known whether Sargon built a large empire. Akkadian tradition itself saw it in this light, however, and a learned treatise of the late eighth or the seventh century lists no fewer than 65 cities and lands belonging to that empire. Yet, even if Magan and Kapturu (Crete) are given as the eastern and western limits of the conquered territories, it is impossible to transpose this to the third millennium.

Sargon appointed one of his daughters priestess of the moon god in Ur. She took the name of Enheduanna and was succeeded in the same office by Enmenanna, a daughter of Naram-Sin. Enheduanna must have been a very gifted woman; two Sumerian hymns by her have been preserved, and she is also said to have been instrumental in starting a collection of songs dedicated to the temples of Babylonia.

Sargon died at a very old age. The inscriptions, also preserved only in copies, of his son Rimush are full of reports about battles fought in Sumer and Iran, just as if there had never been a Sargonic empire. It is not known in detail how rigorously Akkad wished to control the cities to the south and how much freedom had been left to them; but they presumably clung tenaciously to their inherited local autonomy. From a practical point of view, it was probably in any case impossible to organize an empire that would embrace all Mesopotamia.

Since the reports (i.e., copies of inscriptions) left by Manishtusu, Naram-Sin, and Shar-kali-sharri speak time and again of rebellions and victorious battles and since Rimush, Manishtusu, and Shar-kali-sharri are themselves said to have died violent deaths, the problem of what remained of Akkad's greatness obtrudes.

Wars and disturbances, the victory of one and the defeat of another, and even regicide constitute only some of the aspects suggested to us by the sources. Whenever they extended beyond the immediate Babylonian neighbourhood, the military campaigns of the Akkadian kings were dictated primarily by trade interests instead of being intended to serve the conquest and safeguarding of an empire. Akkad, or more precisely the king, needed merchandise, money, and gold in order to finance wars, buildings, and the system of administration that he had instituted.

On the other hand, the original inscriptions that have been found so far of a king like Naram-Sin are scattered at sites covering a distance of some 620 miles (998 km) as the crow flies, following the Tigris downriver: Diyarbakır on the upper Tigris, Nineveh, Tall Birāk (Tell Brak) on the upper Khābūr River (which had an Akkadian fortress and garrison), Susa in Elam, as well as Marad, Puzrish-Dagan, Adab (Bismāyah), Nippur, Ur, and Girsu in Babylonia. Even if all this was not part of an empire, it surely constituted an impressive sphere of influence.

Also to be considered are other facts that weigh more heavily than high-sounding reports of victories that cannot be verified. After the first kings of the dynasty had borne the title of king of Kish, Naram-Sin assumed the title "king of the four quarters of the earth"—that is, of the universe. As if he were in fact divine, he also had his name written with the cuneiform sign "god," the divine determinative that was customarily used in front of the names of gods; furthermore, he assumed the title of "god of Akkad." It is legitimate to ask whether the concept of deification may be used in the sense of elevation to a rank equal to that of the gods. At the very least it must be acknowledged that, in relation to his city and his subjects, the king saw himself in the role played by the local divinity as protector of the city and guarantor of its well-being. In contemporary judicial documents from Nippur, the oath is often taken "by Naram-Sin," with a formula identical with that used in swearing by a divinity. Documents from Girsu contain Akkadian date formulas of the type "in the year in which Naram-Sin laid the foundations of the Enlil temple at Nippur and of the Inanna temple at Zabalam." As evidenced by the dating procedures customary in Ur III and in the Old Babylonian period, the use of such formulas presupposes that the respective city acknowledged as its overlord the ruler whose name is invoked.

ASCENDANCY OF AKKAD

Under Akkad, the Akkadian language acquired a literary prestige that made it the equal of Sumerian. Under the influence, perhaps, of an Akkadian garrison at Susa, it spread beyond the borders of Mesopotamia. After having employed for several centuries an indigenous script patterned after cuneiform writing, Elam adopted Mesopotamian script during the Akkadian period and with a few exceptions used it even when writing in Elamite rather than Sumerian or Akkadian. The so-called Old Akkadian manner of writing is extraordinarily appealing from the aesthetic point of view; as late as the Old Babylonian era it served as a model for monumental inscriptions. Similarly, the plastic and graphic arts, especially sculpture in the round, relief work, and cylinder seals, reached a high point of perfection.

Thus the reign of the five kings of Akkad may be considered one of the most productive periods of Mesopotamian history. Although separatist forces opposed all unifying tendencies, Akkad brought about a broadening of political horizons and dimensions. The period of Akkad fascinated historiographers as did few other eras. Having contributed its share to the storehouse of legend, it has never disappeared from memory. With phrases such as "There will come a king of the four quarters of the earth," liver omens (soothsaying done by analyzing the shape of a sheep's liver) of the Old Babylonian period express the yearning for unity at a time when Babylonia had once again disintegrated into a dozen or more small states.

THE END OF THE DYNASTY

Of the kings after Shar-kali-sharri (c. 2217–c. 2193), only the names and a few brief inscriptions have survived. Quarrels arose over the succession, and the dynasty went under, although modern scholars know as little about the individual stages of this decline as about

the rise of Akkad. Two factors contributed to its downfall: the invasion of the nomadic Amurrus (Amorites), called Martu by the Sumerians, from the northwest, and the infiltration of the Gutians, who came, apparently, from the region between the Tigris and the Zagros Mountains to the east. This argument, however, may be a vicious circle, as these invasions were provoked and facilitated by the very weakness of Akkad. In Ur III the Amorites, in part already sedentary, formed one ethnic component along with Sumerians and Akkadians. The Gutians, on the other hand, played only a temporary role, even if the memory of a Gutian dynasty persisted until the end of the 17th century BC. As a matter of fact, the wholly negative opinion that even some modern historians have of the Gutians is based solely on a few stereotyped statements by the Sumerians and Akkadians, especially on the victory inscription of Utu-hegal of Erech (c. 2116–c. 2110). While Old Babylonian sources give the region between the Tigris and the Zagros Mountains as the home of the Gutians, these people probably also lived on the middle Euphrates during the third millennium. According to the Sumerian king list, the Gutians held the "kingship" in southern Mesopotamia for about 100 years. It has long been recognized that there is no question of a whole century of undivided Gutian rule and that some 50 years of this rule coincided with the final half century of Akkad. From this period there has

SOCIAL AND CULTURAL RECORDS

Sumerian inscription, detail of a diorite statue of Gudea of Lagash, 22nd century BC; in the Louvre, Paris. Archives Photographiques

Surviving epigraphic matter from the third and early second millennia BC includes both historical and quasi-historical material. The Sumerian king list is a compilation of names, places, and wholly fabulous dates and exploits, apparently edited to show and promote time-hallowed oneness of kingship in the face of the splintered city-states of the period. The Sargon Chronicle is a piece of literary legendry concentrating on spectacular figures and feats of the past, whereas contemporary royal inscriptions, notably by Sargon I of Akkad and Gudea of Lagash, are historical documents in the proper sense.

Both kinds of texts are preserved also from the Babylonian and Assyrian periods, from the reign of Hammurabi (1792–1750 BC) to the sixth century BC. There are lists of date formulas and year names from Hammurabi's reign and from that of his son Samsuiluna; lists of Assyrian eponymous year names, based on those of dignitaries; the Babylonian king lists, running from Hammurabi through the Kassite era and the Assyrian domination of Babylon to the last flicker of Babylonian self-assertion in the early sixth century BC; the Assyrian king list from Khorsabad, which made good use of earlier compilations; and notably the so-called Synchronistic Chronicle, which juxtaposed the kings of Assyria and Babylonia in the same millennial sequence. Historical documents comprise, above all, the stately sequence of annals by the kings of Assyria, recorded on stone slabs, stelae, foundation markers of buildings, bronze gates, statues, and obelisks and in clay archives (prisms, cylinders, tablets). Starting in the Old Assyrian period, they were especially extensive in the reigns of Tiglath-pileser I (1115–1077 BC), Ashurnasirpal II (883–859 BC), Shalmaneser III (858–824 BC), Adad-nirari III (810–783 BC), Tiglath-pileser III (744–727 BC), Shalmaneser V (726–722 BC), Sargon II (721–705 BC), Sennacherib (704–681 BC), Esarhaddon (c. 680–669 BC), and Ashurbanipal (668–627 BC).

For all their swaggering bombast and flaunting of deliberate cruelty, the annals provide prime historical source material. The detail of the Assyrian conquest of Syria, Palestine, parts of Asia Minor, Cyprus, Arabia, and Egypt would be spotty indeed without recourse to these annals, for they show the centre of political power, unlike such provincial records as those from contemporary Egypt or the Bible.

also been preserved a record of a "Gutian interpreter." As it is altogether doubtful whether the Gutians had made any city of southern Mesopotamia their "capital" instead of controlling Babylonia more or less informally from outside, scholars cautiously refer to "viceroys" of this people. The Gutians have left no material records, and the original inscriptions about them are so scanty that no binding statements about them are possible.

The Gutians' influence probably did not extend beyond Umma. The neighbouring state of Lagash enjoyed a century of complete independence, between Shar-kali-sharri and the beginning of Ur III, during which time it showed expansionist tendencies and had widely ranging trade connections. Of the *ensi* Gudea, a contemporary of Ur-Nammu of Ur III, there are extant writings, exclusively Sumerian in language, which are of inestimable value. He had the time, power, and means to carry out an extensive program of temple construction during his reign, and in a hymn divided into two parts and preserved in two clay cylinders 12 inches (30 centimetres) high he describes explicitly the reconstruction of Eninnu, the temple of the god Ningirsu. Comprising 1,363 lines, the text is second in length only to Eannatum's Stele of Vultures among the literary works of the Sumerians up to that time. While Gudea forges a link, in his literary style, with his country's pre-Sargonic period, his work also bears the unmistakable stamp of the period of Akkad. Thus, the regions that

furnish him building materials reflect the geographic horizon of the empire of Akkad, and the *ensi*'s title "god of his city" recalls the "god of Akkad" (Naram-Sin). The building hymn contains interesting particulars about the work force deployed. "Levies" were organized in various parts of the country, and the city of Girsu itself "followed the *ensi* as though it were a single man." Unfortunately lacking are synchronous administrative archives of sufficient length to provide less summarily compiled information about the social structure of Lagash at the beginning of the third dynasty of Ur. After the great pre-Sargonic archives of the Baba temple at Girsu, only the various administrative archives of the kings of Ur III give a closer look at the functioning of a Mesopotamian state.

THE THIRD DYNASTY OF UR

Utu-hegal of Erech (Uruk) is given credit for having overthrown Gutian rule by vanquishing their king Tiriqan along with two generals. Utu-hegal calls himself lord of the four quarters of the earth in an inscription, but this title, adopted from Akkad, is more likely to signify political aspiration than actual rule. Utu-hegal was a brother of the Ur-Nammu who founded the third dynasty of Ur ("third" because it is the third time that Ur is listed in the Sumerian king list). Under Ur-Nammu and his successors Shulgi, Amar-Su'ena, Shu-Sin, and Ibbi-Sin, this dynasty lasted for a century (c. 2112–c. 2004). Ur-Nammu was at first "governor" of the city of Ur under Utu-hegal. How he became king is not known, but there may well be some parallels between his rise and the career of Ishbi-Erra of Isin or, indeed, that of Sargon. By eliminating the state of Lagash, Ur-Nammu caused the coveted overseas trade (Dilmun, Magan, and Meluhha) to flow through Ur. As evidenced by a new royal title that he was the first to bear—that of "king of Sumer and Akkad"—he had built up a state that comprised at least the southern part of Mesopotamia. Like all great rulers, he built much, including the very impressive ziggurats of Ur and Erech, which acquired their final monumental dimensions in his reign.

Assyriologists have given the name of Code of Ur-Nammu to a literary monument that is the oldest known example of a genre extending through the Code of Lipit-Ishtar in Sumerian to the Code of Hammurabi, written in Akkadian. (Some scholars have attributed it to Ur-Nammu's son Shulgi.) It is a collection of sentences or verdicts mostly following the pattern of "If A [assumption], it follows that B [legal consequence]." The collection is framed by a prologue and an epilogue. The original was most likely a stela, but all that is known of the Code of Ur-Nammu so far are Old Babylonian copies. The term code as used here is conventional terminology and should not give the impression of any kind of "codified" law;

furthermore, the content of the Code of Ur-Nammu is not yet completely known. It deals, among other things, with adultery by a married woman, the defloration of someone else's female slave, divorce, false accusation, the escape of slaves, bodily injury, and the granting of security, as well as with legal cases arising from agriculture and irrigation.

Before its catastrophic end under Ibbi-Sin, the state of Ur III does not seem to have suffered setbacks and rebellions as grievous as those experienced by Akkad. There are no clear indications pointing to inner unrest, although it must be remembered that the first 20 years of Shulgi's reign are still hidden in darkness. However, from that point on until the beginning of Ibbi-Sin's reign, or for a period of 50 years at least, the sources give the impression of peace enjoyed by a country that lived undisturbed by encroachments from abroad. Some expeditions were sent into foreign lands, to the region bordering on the Zagros, to what later became Assyria, and to the vicinity of Elam, in order to secure the importation of raw materials, in a fashion reminiscent of Akkad. Force seems to have been employed only as a last resort, and every attempt was made to bring about peaceful conditions on the other side of the border through the dispatch of embassies or the establishment of family bonds—for example, by marrying the king's daughters to foreign rulers.

Shulgi, too, called himself king of the four quarters of the earth. Although he resided in Ur, another important centre was in Nippur, whence—according to the prevailing ideology—Enlil, the chief god in the Sumerian state pantheon, had bestowed on Shulgi the royal dignity. Shulgi and his successors enjoyed divine honours, as Naram-Sin of Akkad had before them; by now, however, the process of deification had taken on clearer outlines in that sacrifices were offered and chapels built to the king and his throne, while the royal determinative turned up in personal names. Along with an Utu-hegal ("The Sun God Is Exuberance") there appears a Shulgi-hegal ("Shulgi Is Exuberance"), and so forth.

ADMINISTRATION

The highest official of the state was the *sukkal-mah*, literally "supreme courier," whose position may be described as "(state) chancellor." The empire was divided into some 40 provinces ruled by as many *ensi*s, who, despite their far-reaching authority (civil administration and judicial powers), were no longer autonomous, even if only indirectly, although the office was occasionally handed down from father to son. They could not enter into alliances or wage wars on their own. The *ensi*s were appointed by the king and could probably also be transferred by him to other provinces. Each of these provinces was obliged to pay a yearly tribute, the amount of which was negotiated by emissaries. Of special significance in this was a system called *bala*, "cycle" or "rotation," in which the *ensi*s of the southern provinces took part; among other things, they had to keep the state stockyards supplied with sacrificial animals. Although the "province" often corresponded to a former city-state, many others were no doubt newly established. The so-called land-register text of Ur-Nammu describes four such provinces north of Nippur, giving the precise boundaries and ending in each case with the statement, "King Ur-Nammu has confirmed the field of the god XX for the god XX." In some cities, notably in Erech, Mari, or Dēr (near what is now Badrah, Iraq), the administration was in the hands of a *šakkana*, a man whose title is rendered partly by "governor" and partly by "general."

The available histories are practically unanimous in seeing in Ur III a strongly centralized state marked by the king's position as absolute ruler. Nevertheless, some caution is indicated. For one thing, the need to deal as carefully as possible with the *ensi*s must not be underestimated. A further question arises from the borders between and relative extent of the "public" and the "private" sector; the latter's importance may have been underrated as well. What is meant by "private" sector is a population group with land of its own and with revenues not directly granted by a temple or a "palace," such as by the king's or an *ensi*'s household. The traditional picture is derived from the sources, the state archives of Puzrish-Dagan, a gigantic "stockyard" situated outside the gates of Nippur, which supplied the city's temples with sacrificial animals but inevitably also comprised a major wool and leather industry; other such archives are those of Umma, Girsu, Nippur, and Ur. All these activities were overseen by a finely honed bureaucracy that stressed the use of official channels, efficient administration, and precise accounting. The various administrative organs communicated with one another by means of a smoothly functioning network of messengers. Although almost 24,000 documents referring to the economy of Ur III have so far been published, the majority of them are still waiting to be properly evaluated. Nor is there yet a serviceable typology for them; only when that has been drawn up will it be possible to write a book entitled "The Economic System of Ur III." Represented in the main by contracts (loans, leases of temple land, the purchase of slaves, and the like), the "private" sector makes up only a small part of this mass of textual material. Neither can the sites at which discoveries have been made so far be taken as representative. In northern Babylonia, for example, scarcely any contemporary written documents have yet been recovered.

ETHNIC, GEOGRAPHIC, AND INTELLECTUAL CONSTITUENTS

From the ethnic point of view, Mesopotamia was as heterogeneous at the end of the third millennium as it had been earlier. The Akkadian element predominated, and the proportion of speakers of Akkadian to speakers of Sumerian continued to change in favour of the former. The third group, first mentioned under Shar-kali-sharri of Akkad, are the Amorites. In Ur III some members of this people are already found in the higher echelons of the administration, but most of them, organized in tribes, still led a nomadic life. Their great days came in the Old Babylonian period. While clearly differing linguistically from Akkadian, the Amorite language, which can be reconstructed to some extent from more than a thousand proper names, is fairly closely related to the so-called Canaanite branch of the Semitic languages, of which it may in fact represent an older form. The fact that King Shu-Sin had a regular wall built clear across the land, the "wall that keeps out the Tidnum" (the name of a tribe), shows how strong the pressure of the nomads was in the 21st century and what efforts were made to check their influx. The fourth major ethnic group was the Hurrians, who were especially important in northern Mesopotamia and in the vicinity of modern Kirkūk.

It is likely that the geographic horizon of the empire of Ur III did not materially exceed that of the empire of Akkad. No names of localities in the interior of Anatolia have been found, but there was much coming and going of messengers between Mesopotamia and Iran, far beyond Elam. There is also one mention of Gubla (Byblos) on the Mediterranean coast. Oddly enough, there is no evidence of any relations with Egypt, either in Ur III or in the Old Babylonian period. It is odd if no contacts existed at the end of the third millennium between the two great civilizations of the ancient Middle East.

Intellectual life at the time of Ur III must have been very active in the cultivation and transmission of older literature, as well as in new creations. Although its importance as a spoken tongue was slowly diminishing, Sumerian still flourished as a written language, a state of affairs that continued into the Old Babylonian period. As shown by the hymn to the deified king, new literary genres arose in Ur III. If Old Babylonian copies are any indication, the king's correspondence with leading officials was also of a high literary level.

In the long view, the third dynasty of Ur did not survive in historical memory as vigorously as did Akkad. To be sure, Old Babylonian historiography speaks of Ur III as *bala-Šulgi*, the "(reigning) cycle of Shulgi"; however, there is nothing that would correspond to the epic poems about Sargon and Naram-Sin. The reason is not clear, but it is conceivable that the later, purely Akkadian population felt a closer identification with Akkad than with a state that to a large extent still made use of the Sumerian language.

Ur III in Decline

The decline of Ur III is an event in Mesopotamian history that can be followed in greater detail than other stages of that history thanks to sources such as the royal correspondence, two elegies on the destruction of Ur and Sumer, and an archive from Isin that shows how Ishbi-Erra, as usurper and king of Isin, eliminated his former overlord in Ur. Ibbi-Sin was waging war in Elam when an ambitious rival came forward in the person of Ishbi-Erra from Mari, presumably a general or high official. By emphasizing to the utmost the danger threatening from the Amorites, Ishbi-Erra urged the king to entrust to him the protection of the neighbouring cities of Isin and Nippur. Ishbi-Erra's demand came close to extortion, and his correspondence shows how skillfully he dealt with the Amorites and with individual *ensis*, some of whom soon went over to his side. Ishbi-Erra also took advantage of the depression that the king suffered because the god Enlil "hated him," a phrase presumably referring to bad omens resulting from the examination of sacrificed animals, on which procedure many rulers based their actions (or, as the case may be, their inaction).

Ishbi-Erra fortified Isin and, in the 10th year of Ibbi-Sin's reign, began to employ his own dating formulas on documents, an act tantamount to a renunciation of loyalty. Ishbi-Erra, for his part, believed himself to be the favourite of Enlil, the more so as he ruled over Nippur, where the god had his sanctuary. In the end he claimed suzerainty over all of southern Mesopotamia, including Ur.

While Ishbi-Erra purposefully strengthened his domains, Ibbi-Sin continued for 14 more years to rule over a decreasing portion of the land. The end of Ur came about through a concatenation of misfortunes. A famine broke out, and Ur was besieged, taken, and destroyed by the invading Elamites and their allies among the Iranian tribes. Ibbi-Sin was led away captive, and no more was heard of him. The elegies record in moving fashion the unhappy end of Ur, the catastrophe that had been brought about by the wrath of Enlil.

CHAPTER 3

THE OLD BABYLONIAN PERIOD

During the collapse of Ur III, Ishbi-Erra established himself in Isin and founded a dynasty there that lasted from 2017 to 1794. His example was followed elsewhere by local rulers, as in Dēr, Eshnunna, Sippar, Kish, and Larsa. In many localities an urge was felt to imitate the model of Ur; Isin probably took over unchanged the administrative system of that state. Ishbi-Erra and his successors had themselves deified, as did one of the rulers of Dēr, on the Iranian border. For almost a century Isin predominated within the mosaic of states that were slowly reemerging. Overseas trade revived after Ishbi-Erra had driven out the Elamite garrison from Ur, and under his successor, Shu-ilishu, a statue of the moon god Nanna, the city god of Ur, was recovered from the Elamites.

Up to the reign of Lipit-Ishtar (c. 1934–c. 1924), the rulers of Isin so resembled those of Ur, as far as the king's assessment of himself in the hymns is concerned, that it seems almost arbitrary to postulate a break between Ibbi-Sin and Ishbi-Erra. As a further example of continuity it might be added that the Code of Lipit-Ishtar stands exactly midway chronologically between the Code of Ur-Nammu and the Code of Hammurabi. Yet it is much closer to the former in language and especially in legal philosophy than to Hammurabi's compilation of judgments. For example, the Code of Lipit-Ishtar does not know the lex talionis ("an eye for an eye and a tooth for a tooth"), the guiding principle of Hammurabi's penal law.

POLITICAL FRAGMENTATION

It is probable that the definitive separation from Ur III came about through changing components of the population, from "Sumerians and Akkadians" to "Akkadians and Amorites." An Old Babylonian liver omen states that "he of the steppes will enter, and chase out the one in the city." This is indeed an abbreviated formula for an event that took place more than once, the usurpation of the king's throne in the city by the "sheikh" of some Amorite tribe. These usurpations were regularly carried out as part of the respective tribes became settled, although this was not so in the case of Isin because the house of Ishbi-Erra came from Mari and was of Akkadian origin, to judge by the rulers' names. By the same linguistic token the dynasty of Larsa was Amorite. The fifth ruler of the latter dynasty, Gungunum (ruled c. 1932–c. 1906), conquered Ur and established himself as the equal and rival of Isin; at this stage—the end of the 20th century BC—if not before, Ur had certainly outlived itself.

From Gungunum until the temporary unification of Mesopotamia under Hammurabi, the political picture was determined by the disintegration of the balance of power, by incessant vacillation of alliances, by the presumption of the various rulers, by the fear of encroachments by the Amorite nomads, and by increasingly wretched social conditions. The extensive archive of correspondence from the royal palace of Mari (c. 1810–1750) is the best source of information about the political and diplomatic game and its rules, whether honoured or broken. It covers treaties, the dispatch and reception of embassies, agreements about the integration of allied armies, espionage, and "situation reports" from "foreign" courts. Devoid of exaggeration or stylization, these letters, dealing as they do with everyday events, are preferable to the numerous royal inscriptions on buildings, even when the latter contain historical allusions.

LITERARY TEXTS AND INCREASING DECENTRALIZATION

Another indirect but far from negligible source for the political and socioeconomic situation in the 20th–18th centuries BC is the literature of omens. These are long compendiums in which the condition of a sheep's liver or some other divinatory object (for instance, the behaviour of a drop of oil in a beaker filled with water, the appearance of a newborn baby, and the shape of rising clouds of incense) is described at length and commented on with the appropriate prediction: "The king will kill his dignitaries and distribute their houses and property among the temples"; "A powerful man will ascend the throne in a foreign city"; "The land that rose up against its 'shepherd' will continue to be ruled by that 'shepherd'"; "The king will depose his chancellor"; and "They will lock the city gate and there will be a calamity in the city."

Beginning with Gungunum of Larsa, the texts allow greater insight into the private sector than in any other previous period. There is a considerable increase in the number of private contracts and private correspondences. Especially frequent among the private contracts are those concluded about loans of silver or grain (barley), illustrating the common man's plight, especially when driven to seek out a creditor, the first step on a road that in many instances led to ruin. The rate of interest, fixed at 20 percent in the case of silver and 33 percent in that of grain, increased further if the deadline for repayment, usually at harvest time, was not kept. Insolvency resulted in imprisonment for debt, slavery by mortgage, and even the sale of children and the debtor's own person. Many private letters contain entreaties for the release of family members from imprisonment at the creditor's hands. Yet considerable fortunes were also made, in "liquid" capital as well as landed property. As these tendencies threatened to end in economic disaster, the kings prescribed as a corrective the liquidation of debts, by way of temporary alleviation at least. The exact wording of one such decree is known from the time of Ammiṣaduqa of Babylon.

Until the Ur III period, the only archives so far recovered dealt with temples or the palace. However, belonging to the Old Babylonian period, along with documents pertaining to civil law, were an increasing number of administrative records of privately managed households, inns, and farms: settlements of accounts, receipts, and notes on various transactions. Here was clearly a regular bourgeoisie, disposing of its own land and possessing means independent of temple and palace. Trade, too, was now chiefly in private hands. The merchant traveled (or sent his partners) at his own risk, not on behalf of the state. Among the civil-law contracts there was a substantial increase in records of land purchases.

Also significant for the economic situation in the Old Babylonian era was a process that might be summarized as "secularization of the temples," even if all the stages of this development cannot be traced. The palace had probably possessed for centuries the authority to dispose of temple property, but, whereas UruKAgina of Lagash had still branded the tendency as leading to abuses, the citizen's relationship to the temple now took on individual traits. Revenues from certain priestly offices—benefices, in other words—went to private individuals and were sold and inherited. The process had begun in Ur, where the king bestowed benefices, although the recipients could not own them. The archives of the "canonesses" of the sun god of Sippar furnish a particularly striking example of the fusion of religious service and private economic interest. These women, who lived in a convent called *gagûm*, came from the city's leading families and were not allowed to marry. With their property, consisting of land and silver, they engaged in a lively and remunerative business by granting loans and leasing out fields.

The tendency toward decentralization had begun in the Old Babylonian period with Isin. It concluded with the 72-year reign of the house of Kudur-Mabuk in Larsa (c. 1834–c. 1763). Kudur-Mabuk, sheikh of the Amorite tribe of the Jamutbal, despite his Elamite name, helped his son Warad-Sin to secure the throne. This usurpation allowed Larsa, which had passed through a period of internal unrest, to flourish one more time. Under Warad-Sin and in the long reign of his brother Rim-Sin, large portions of southern Babylonia, including Nippur, were once again united in one state of Larsa in 1794. Larsa was conquered by Hammurabi in 1763.

EARLY HISTORY OF ASSYRIA

Strictly speaking, the use of the name "Assyria" for the period before the latter half of the second millennium BC is anachronistic. Assyria—as against the city-state of Ashur—did not become an independent state until about 1400 BC. For convenience, however, the term is used throughout this section.

In contrast to southern Mesopotamia or the mid-Euphrates region (Mari), written sources in Assyria do not begin until very late, shortly before Ur III. By Assyria—a region that does not lend itself to precise geographic delineation—is understood the territory on the Tigris north of the river's passage through the mountains of the Jabal Ḥamrīn to a point north of Nineveh, as well as the area between Little and Great Zab (a tributary of the Tigris in northeast Iraq) and to the north of the latter. In the north, Assyria was later bordered by the mountain state of Urartu; to the east and southeast its neighbour was the region around ancient Nuzu (near modern Kirkūk, "Arrapchitis" [Arrapkha] of the Greeks). In the early second millennium the main cities of this region were Ashur (160 miles [257 km] north-northwest of modern Baghdad), the capital (synonymous with the city god and national divinity); Nineveh, lying opposite modern Mosul; and Urbilum, later Arbela (modern Irbīl, some 200 miles [322 km] north of Baghdad).

In Assyria, inscriptions were composed in Akkadian from the beginning. Under Ur III, Ashur was a provincial capital. Assyria as a whole, however, is not likely to have been a permanently secured part of the empire, since two date formulas of Shulgi and Amar-Su'ena mention the destruction of Urbilum. Ideas of the population of Assyria in the third millennium are necessarily very imprecise. It is not known how long Semitic tribes had been settled there. The inhabitants of southern Mesopotamia called Assyria Shubir in Sumerian and Subartu in Akkadian; these names may point to a Subarian population that was related to the Hurrians. Gasur, the later Nuzu, belonged to the Akkadian language region about the year 2200, but was lost to the Hurrians in the first quarter of the second millennium. The Assyrian dialect of Akkadian found in the beginning of the second millennium differs strongly from the dialect of Babylonia. These two versions of the Akkadian language continue into the first millennium.

In contrast to the kings of southern Mesopotamia, the rulers of Ashur styled themselves not king but partly *iššiakum*, the Akkadian equivalent of the Sumerian word *ensi*, partly *rubā'um*, or "great one." Unfortunately, the rulers cannot be synchronized precisely with the kings of southern Mesopotamia before Shamshi-Adad I (*c.* 1813–*c.* 1781 BC). For instance, it has not yet been established just when Ilushuma's excursion toward the southeast, recorded in an inscription, actually took place. Ilushuma boasts of having freed of taxes the "Akkadians and their children." While he mentions the cities of Nippur and Ur, the other localities listed were situated in the region east of the Tigris. The event itself may have taken place in the reign of Ishme-Dagan of Isin (*c.* 1953–*c.* 1935 BC), although how far Ilushuma's words correspond to the truth cannot be checked. In the Babylonian texts, at any rate, no reference is made to Assyrian intervention. The whole problem of dating is aggravated by the fact that the Assyrians did not, unlike the Babylonians, use date formulas that often contain interesting historical details; instead, every year was designated by the name of a high official (eponymic dating). The conscious cultivation of an old tradition is mirrored in the fact that two rulers of 19th-century Assyria called themselves Sargon and Naram-Sin after famous models in the Akkadian dynasty.

Aside from the generally scarce reports on projected construction, there is at present no information about the city of Ashur and its surroundings. There exists, however, unexpectedly rewarding source material from the trading colonies of Ashur in Anatolia. The texts come mainly from Kanesh (modern Kültepe, near Kayseri, in Turkey) and from Hattusa (modern Boğazköy, Tur.), the later Hittite capital. In the 19th century BC three generations of Assyrian merchants engaged in a lively commodity trade (especially in textiles and metal) between the homeland and Anatolia, also taking part profitably in internal Anatolian trade. Like their contemporaries in southern Mesopotamia, they did business privately and at their own risk, living peacefully and occasionally intermarrying with the "Anatolians." As long as they paid taxes to the local rulers, the Assyrians were given a free hand.

Clearly these forays by Assyrian merchants led to some transplanting of Mesopotamian culture into Anatolia. Thus the Anatolians adopted cuneiform writing and used the Assyrian language. While this influence doubtless already affected the first Hittites arriving in Anatolia, a direct line from the period of these trading colonies to the Hittite empire cannot yet be traced.

From about 1813 to about 1781 Assyria was ruled by Shamshi-Adad I, a contemporary of Hammurabi and a personality in no way inferior to him. Shamshi-Adad's father—an Amorite, to judge by the name—had ruled near Mari. The son, not being of Assyrian origin, ascended the throne of Assyria as a foreigner and on a detour, as it were, after having spent some time as an exile in Babylonia. He had his two sons rule as viceroys, in Ekallātum on the Tigris and in Mari, respectively, until the older of the two, Ishme-Dagan, succeeded his father on the throne. Through the archive of correspondence in the palace at Mari, scholars are particularly well informed about Shamshi-Adad's reign and many aspects of his personality. Shamshi-Adad's state had a common border for some time with the Babylonia of Hammurabi.

Soon after Shamshi-Adad's death, Mari broke away, regaining its independence under an Amorite dynasty that had been living there for generations. In the end, Hammurabi conquered and destroyed Mari. After Ishme-Dagan's death, Assyrian history is lost sight of for more than 100 years.

THE OLD BABYLONIAN EMPIRE

Hammurabi (c. 1792–c. 1750 BC) is surely the most impressive and by now the best-known figure of the ancient Middle East of the first half of the second millennium BC. He owes his posthumous reputation to the great stela into which the Code of Hammurabi was carved and indirectly also to the fact that his dynasty has made the name of Babylon famous for all time. In much the same way in which pre-Sargonic Kish exemplified the non-Sumerian area north of Sumer and Akkad lent its name to a country and a language, Babylon became the symbol of the whole country that the Greeks called Babylonia.

This term is used anachronistically by Assyriologists as a geographic concept in reference to the period before Hammurabi. Originally the city's name was probably Babilla, which was reinterpreted in popular etymology as Bāb-ili ("Gate of the God").

The first dynasty of Babylon rose from insignificant beginnings. The history of the erstwhile province of Ur is traceable from about 1894 onward, when the Amorite Sumuabum came to power there. What is known of these events fits altogether into the modest proportions of the period when Mesopotamia was a mosaic of small states. Hammurabi played skillfully on the instrument of coalitions and became more powerful than his predecessors had been. Nonetheless, it was only in the 30th year of his reign, after his conquest of Larsa, that he gave concrete expression to the idea of ruling all of southern Mesopotamia by "strengthening the foundations of Sumer and Akkad," in the words of that year's dating formula. In the prologue to the Code of Hammurabi the king lists the following cities as belonging to his dominions: Eridu near Ur, Ur, Lagash and Girsu, Zabalam, Larsa, Erech, Adab, Isin, Nippur, Keshi, Dilbat, Borsippa, Babylon itself, Kish, Malgium, Mashkan-shapir, Kutha, Sippar, Eshnunna in the Diyālā region, Mari, Tuttul on the lower Balīkh (a tributary of the Euphrates), and finally Ashur and Nineveh. This was on a scale reminiscent of Akkad or Ur III. Yet Ashur and Nineveh cannot have formed part of this empire for long because at the end of Hammurabi's reign mention is made again of wars against Subartu—that is, Assyria.

Under Hammurabi's son Samsuiluna (c. 1749–c. 1712 BC) the Babylonian empire greatly shrank in size. Following what had almost become a tradition, the south rose up in revolt. Larsa regained its autonomy for some time, and the walls of Ur, Erech, and Larsa were leveled. Eshnunna, which evidently had also seceded, was vanquished about 1730. Later chronicles mention the existence of a state in the Sealand, with its own dynasty (by "Sealand" is understood the marshlands of southern Babylonia). Knowledge of this new dynasty is unfortunately very vague, only one of its kings being documented in contemporary texts. About 1741 Samsuiluna mentions the Kassites for the first time; about 1726 he constructed a stronghold, "Fort Samsuiluna," as a bulwark against them on the Diyālā near its confluence with the Tigris.

Like the Gutians before them, the Kassites were at first prevented from entering Babylonia and pushed into the mid-Euphrates region; there, in the kingdom of Khana (centred on Mari and Terqa, both below the junction with the Khābūr River), a king appears with the Kassite name of Kashtiliashu, who ruled toward the end of the Babylonian dynasty. From Khana the Kassites moved south in small groups, probably as harvest workers. After the Hittite invasion under Mursilis I, who is said to have dethroned the last king of Babylon, Samsuditana, in 1595, the Kassites assumed the royal power in Babylonia. So far, the contemporary sources do not mention this epoch, and the question remains unresolved as to how the Kassite rulers named in king lists mesh with the end of the second millennium BC.

BABYLONIAN LAW

The Code of Hammurabi is the most frequently cited cuneiform document in specialized literature. Its first scholarly publication in 1902 led to the development of a special branch of comparative jurisprudence, the study of cuneiform law. Following the division made by the first editor, Jean-Vincent Scheil, the Code of Hammurabi contains 280 judgments, or "paragraphs," on civil and criminal law, dealing in the main with cases from everyday life in such a manner that it becomes obvious that the "lawgiver" or compiler had no intention of covering all possible contingencies.

In broad outline, the themes treated in the Code of Hammurabi are libel; corrupt administration of justice; theft, receiving stolen goods, robbery, looting, and burglary; murder, manslaughter, and bodily injury; abduction; judicature of tax lessees; liability for negligent damage to fields and crop damage caused by grazing cattle; illegal felling of palm trees; legal problems of trade enterprises, in particular, the relationship between the merchant and his employee traveling overland, and embezzlement of merchandise; trust monies; the proportion of interest to loan money; the legal position of the female publican; slavery and ransom, slavery for debt, runaway slaves, the sale and manumission of slaves, and the contesting of slave status; the rent of persons, animals, and ships and their respective tariffs, offenses committed by hired labourers, and the vicious bull; family law: the price of a bride, dowry, the married woman's property, wife and concubine, and the legal position of the respective issue, divorce, adoption, the wet nurse's contract, and inheritance; and the legal position of certain priestesses. A similar if much shorter compendium of judgments, probably antedating that of Hammurabi by a generation or two, has been discovered in Eshnunna.

Hammurabi, who called his own work *dīnāt mīŷarim,* or "verdicts of the just order," states in the epilogue that it was intended as legal aid for persons in search of advice. Whether these judgments

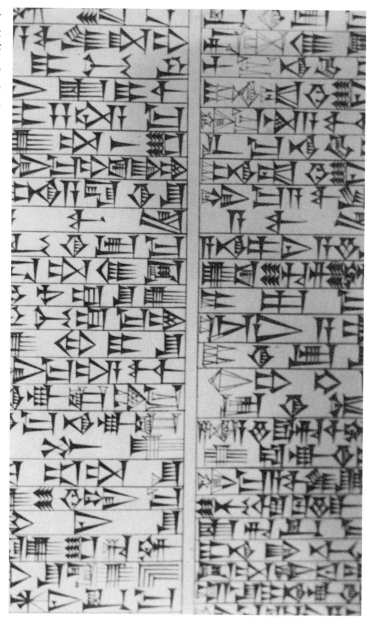

Transcribed copy of a section of the Code of Hammurabi, the ancient record of Babylonian laws named for the king whose nearly 300 legal decisions are collected therein. Kean Collection/Hulton Archive/Getty Images

were meant to have binding force in the sense of modern statutes, however, is a matter of controversy. The Code of Hammurabi differs in many respects from the Code of Lipit-Ishtar, which was written in Sumerian. Its most striking feature lies in the extraordinary severity of its penalties and in the principle of the lex talionis. The same attitude is reflected in various Old Babylonian contracts in which defaulters are threatened with bodily punishment. It is often said, and perhaps rightly so, that this severity, which so contrasts with Sumerian judicial tradition, can be traced back to the Amorite influence.

There is yet another way in which the Code of Hammurabi has given rise to much discussion. Many of its "paragraphs" vary according to whether the case concerns an *awīlum*, a *muškēnum*, or a *wardum*. A threefold division of the populace had been postulated on the basis of these distinctions. The *wardum* is the least problematic: he is the slave—that is, a person in bondage who could be bought and sold, unless he was able to regain his freedom under certain conditions as a debtor-slave. The *muškēnum* were, under King Hammurabi at least, persons employed by the palace who could be given land in usufruct without receiving it as property. *Awīlum* were the citizens who owned land in their own right and depended neither on the palace nor on the temple. As the Soviet scholar Igor M. Diakonov has pointed out, the distinction cannot have been very sharply drawn, because the classes *awīlum* and *muškēnum* are not mutually exclusive. A man in high palace office could fairly easily purchase land as private property, whereas the free citizen who got into debt as a result of a bad harvest or some other misfortune had one foot in the slave class. Still unanswered is the question as to which segment of the population could be conscripted to do public works, a term that included the levy in case of war.

Ammiṣaduqa (c. 1646–c. 1626 BC) comes a century and a half after Hammurabi. His edict, already referred to, lists, among others, the following social and economic factors: private debts in silver and grain, if arising out of loans, were canceled; also canceled were back taxes that certain officials owed the palace and that had to be collected from the people; the female publican had to renounce the collection of outstanding debts in beer and barley and was, in turn, excused from paying amounts of silver and barley to the king; taxes on leased property were reduced; debt slaves who had formerly been free (as against slaves made over from debtor to creditor) were ransomed; and high officials were forbidden on pain of death to press those who held property in fee into harvest work by prepayment of wages. The phrase "because the king gave the land a just order" serves as a rationale for many of these instances. In contrast to the codes, about whose binding force there is much doubt, edicts such as those of Ammiṣaduqa had legal validity since

BACKGROUND: CODE OF HAMMURABI

The most complete and perfect extant collection of Babylonian laws, the Code of Hammurabi consists of legal decisions inscribed on a diorite stela set up in Babylon's temple of Marduk, the national god of Babylonia.

The background of the code is a body of Sumerian law under which civilized communities had lived for many centuries. The existing text is in the Akkadian language. Yet even though no Sumerian version is known to survive, the code was meant to be applied to a wider realm than any single country and to integrate Semitic and Sumerian traditions and peoples. Moreover, despite a few primitive survivals relating to family solidarity, district responsibility, trial by ordeal, and the lex talionis (i.e., an eye for an eye, a tooth for a tooth), the code was advanced far beyond tribal custom and recognized no blood feud, private retribution, or marriage by capture.

The principal (and only considerable) source of the Code of Hammurabi is the stela discovered at Susa in 1901 by the French Orientalist Jean-Vincent Scheil and now preserved in the Louvre.

there are references to the edicts of other kings in numerous legal documents of the Old Babylonian period.

BABYLONIAN LITERATURE

The literature and the literary languages of Babylonia during the three centuries following Ur III deserve attention. When commenting on literary and historical texts such as the inscriptions of the kings of Akkad, it was pointed out that these were not originals but copies of Old Babylonian vintage. So far, such copies are the main source for Sumerian literature. Yet, while the Old Babylonian period witnessed the creation of much literature (royal hymns of the kings of Isin, Larsa, and Babylon and elegies), it was above all a time of intensive cultivation of traditional literature. The great Sumerian poems, whose origins or first written version, respectively, can now be traced back to about 2600, were copied again and again. After 2000, when Sumerian as a spoken language rapidly receded to isolated regions and eventually disappeared altogether, texts began to be translated, line by line, into Akkadian until there came to be bilingual versions.

An important part of this, especially in the instructional program in schools, were the so-called lexicographical texts. Sumerian word lists are almost as old as cuneiform writing itself; they formed the perfect material for those learning to write. In the Old Babylonian period, the individual lexical entries were translated and often annotated with phonetic signs. This led to the creation of "dictionaries," the value of which to the modern philologist cannot be exaggerated. Since Sumerian had to be taught much more than before, regular "grammatical treatises" also came into being. So far as it was possible, in view of the radically different structures of the two languages, Sumerian pronouns, verb forms, and the like were translated into Akkadian, including entire "paradigms" of individual verbs.

In belles lettres, Sumerian still predominates, although there is no lack of Akkadian masterpieces, including the oldest Akkadian version of the epic of Gilgamesh. The very high prestige still enjoyed by Sumerian should not be underestimated, and it continued to be used for inscriptions on buildings and the yearly dating formulas. Aside from being the language of practical affairs (i.e., letters and contracts), there was a high incidence of Akkadian in soothsaying and divinatory literature. To be sure, the Sumerians also practiced foretelling the future from the examination of animal entrails, but as far as is known they did not write down the results. In Akkadian, on the other hand, there are extensive and "scientifically" arranged compendiums of omens based on the liver (as well as other omens), reflecting the importance that the divination of the future had in religion, in politics, and in all aspects of daily life.

Judging by its increasingly refined juridical thought, its ability to master in writing ever more complicated administrative procedures, its advanced knowledge of mathematics, and the fact that it marks the beginning of the study of astronomy, the Old Babylonian period appears to have been a time of exceedingly active intellectual endeavour—despite, if not because of, its lack of political cohesiveness.

THE HURRIANS

The Hurrians enter the orbit of ancient Middle Eastern civilization toward the end of the third millennium BC. They arrived in Mesopotamia from the north or the east, but it is not known how long they had lived in the peripheral regions. There is a brief inscription in Hurrian language from the end of the period of Akkad, while that of King Arishen (or Atalshen) of Urkish and Nawar is written in Akkadian. The language of the Hurrians must have belonged to a widespread group of ancient Middle Eastern languages. The relationship between Hurrian and Subarian has already been mentioned, and the language of the Urartians, who played an important role from the end of the second millennium to the eighth century BC, is likewise closely related to Hurrian.

It is not known whether the migrations of the Hurrians ever took the form of aggressive invasion. Texts from 18th century BC Mari speak of battles with the Hurrian tribe of Turukku south of Lake Urmia (some 150 miles [241 km] from the Caspian Sea's southwest corner), but

HURRIAN LANGUAGE

The Hurrian language was spoken from the last centuries of the third millennium BC until at least the latter years of the Hittite empire (c. 1400–c. 1190 BC). Hurrian is neither an Indo-European language nor a Semitic language, It is generally believed that the speakers of Hurrian originally came from the Armenian mountains and spread over southeast Anatolia and northern Mesopotamia at the beginning of the second millennium BC. Before the middle of the second millennium BC, parts of Hurrian territory were under the control of an Indo-Aryan ruling class, the Mitanni, whose name was incorrectly applied to the Hurrians by early researchers.

Many sources for the language exist, including an extensive Hurrian-Hittite bilingual and numerous passages marked hurlili 'in Hurrian' found among the cuneiform tablets discovered in the ruins of the Hittite archives at Hattusa (near the modern town of Boğazkale, formerly Boğazköy, Tur.). Other Hurrian texts have been found in the cities of Urkish (Mardin region, c. 1970 BC), Mari (on the middle Euphrates, 18th century BC), Amarna (Egypt, c. 1400 BC), and Ugarit (on the coastline of northern Syria, 14th century BC). Amarna yielded the most important Hurrian document, a political letter sent to Pharaoh Amenhotep III.

Hurrian constitutes the sixth language of the Hittite archives—after Sumerian, Akkadian, Hattian, Palaic, and Luwian. The later Urartian language is thought to be descended from the same parent language as Hurrian.

these were mountain campaigns, not the warding off of an offensive. Proper names in cuneiform texts, their frequency increasing in the period of Ur III, constitute the chief evidence for the presence of Hurrians. Nevertheless, there is no clear indication that the Hurrians had already advanced west of the Tigris at that time.

An entirely different picture results from the 18th-century palace archives of Mari and from texts originating near the upper Khābūr River. Northern Mesopotamia, west of the Tigris, and Syria appear settled by a population that is mainly Amorite and Hurrian. The later had already reached the Mediterranean littoral, as shown by texts from Alalakh on the Orontes. In Mari, literary texts in Hurrian also have been found, indicating that Hurrian had by then become a fully developed written language as well.

The high point of the Hurrian period was not reached until about the middle of the second millennium. In the 15th century, Alalakh was heavily Hurrianized; and in the empire of Mitanni the Hurrians represented the leading and perhaps the most numerous population group.

CHAPTER 4

MESOPOTAMIA TO THE END OF THE ACHAEMENIAN PERIOD

About 150 years after the death of Hammurabi, his dynasty was destroyed by an invasion of new peoples. Because there are very few written records from this era, the time from about 1560 BC to about 1440 BC (in some areas until 1400 BC) is called the dark ages. The remaining Semitic states, such as the state of Ashur, became minor states within the sphere of influence of the new states of the Kassites and the Hurrians/Mitanni. The languages of the older cultures, Akkadian and Sumerian, continued or were soon reestablished, however. The cuneiform script persisted as the only type of writing in the entire area. Cultural continuity was not broken off, either, particularly in Babylonia. A matter of importance was the emergence of new Semitic leading classes from the ranks of the priesthood and the scribes. These gained increasing power.

THE KASSITES IN BABYLONIA

The Kassites had settled by 1800 BC in what is now western Iran in the region of Hamadan-Kermanshah. The first to feel their forward thrust was Samsuiluna, who had to repel groups of Kassite invaders. Increasing numbers of Kassites gradually reached Babylonia and other parts of Mesopotamia.

There they founded principalities, of which little is known. No inscription or document in the Kassite language has been preserved. Some 300 Kassite words have been found in Babylonian documents. Nor is much known about the social structure of the Kassites or their culture. There seems to have been no hereditary kingdom. Their religion was polytheistic; the names of some 30 gods are known.

The beginning of Kassite rule in Babylonia cannot be dated exactly. A king called Agum II ruled over a state that stretched from western Iran to the middle part of the Euphrates valley; 24 years after the Hittites had carried off the statue of the Babylonian god Marduk, he regained possession of the statue, brought it back to Babylon, and renewed the cult, making the god Marduk the equal of the corresponding Kassite god, Shuqamuna. Meanwhile, native princes continued to reign in southern Babylonia. It may have been Ulamburiash who finally annexed this area around 1450 and began negotiations with Egypt in Syria. Karaindash built a temple with bas-relief tile ornaments in Erech (Uruk) about 1420. A new capital west of Baghdad, Dur-Kurigalzu, competing with Babylon, was founded and named after Kurigalzu I (c. 1400–c. 1375). His successors Kadashman-Enlil I (c. 1375–c. 1360) and Burnaburiash II (c. 1360–c. 1333) were in correspondence with the Egyptian rulers Amenhotep III and Akhenaton (Amenhotep IV) regarding trading their lapis lazuli and other items for gold, as well as in planning political marriages.

Kurigalzu II (c. 1332–c. 1308) fought against the Assyrians but was defeated by them. His successors sought to ally themselves with the Hittites in order to stop the expansion of the Assyrians. During the reign of Kashtiliash IV (c. 1232–c. 1225), Babylonia waged war on two fronts at the same time—against Elam and Assyria—ending in the catastrophic invasion and destruction of Babylon by Tukulti-Ninurta I. Not until the time of the kings Adad-shum-uṣur (c. 1216–c. 1187) and Melishipak (c. 1186–c. 1172) was Babylon able to experience a period of prosperity and peace. Their successors were again forced to fight, facing the conqueror King Shutruk-Nahhunte of Elam (c. 1185–c. 1155). Cruel and fierce, the Elamites finally destroyed the dynasty of the Kassites during these wars (about 1155). Some poetical works lament this catastrophe.

Letters and documents of the time after 1380 show that many things had changed after the Kassites took power. The Kassite upper class, always a small minority, had been largely "Babylonianized." Babylonian names were to be found even among the royalty, and they predominated among the civil servants and the officers. The new feudal character of the social structure showed the influence of the Kassites. Babylonian town life had revived on the basis of commerce and handicrafts. The Kassitic nobility, however, maintained the upper

An example of kudurru, or an inscribed tablet used as a boundary stone. This stone, on exhibit at the Louvre in Paris and dating back to c. 1200 B.C., remains unfinished. Louvre, Paris, France/ The Bridgeman Art Library/Getty Images

grants. From the time of Kurigalzu II these were registered on stone tablets or, more frequently, on boundary stones called *kudurru*s. After 1200 the number of these increased substantially, because the kings needed a steadily growing retinue of loyal followers. The boundary stones had pictures in bas-relief, very often a multitude of religious symbols, and frequently contained detailed inscriptions giving the borders of the particular estate. Sometimes the deserts of the recipient were listed and his privileges recorded; trespassers were threatened with the most terrifying curses. Agriculture and cattle husbandry were the main pursuits on these estates, and horses were raised for the light war chariots of the cavalry. There was an export trade in horses and vehicles in exchange for raw material. As for the king, the idea of the social-minded ruler continued to be valid.

The decline of Babylonian culture at the end of the Old Babylonian period continued for some time under the Kassites. Not until approximately 1420

hand in the rural areas, their wealthiest representatives holding very large landed estates. Many of these holdings came from donations of the king to deserving officers and civil servants, considerable privileges being connected with such

KUDURRUS

Kudurrus (Akkadian: "frontier," or "boundary") are a type of boundary stone used by the Kassites of ancient Mesopotamia. A stone block or slab, it served as a record of a grant of land made by the king to a favoured person.

The original kudurrus were kept in temples, while clay copies were given to the landowners. On the stone were engraved the clauses of the contract, the images or symbols of the gods under whose protection the gift was placed, and the curse on those who violated the rights conferred. The kudurrus are important not only for economic and religious reasons but also as almost the only works of art surviving from the period of Kassite rule in Babylonia (c. 16th–c. 12th century BC).

did the Kassites develop a distinctive style in architecture and sculpture. Kurigalzu I played an important part, especially in Ur, as a patron of the building arts. Poetry and scientific literature developed only gradually after 1400. The existence of earlier work is clear from poetry, philological lists, and collections of omens and signs that were in existence by the 14th century or before and that have been discovered in the Hittite capital of Hattusa, in the Syrian capital of Ugarit, and even as far away as Palestine. Somewhat later, new writings appear: medical diagnoses and recipes, more Sumero-Akkadian word lists, and collections of astrological and other omens and signs with their interpretations.

Most of these works are known today only from copies of more recent date. The most important is the Babylonian epic of the creation of the world, *Enuma elish*. Composed by an unknown poet, probably in the 14th century, it tells the story of the god Marduk. He began as the god of Babylon and was elevated to be king over all other gods after having successfully accomplished the destruction of the powers of chaos. For almost 1,000 years this epic was recited during the New Year's festival in the spring as part of the Marduk cult in Babylon. The literature of this time contains very few Kassitic words. Many scholars believe that the essential groundwork for the development of the subsequent Babylonian culture was laid during the later epoch of the Kassite era.

THE HURRIAN AND MITANNI KINGDOMS

The weakening of the Semitic states in Mesopotamia after 1550 enabled the Hurrians to penetrate deeper into this region, where they founded numerous small states in the eastern parts of Anatolia, Mesopotamia, and Syria. The Hurrians came from northwestern Iran, but until recently very little was known about their early history. After 1500, isolated dynasties appeared with Indo-Aryan names, but the significance of this is disputed. The presence of Old Indian technical terms in later records about horse breeding and the use of the names of Indian gods (such as, for example, Indra and Varuna) in some compacts of state formerly led several scholars to assume that numerous groups of Aryans, closely related to the Indians, pushed into Anatolia from the northeast. They were also credited with the introduction of the light war chariot with spoked wheels. This conclusion, however, is by no means established fact. So far it has not been possible to appraise the numbers and the political and cultural influence of the Aryans in Anatolia and Mesopotamia relative to those of the Hurrians.

Some time after 1500 the kingdom of Mitanni (or Mittani) arose near the sources of the Khābūr River in Mesopotamia. Since no record or inscription of their kings has been unearthed, little is known about the development and history of the Mitanni kingdom before King Tushratta. The Mitanni empire was known to the Egyptians under the name of Naharina, and Thutmose III fought frequently against it after 1460 BC. By 1420 the domain of the Mitanni king Saustatar (Saushatar) stretched from the Mediterranean all the way to the northern Zagros Mountains, in western Iran, including Alalakh, in northern Syria, as well as Nuzu, Kurrukhanni, and Arrapkha. The northern boundary dividing Mitanni from the Hittites and the other Hurrian states was never fixed, even under Saustatar's successors Artatama I and Shuttarna II, who married their daughters to the pharaohs Thutmose IV (1400–1390) and Amenhotep III (1390–1353). Tushratta (c. 1365–c. 1330), the son of Shuttarna, was able to maintain the kingdom he had inherited for many years. In his sometimes very long letters—one of them written in Hurrian—to Amenhotep III and Akhenaton (1353–1336), he wrote about commerce, his desire for gold, and marriage. Weakened by internal strife, the Mitanni kingdom eventually became a pawn between the rising kingdoms of the Hittites and the Assyrians.

The kingdom of Mitanni was a feudal state led by a warrior nobility of Aryan or Hurrian origin. Frequently horses were bred on their large landed estates. Documents and contract agreements in Syria often mention a chariot-warrior caste that also constituted the social upper class in the cities. The aristocratic families usually received their landed property as an inalienable fief. Consequently, no documents on the selling of landed property are to be found in the great archives of Akkadian documents and letters discovered in Nuzu, near Kirkūk. The prohibition against selling landed property was often dodged, however, with a stratagem: the previous owner "adopted" a willing buyer against an appropriate sum of money. The wealthy lord Tehiptilla was "adopted" almost 200 times, acquiring tremendous holdings of landed property in this way without interference by the local governmental authorities. He had gained his wealth through trade and commerce and through a productive two-field system of agriculture (in which each field was cultivated only once in two years).

For a long time, Prince Shilwa-Teshub was in charge of the royal governmental administration in the district capital. Sheep breeding was the basis for a woolen industry, and textiles collected by the palace were exported on a large scale. Society was highly structured in classes, ranks, and professions. The judiciary, patterned after the Babylonian model, was well organized; the documents place heavy emphasis on correct procedure.

Native sources on the religion of the Hurrians of the Mitanni kingdom are limited. About their mythology, however, much is known from related Hittite and Ugaritic myths. Like the other peoples of the ancient Middle East, the Hurrians worshiped gods of various origins. The king of the gods was the weather god Teshub. According to the myths, he violently deposed his father Kumarbi; in this respect he resembled the Greek god Zeus, who deposed his father Kronos. The war chariot of Teshub was drawn by the bull gods Seris ("Day") and Hurris ("Night"). Major sanctuaries of Teshub were located at Arrapkha (modern Kirkūk) and at Halab (modern Aleppo) in Syria. In the east his consort was the goddess of love and war Shaushka, and in the west the goddess Hebat (Hepat); both were similar to the Ishtar-Astarte of the Semites.

The sun god Shimegi and the moon god Kushuh, whose consort was Nikkal, the Ningal of the Sumerians, were of lesser rank. More important was the position of the Babylonian god of war and the underworld, Nergal. In northern Syria the god of war Astapi and the goddess of oaths Ishara are attested as early as the third millennium BC.

In addition, a considerable importance was attributed to impersonal numina such as heaven and earth as well as to deities of mountains and rivers. In the myths the terrible aspect of the gods often prevails over indications of a benevolent attitude. The cults of sacrifices and other rites are similar to those known from the neighbouring countries; many Hurrian rituals were found in Hittite Anatolia. There is abundant evidence for magic and oracles.

Temple monuments of modest dimensions have been unearthed; in all probability, specific local traditions were a factor in their design. The dead were probably buried outside the settlement. Small artifacts, particularly seals, show a peculiar continuation of Babylonian and Assyrian traditions in their preference for the naturalistic representation of figures. There were painted ceramics with finely drawn decorations (white on a dark background). The strong position of the royal house was evident in the large palaces, existing even in district capitals. The palaces were decorated with frescoes. Because only a few Mitanni settlements have been unearthed in Mesopotamia, knowledge of Mitanni arts and culture is as yet insufficient.

THE RISE OF ASSYRIA

Very little can be said about northern Assyria during the second millennium BC. Information on the old capital, Ashur, located in the south of the country, is somewhat more plentiful. The old lists of kings suggest that the same dynasty ruled continuously over Ashur from about 1600. All the names of the kings are given, but little else is known about Ashur before 1420. Almost all the princes had Akkadian names, and it can be assumed that their sphere of influence was rather small. Although Assyria belonged to the kingdom of the Mitanni for a long time, it seems that Ashur retained a certain autonomy. Located close to the boundary with Babylonia, it played that empire off against Mitanni whenever possible. Puzur-Ashur III concluded a border treaty with Babylonia about 1480, as did Ashur-bel-nisheshu about 1405. Ashur-nadin-ahhe II (c. 1392–c. 1383) was even able to obtain support from Egypt, which sent him a consignment of gold.

Ashur-uballit I (c. 1354–c. 1318) was at first subject to King Tushratta of Mitanni. After 1340, however, he attacked Tushratta, presumably together with Suppiluliumas I of the Hittites. Taking away from Mitanni parts of northeastern Mesopotamia, Ashur-uballit now called himself "Great King" and socialized with the king of Egypt on equal terms, arousing the indignation of the king of Babylonia. Ashur-uballit was the first to name Assyria the Land of Ashur, because the old name, Subartu, was often used in a derogatory sense in Babylonia. He ordered his short inscriptions to be partly written in the Babylonian dialect rather than the Assyrian, since this was considered refined. Marrying his daughter to a Babylonian, he intervened there energetically when Kassite nobles murdered his grandson. Future generations came to consider him rightfully as the real founder of the Assyrian empire. His son Enlil-nirari (c. 1326–c. 1318) also fought against Babylonia. Arik-den-ili (c. 1308–c. 1297) turned westward, where he encountered Semitic tribes of the so-called Akhlamu group.

Still greater successes were achieved by Adad-nirari I (c. 1295–c. 1264). Defeating the Kassite king Nazimaruttash, he forced him to retreat. After that he defeated the kings of Mitanni, first Shattuara I, then Wasashatta. This enabled him for a time to incorporate all Mesopotamia into his empire as a province, although in later struggles he lost large parts to the Hittites. In the east, he was satisfied with the defense of his lands against the mountain tribes.

Adad-nirari's inscriptions were more elaborate than those of his predecessors and were written in the Babylonian dialect. In them he declares that he feels called to these wars by the gods, a statement that was to be repeated by other kings after him. Assuming the old title of great king, he called himself "King of All." He enlarged the temple and the palace in Ashur and also developed the fortifications there, particularly at the banks of the Tigris River. He worked on large building projects in the provinces.

His son Shalmaneser I (Shulmanu-asharidu; *c.* 1263–*c.* 1234) attacked Uruatru (later called Urartu) in southern Armenia, which had allegedly broken away. Shattuara II of Hanigalbat, however, put him into a difficult situation, cutting his forces off from their water supplies. With courage born of despair, the Assyrians fought themselves free. They then set about reducing what was left of the Mitanni kingdom into an Assyrian province. The king claimed to have blinded 14,400 enemies in one eye—psychological warfare of a similar kind was used more and more as time went by. The Hittites tried in vain to save Hanigalbat. Together with the Babylonians they fought a commercial war against Ashur for many years. Like his father, Shalmaneser was a great builder. At the juncture of the Tigris and Great Zab rivers, he founded a strategically situated second capital, Kalakh (biblical Calah; modern Nimrūd).

His son was Tukulti-Ninurta (*c.* 1233–*c.* 1197), the Ninus of Greek legends. Gifted but extravagant, he made his nation a great power. He carried off thousands of Hittites from eastern Anatolia. He fought particularly hard against Babylonia, deporting Kashtiliash IV to Assyria. When the Babylonians rebelled again, he plundered the temples in Babylon, an act regarded as a sacrilege, even in Assyria. The relationship between the king and his capital deteriorated steadily. For this reason the king began to build a new city, Kar-Tukulti-Ninurta, on the other side of the Tigris River. Ultimately, even his sons rebelled against him and laid siege to him in his city; in the end he was murdered. His victorious wars against Babylonia were glorified in an epic poem, but his empire broke up soon after his death. Assyrian power declined for a time, while that of Babylonia rose.

Assyria had suffered under the oppression of both the Hurrians and the Mitanni kingdom. Its struggle for liberation and the bitter wars that followed had much to do with its development into a military power. In his capital of Ashur, the king depended on the citizen class and the priesthood, as well as on the landed nobility that furnished him with the war-chariot troops.

Documents and letters show the important role that agriculture played in the development of the state. Assyria was less dependent on artificial irrigation than was Babylonia. The breeding of horses was carried on intensively; remnants of elaborate directions for their training are extant. Trade and commerce also were of notable significance: metals were imported from Anatolia or Armenia, tin from northwestern Iran, and lumber from the west. The opening up of new trade routes was often a cause and the purpose of war.

Assyrian architecture, derived from a combination of Mitannian and

Babylonian influences, developed early quite an individual style. The palaces often had colourful wall decorations. The art of seal cutting, taken largely from Mitanni, continued creatively on its own. The schools for scribes, where all the civil servants were trained, taught both the Babylonian and the Assyrian dialects of the Akkadian language. Babylonian works of literature were assimilated into Assyrian, often reworked into a different form. The Hurrian tradition remained strong in the military and political sphere while at the same time influencing the vocabulary of language.

BABYLONIA UNDER THE SECOND DYNASTY OF ISIN

In a series of heavy wars about which not much is known, Marduk-kabit-ahheshu (c. 1152–c. 1135) established what came to be known as the second dynasty of Isin. His successors were often forced to continue the fighting. The most famous king of the dynasty was Nebuchadrezzar I (Nabu-kudurri-uṣur; c. 1119–c. 1098). He fought mainly against Elam, which had conquered and ravaged a large part of Babylonia. His first attack miscarried because of an epidemic among his troops, but in a later campaign he conquered Susa, the capital of Elam, and returned the previously removed statue of the god Marduk to its proper place. Soon thereafter the king of Elam was assassinated, and his kingdom once again fell apart into small states. This enabled

Nebuchadrezzar to turn west, using the later years of peace to start extensive building projects.

After him, his son became king, succeeded by his brother Marduk-nadin-ahhe (c. 1093–c. 1076). At first successful in his wars against Assyria, he later experienced heavy defeat. A famine of catastrophic proportions triggered an attack from Aramaean tribes, the ultimate blow. His successors made peace with Assyria, but the country suffered more and more from repeated attacks by Aramaeans and other Semitic nomads. Even though some of the kings still assumed grand titles, they were unable to stem the progressive disintegration of their empire. There followed the era known as the second dynasty of the Sealand (c. 1020–c. 1000), which included three usurpers. The first of these had the Kassitic name of Simbar-Shihu (or Simbar-Shipak; c. 1020–c. 1003).

Toward the end of its reign, the dynasty of the Kassites became completely Babylonianized. The changeover to the dynasty of Isin, actually a succession of kings from different families, brought no essential transformation of the social structure. The feudal order remained. New landed estates came into existence in many places through grants to deserving officers; many boundary stones (kudurrus) have been found that describe them. The cities of Babylonia retained much of their former autonomy. The border provinces, however, were administered by royally appointed governors with civil and military functions.

In the literary arts this was a period of creativity; thus the later Babylonians with good reason regarded the time of Nebuchadrezzar I as one of the great eras of their history. A heroic epic, modeled upon older epics, celebrates the deeds of Nebuchadrezzar I, but unfortunately little of it is extant. Other material comes from the ancient myths. The poet of the later version of the epic of Gilgamesh, Sin-leqe-unnini (c. 1150–?) of Erech (Uruk), is known by name. This version of the epic is known as the Twelve-Tablet Poem; it contains about 3,000 verses. It is distinguished by its greater emphasis on the human qualities of Gilgamesh and his friend Enkidu; this quality makes it one of the great works of world literature.

Another poet active at about the same time was the author of a poem of 480 verses called *Ludlul bēl nēmeqi* ("Let Me Praise the Possessor of Wisdom"). The poem meditates on the workings of divine justice, which sometimes appear strange and inexplicable to suffering human beings; this subject had acquired an increasing importance in the contemporary religion of Babylon. The poem describes the multifarious sufferings of a high official and his subsequent salvation by the god Marduk.

The gradual reduction of the Sumerian pantheon of about 2,000 gods by the identification and integration of originally distinct gods and goddesses of similar functions resulted in a growing number of surnames or compound names for the main gods (Marduk, for example, had about 50 such names) and later in a conception of "the god" and "the goddess" with interchangeable names in the cults of the great temples. There was a theology of identifications of gods, which was documented by god lists in two columns with hundreds of entries in the form "Enzag = Nabû of (the island of) Dilmun," as well as by many hymns and prayers of the time and by later compositions.

As a consequence of the distinction of an enormous number of multifarious sins, the concept of a universal sinfulness of humankind is increasingly observed in this period and later. All human beings, therefore, were believed to be in need of the forgiveness afforded by the deities to sincere worshipers. Outside of Israel, the concept of sinfulness can be found in ancient times only in Babylonia and Assyria.

ASSYRIA BETWEEN 1200 AND 1000 BC

After a period of decline following Tukulti-Ninurta I, Assyria was consolidated and stabilized under Ashur-dan I (c. 1179–c. 1134) and Ashur-resh-ishi I (c. 1133–c. 1116). Several times forced to fight against Babylonia, the latter was even able to defend himself against an attack by Nebuchadrezzar I. According to the inscriptions, most of his building efforts were in Nineveh, rather than in the old capital of Ashur.

His son Tiglath-pileser I (Tukulti-apil-Esharra; c. 1115–c. 1077) raised the power of Assyria to new heights. First he turned against a large army of the Mushki that had entered into southern Armenia from Anatolia, defeating them decisively. After this, he forced the small Hurrian states of southern Armenia to pay him tribute. Trained in mountain warfare themselves and helped by capable pioneers, the Assyrians were now able to advance far into the mountain regions. Their main enemies were the Aramaeans, the Semitic Bedouin nomads whose many small states often combined against the Assyrians. Tiglath-pileser I also went to Syria and even reached the Mediterranean, where he took a sea voyage. After 1100 these campaigns led to conflicts with Babylonia. Tiglath-pileser conquered northern Babylonia and plundered Babylon, without decisively defeating Marduk-nadin-ahhe. In his own country the king paid particular attention to agriculture and fruit growing, improved the administrative system, and developed more thorough methods of training scribes.

Three of his sons reigned after Tiglath-pileser, including Ashur-bel-kala (c. 1074–c. 1057). Like his father, he fought in southern Armenia and against the Aramaeans with Babylonia as his ally. Disintegration of the empire could not be delayed, however. The grandson of Tiglath-pileser, Ashurnasirpal I (c. 1050–c. 1032), was sickly and unable to do more than defend Assyria proper against his enemies. Fragments of three of his prayers to Ishtar are preserved; among them is a penitential prayer in which he wonders about the cause of so much adversity. Referring to his many good deeds, but admitting his guilt at the same time, he asks for forgiveness and health. According to the king, part of his guilt lay in neglecting to teach his subjects the fear of god. After him, little is known for 100 years.

State and society during the time of Tiglath-pileser were not essentially different from those of the 13th century. Collections of laws, drafts, and edicts of the court exist that go back as far as the 14th century BC. Presumably, most of these remained in effect. One tablet defining the marriage laws shows that the social position of women in Assyria was lower than in Babylonia or Israel or among the Hittites. A man was allowed to send away his wife at his own pleasure with or without divorce money. In the case of adultery, he was permitted to kill or maim her. Outside her house the woman was forced to observe many restrictions, such as the wearing of a veil. It is not clear whether these regulations carried the weight of law, but they seem to have represented a reaction against practices that were more favourable to women. Two somewhat older marriage contracts, for example, granted equal rights to both partners, even in divorce. The women of the king's harem were subject to severe punishment, including beating, maiming, and death, along with those who guarded and looked after them. The penal laws of the time were generally more severe in Assyria than in other countries of the East. The death penalty was not uncommon. In less serious cases the penalty was forced labour after flogging. In certain cases there was trial by ordeal. One tablet treats the subject of landed property rights. Offenses against the established boundary lines called for extremely severe punishment. A creditor was allowed to force his debtor to work for him, but he could not sell him.

The greater part of Assyrian literature was either taken over from Babylonia or written by the Assyrians in the Babylonian dialect, who modeled their works on Babylonian originals. The Assyrian dialect was used in legal documents, court and temple rituals, and collections of recipes—as, for example, in directions for making perfumes. A new art form was the picture tale: a continuing series of pictures carved on square stelae of stone. The pictures, showing war or hunting scenes, begin at the top of the stela and run down around it, with inscriptions under the pictures explaining them. These and the finely cut seals show that the fine arts of Assyria were beginning to surpass those of Babylonia. Architecture and other forms of the monumental arts also began a further development, such as the double temple with its two towers (ziggurat). Colourful enameled tiles were used to decorate the facades.

ASSYRIA AND BABYLONIA UNTIL ASHURNASIRPAL II

The most important factor in the history of Mesopotamia in the 10th century was the continuing threat from the Aramaean seminomads. Again and again, the kings of both Babylonia and Assyria were forced to repel their invasions. Even though the Aramaeans were not able to gain a foothold in the main cities, there are evidences of them in many rural areas. Ashur-dan II (934–912) succeeded in suppressing the Aramaeans and the mountain people, in this way stabilizing the Assyrian boundaries. He reintroduced the use of the Assyrian dialect in his written records.

Adad-nirari II (c. 911–891) left detailed accounts of his wars and his efforts to improve agriculture. He led six campaigns against Aramaean intruders from northern Arabia. In two campaigns against Babylonia he forced Shamash-mudammiq (c. 930–904) to surrender extensive territories. Shamash-mudammiq was murdered, and a treaty with his successor, Nabu-shum-ukin (c. 904–888), secured peace for many years. Tukulti-Ninurta II (c. 890–884), the son of Adad-nirari II, preferred Nineveh to Ashur. He fought campaigns in southern Armenia. He was portrayed on stelae in blue and yellow enamel in the late Hittite style, showing him under a winged sun—a theme adopted from Egyptian art. His son Ashurnasirpal II (883–859) continued the policy of conquest and expansion. He left a detailed account of his campaigns, which were impressive in their cruelty. Defeated enemies were impaled, flayed, or beheaded in great numbers. Mass deportations, however, were found to serve the interests of the growing empire better than terror. Through the systematic exchange of native populations, conquered regions were denationalized. The result was a submissive, mixed population in which the Aramaean element became the majority. This provided the labour force for the various public works in the metropolitan centres of the Assyrian empire. Ashurnasirpal II rebuilt Kalakh, founded by Shalmaneser I, and made it his capital. Ashur remained the centre of the worship of the god Ashur—in whose name all the wars of conquest were fought. A third capital was Nineveh.

Ashurnasirpal II was the first to use cavalry units to any large extent in addition to infantry and war-chariot troops. He also was the first to employ heavy, mobile battering rams and wall breakers in his sieges. Following after the conquering troops came officials from all branches of the civil service, because the king wanted to lose no time in incorporating the new lands into his empire. The supremacy of Assyria over its neighbouring states owed much to the proficiency of the government service under the leadership of the minister Gabbilani-eresh. The campaigns of Ashurnasirpal II led him mainly to southern Armenia and Mesopotamia. After a series of heavy wars, he incorporated Mesopotamia as far as the Euphrates River. A campaign to Syria encountered little resistance. There was no great war against Babylonia. Ashurnasirpal, like other Assyrian kings, may have been moved by religion not to destroy Babylonia, which had almost the same gods as Assyria. Both empires must have profited from mutual trade and cultural exchange. The Babylonians, under the energetic Nabu-apla-iddina (c. 887–855) attacked the Aramaeans in southern Mesopotamia and occupied the valley of the Euphrates River to about the mouth of the Khābūr River.

Ashurnasirpal, so brutal in his wars, was able to inspire architects, structural engineers, and artists and sculptors to heights never before achieved. He built and enlarged temples and palaces in several cities. His most impressive monument was his own palace in Kalakh, covering a space of 269,000 square feet (25,000 square metres). Hundreds of large limestone slabs were used in murals in the staterooms and living quarters. Most of the scenes were done in relief, but painted murals also have been found. Most of them depict mythological themes and symbolic fertility rites, with the king participating. Brutal war pictures were aimed to discourage enemies. The chief god of Kalakh was Ninurta, god of war and the hunt. The tower of the temple dedicated to Ninurta also served as an astronomical observatory. Kalakh soon became the cultural centre of the empire. Ashurnasirpal claimed to have entertained 69,574 guests at the opening ceremonies of his palace.

SHALMANESER III AND SHAMSHI-ADAD V OF ASSYRIA

The son and successor of Ashurnasirpal was Shalmaneser III (858–824). His father's equal in both brutality and energy, he was less realistic in his undertakings. His inscriptions, in a peculiar blend of Assyrian and Babylonian, record his considerable achievements, but are not always able to conceal his failures. His campaigns were directed mostly against Syria. While he was able to conquer northern Syria and make it a province, in the south he could only weaken the strong state of Damascus and was unable, even after several wars, to eliminate it. In 841 he laid unsuccessful siege to Damascus. Also in 841 King Jehu of Israel was forced to pay tribute. In his invasion of Cilicia, Shalmaneser had only partial success. The same was true of the kingdom of Urartu in Armenia, from which, however, the troops returned with immense quantities of lumber and building stone. The king and, in later years, the general Dayyan-Ashur went several times to western Iran, where they found such states as Mannai in northwestern Iran and, farther away in the southeast, the Persians. They also encountered the Medes during these wars. Horse tribute was collected.

In Babylonia, Marduk-zakir-shumi I ascended the throne about the year 855. His brother Marduk-bel-usati rebelled against him, and in 851 the king was forced to ask Shalmaneser for help. Shalmaneser was only too happy to oblige; when the usurper had been finally eliminated (850), Shalmaneser went to southern Babylonia, which at that time was almost completely dominated by Aramaeans. There he encountered, among others, the Chaldeans, mentioned for the first time in 878 BC, who were to play a leading role in the history of later times; Shalmaneser made them tributaries.

During his long reign he built temples, palaces, and fortifications in Assyria as well as in the other capitals of his provinces. His artists created many statues and stelae. Among the best known is the Black Obelisk, which includes a picture of Jehu of Israel paying tribute. The bronze doors from the town of Imgur-Enlil (Balawat) in Assyria portray the course of his campaigns and other undertakings in rows of pictures, often very lifelike. Hundreds of delicately carved ivories were carried away from Phoenicia, and many of the artists along with them; these later made Kalakh a centre for the art of ivory sculpture.

In the last four years of the reign of Shalmaneser, the crown prince Ashurda'in-apla led a rebellion. The old king appointed his younger son Shamshi-Adad as the new crown prince. Forced to flee to Babylonia, Shamshi-Adad V (823–811) finally managed to regain the kingship with the help of Marduk-zakir-shumi I under humiliating conditions. As king he campaigned with varying success in southern Armenia and Azerbaijan, later turning against Babylonia. He won several battles against the Babylonian kings Marduk-balassu-iqbi and Baba-aha-iddina (about 818–12) and pushed through to Chaldea. Babylonia remained independent, however.

ADAD-NIRARI III
AND HIS SUCCESSORS

Shamshi-Adad V died while Adad-nirari III (810–783) was still a minor. His Babylonian mother, Sammu-ramat, took over the regency, governing with great energy until 806. The Greeks, who called her Semiramis, credited her with legendary accomplishments, but historically little is known about her. Adad-nirari later led several campaigns against the Medes and also against Syria and Palestine. In 804 he reached Gaza, but Damascus proved invincible. He also fought in Babylonia, helping to restore order in the north.

Shalmaneser IV (c. 783–773) fought against Urartu, then at the height of its power under King Argishti (c. 780–755). He successfully defended eastern Mesopotamia against attacks from Armenia. On the other hand, he lost most of Syria after a campaign against Damascus in 773. The reign of Ashur-dan III (772–755) was shadowed by rebellions and by epidemics of plague. Of Ashur-nirari V (754–746) little is known.

In Assyria the feudal structure of society remained largely unchanged. Many of the conquered lands were combined to form large provinces. The governors of these provinces sometimes acquired considerable independence, particularly under the weaker monarchs after Adad-nirari III. Some of them even composed their own inscriptions. The influx of displaced peoples into the cities of Assyria created large metropolitan centres. The spoils of war, together with an expanding trade, favoured the development of a well-to-do commercial class. The dense population of the cities gave rise to social tensions that only the strong kings were able to contain. A number of the former capitals of the conquered lands remained important as capitals of provinces. There was much new building. A standing occupational force was needed in the provinces, and these troops grew steadily in proportion to the total military forces. There are no records on the training of officers or on military logistics. The civil service also expanded, the largest administrative body being the royal court, with thousands of functionaries and craftsmen in the several residential cities.

The cultural decline about the year 1000 was overcome during the reigns of Ashurnasirpal II and Shalmaneser III. The arts in particular experienced a tremendous resurgence. Literary works continued to be written in Assyrian and were seldom of great importance. The literature that had been taken over from Babylonia was further developed with new writings, although one can rarely distinguish between works written in Assyria and works written in Babylonia. In religion, the official cults of Ashur and Ninurta continued, while the religion of the common people went its separate way.

In Babylonia not much was left of the feudal structure; the large landed estates almost everywhere fell prey to the inroads of the Aramaeans, who were at first half nomadic. The leaders of their tribes and clans slowly replaced the former landlords. Agriculture on a large scale was no longer possible except on the outskirts of metropolitan areas. The predominance of the Babylonian schools for scribes may have prevented the emergence of an Aramaean literature. In any case, the Aramaeans seem to have been absorbed into the Babylonian culture. The religious cults in the cities remained essentially the same. The Babylonian empire was slowly reduced to poverty, except perhaps in some of the cities.

In 764, after an epidemic, the Erra epic, the myth of Erra (the god of war and pestilence), was written by Kabti-ilani-Marduk. He invented an original plot, which diverged considerably from the old myths. Long discourses of the gods involved in the action form the most important part of the epic. There is a passage in the epic claiming that the text was divinely revealed to the poet during a dream.

THE NEO-ASSYRIAN EMPIRE (746–609)

For no other period of Assyrian history is there an abundance of sources comparable to those available for the interval from roughly 745 to 640. Aside from the large number of royal inscriptions, about 2,400 letters, most of them more or less fragmentary, have been published. Usually the senders and recipients of these letters are the king and high government officials. Among them are reports from royal agents about foreign affairs and letters about cultic matters. Treaties, oracles, queries to the sun god about political matters, and prayers of or for kings contain a great deal of additional information. Last but certainly not least are paintings and wall reliefs, which are often very informative.

TIGLATH-PILESER III AND SHALMANESER V

The decline of Assyrian power after 780 was notable. Syria and considerable lands in the north were lost. A military coup deposed King Ashur-nirari V and raised a general to the throne. Under the name of Tiglath-pileser III (745–727), he brought the empire to its greatest expanse. He reduced the size of the provinces in order to break the partial independence of the governors. He also invalidated the tax privileges of cities such as Ashur and Harran in order to distribute the tax load more evenly over the entire realm. Military equipment was improved substantially. In 746 he went to Babylonia to aid Nabu-nasir (747–734) in his fight against Aramaean tribes. Tiglath-pileser defeated the Aramaeans and then made visits to the large cities of Babylonia. There he tried to secure the support of the priesthood by patronizing their building projects. Babylonia retained its independence.

His next undertaking was to check Urartu. His campaigns in Azerbaijan were designed to drive a wedge between Urartu and the Medes. In 743 he went to

Syria, defeating there an army of Urartu. The Syrian city of Arpad, which had formed an alliance with Urartu, did not surrender so easily. It took Tiglath-pileser three years of siege to conquer Arpad, whereupon he massacred the inhabitants and destroyed the city. In 738 a new coalition formed against Assyria under the leadership of Sam'al (modern Zincirli) in northern Syria. It was defeated, and all the princes from Damascus to eastern Anatolia were forced to pay tribute. Another campaign in 735, this time directed against Urartu itself, was only partly successful. In 734 Tiglath-pileser invaded southern Syria and the Philistine territories in Palestine, going as far as the Egyptian border. Damascus and Israel tried to organize resistance against him, seeking to bring Judah into their alliance. Ahaz of Judah, however, asked Tiglath-pileser for help. In 733 Tiglath-pileser devastated Israel and forced it to surrender large territories. In 732 he advanced upon Damascus, first devastating the gardens outside the city and then conquering the capital and killing the king, whom he replaced with a governor. The queen of southern Arabia, Samsil, was now obliged to pay tribute, being permitted in return to use the harbour of the city of Gaza, which was in Assyrian hands.

The death of King Nabonassar of Babylonia caused a chaotic situation to develop there, and the Aramaean Ukin-zer crowned himself king. In 731 Tiglath-pileser fought and beat him and his allies, but he did not capture Ukin-zer until 729. This time he did not appoint a new king for Babylonia but assumed the crown himself under the name Pulu (Pul in the Hebrew Bible). In his old age he abstained from further campaigning, devoting himself to the improvement of his capital, Kalakh. He rebuilt the palace of Shalmaneser III, filled it with treasures from his wars, and decorated the walls with bas-reliefs. The latter were almost all of warlike character, as if designed to intimidate the onlooker with their presentation of gruesome executions. These pictorial narratives on slabs, sometimes painted, have also been found in Syria, at the sites of several provincial capitals of ancient Assyria.

Tiglath-pileser was succeeded by his son Shalmaneser V (726–722), who continued the policy of his father. As king of Babylonia, he called himself Ululai. Almost nothing is known about his enterprises, since his successor destroyed all his inscriptions. The Bible relates that he marched against Hoshea of Israel in 724 after Hoshea had rebelled. He was probably assassinated during the long siege of Samaria. His successor maintained that the god Ashur had withdrawn his support of Shalmaneser V for acts of disrespect.

SARGON II (721–705) AND MARDUK-APAL-IDDINA OF BABYLONIA

It was probably a younger brother of Shalmaneser who ascended the throne of Assyria in 721. Assuming the old name of Sharru-kin (Sargon in the Bible), meaning "Legitimate King," he assured himself of the support of the priesthood and the merchant class by restoring privileges they had lost, particularly the tax exemptions of the great temples. The change of sovereign in Assyria triggered another crisis in Babylonia. An Aramaean prince from the south, Marduk-apal-iddina II (the biblical Merodach-Baladan), seized power in Babylon in 721 and was able to retain it until 710 with the help of Humbanigash I of Elam. A first attempt by Sargon to recover Babylonia miscarried when Elam defeated him in 721. During the same year the protracted siege of Samaria was brought to a close. The Samarian upper class was deported, and Israel became an Assyrian province. Samaria was repopulated with Syrians and Babylonians. Judah remained independent by paying tribute. In 720 Sargon squelched a rebellion in Syria that had been supported by Egypt. Then he defeated both Hanunu of Gaza and an Egyptian army near the Egyptian border. In 717 and 716 he campaigned in northern Syria, making the hitherto independent state of Carchemish one of his provinces. He also went to Cilicia in an effort to prevent further encroachments of the Phrygians under King Midas (Assyrian: Mitā).

In order to protect his ally, the state of Mannai, in Azerbaijan, Sargon embarked on a campaign in Iran in 719 and incorporated parts of Media as provinces of his empire; however, in 716 another war became necessary. At the same time, he was busy preparing a major attack against Urartu. Under the leadership of the crown prince Sennacherib, armies of agents infiltrated Urartu, which was also threatened from the north by the Cimmerians. Many of their messages and reports have been preserved. The longest inscription ever composed by the Assyrians about a year's enterprise (430 very long lines) is dedicated to this Urartu campaign of 714. Phrased in the style of a first report to the god Ashur, it is interspersed with stirring descriptions of natural scenery. The strong points of Urartu must have been well fortified. Sargon tried to avoid them by going through the province of Mannai and attacking the Median principalities on the eastern side of Lake Urmia. In the meantime, hoping to surprise the Assyrian troops, Rusa of Urartu had closed the narrow pass lying between Lake Urmia and Sahand Mount. Sargon, anticipating this, led a small band of cavalry in a surprise charge that developed into a great victory for the Assyrians. Rusa fled and died. The Assyrians pushed forward, destroying all the cities, fortifications, and even irrigation works of Urartu. They did not conquer Tushpa (the capital) but took possession of the mountain city of Muṣaṣir. The spoils were immense. The following years saw only small campaigns in Media and eastern Anatolia and against Ashdod, in Palestine. King Midas of Phrygia and some cities on Cyprus were quite ready to pay tribute.

Sargon was now free to settle accounts with Marduk-apal-iddina of Babylonia. Abandoned by his ally Shutruk-Nahhunte

Winged bull with a human head, guardian figure from the gate of the palace at Dur-Sharrukin, near Nineveh; in the Louvre. Cliché Musées Nationaux, Paris

At first Sargon resided in Kalakh, but he then decided to found an entirely new capital north of Nineveh. He called the city Dur-Sharrukin— "Sargonsburg" (modern Khorsabad, Iraq). He erected his palace on a high terrace in the northeastern part of the city. The temples of the main gods, smaller in size, were built within the palatial rectangle, which was surrounded by a special wall. This arrangement enabled Sargon to supervise the priests better than had been possible in the old, large temple complexes. One consequence of this design was that the figure of the king pushed the gods somewhat into the background, thereby gaining in importance. Desiring that his palace match the vastness of his empire, Sargon planned it in monumental dimensions. Stone reliefs of two winged bulls with human heads flanked the entrance; they were much larger than anything comparable built before. The walls were decorated with long rows of bas-reliefs showing scenes of war and festive processions. A comparison with a well-executed stela of the Babylonian king Marduk-apal-iddina shows that the fine arts of Assyria had far surpassed those of Babylonia.

II of Elam, Marduk-apal-iddina found it best to flee, first to his native land on the Persian Gulf and later to Elam. Because the Aramaean prince had made himself very unpopular with his subjects, Sargon was hailed as the liberator of Babylonia. He complied with the wishes of the priesthood and at the same time put down the Aramaean nobility. He was satisfied with the modest title of governor of Babylonia.

Sargon never completed his capital, though from 713 to 705 BC tens of thousands of labourers and hundreds of artisans worked on the great city. Yet, with the exception of some magnificent buildings for public officials, only a few durable edifices were completed in the residential section. In 705, in a campaign in northwestern Iran, Sargon was ambushed and killed. His corpse remained unburied, to be devoured by birds of prey. Sargon's son Sennacherib, who had quarreled with his father, was inclined to believe with the priests that his death was a punishment from the neglected gods of the ancient capitals.

SENNACHERIB

Sennacherib (Assyrian: Sin-ahhe-eriba; 704–681) was well prepared for his position as sovereign. With him Assyria acquired an exceptionally clever and gifted, though often extravagant, ruler. His father, interestingly enough, is not mentioned in any of his many inscriptions. He left the new city of Dur-Sharrukin at once and resided in Ashur for a few years until, in 701, he made Nineveh his capital.

Sennacherib had considerable difficulties with Babylonia. In 703 Marduk-apal-iddina

again crowned himself king with the aid of Elam, proceeding at once to ally himself with other enemies of Assyria. After nine months he was forced to withdraw when Sennacherib defeated a coalition army consisting of Babylonians, Aramaeans, and Elamites. The new puppet king of Babylonia was Bel-ibni (702–700), who had been raised in Assyria.

Sennacherib leading a military campaign, detail of a relief from Nineveh, c. 690 BC; in the British Museum. Reproduced by courtesy of the trustees of the British Museum

SARGON II

Sargon II (d. 705 BC) was one of the great kings of Assyria during the last century of its history. During his reign (721–705 BC), he extended and consolidated the conquests of his presumed father, Tiglath-pileser III.

Sargon is the Hebrew rendering (Isaiah chapter 20 verse 1) of Assyrian Sharru-kin, a throne name meaning "the king is legitimate." The name was undoubtedly chosen in reminiscence of two former kings of Assyria, particularly in commemoration of Sargon of Akkad (flourished 2300 BC).

Although Sargon's ancestry is partly veiled in mystery, he was probably a younger son of Tiglath-pileser III and consequently a brother of his predecessor Shalmaneser V, who may have died ignominiously or may have been deposed. It was for Sargon to resume the conquests and to improve the administration of the empire his father had begun to assemble.

Sargon II, detail of a relief from the palace at Khorsabad; in the Louvre, Paris. Courtesy of the Musée du Louvre, Paris; photograph, Maurice Chuzeville

Upon his accession to the throne, he was faced immediately with three major problems: dealing with the Chaldean and Aramaean chieftainships in the southern parts of Babylonia, with the kingdom of Urartu and the peoples to the north in the Armenian highlands, and with Syria and Palestine. By and large, these were the conquests made by Tiglath-pileser III. Sargon's problem was not only to maintain the status quo but to make further conquests to prove the might of the god Ashur, the national god of the Assyrian empire.

When Sargon succeeded to the Assyrian throne, Marduk-apal-iddina II (Merodach-Baladan of the Bible), a dissident chieftain of the Chaldean tribes in the marshes of southern Babylonia, committed the description of his victory over the invading Assyrian armies (720 BC) to writing on a clay cylinder, which he deposited in the city of Erech (modern Tall al-Warkā'). The presence of this record obviously did not suit Sargon. After having discharged other commitments, he uncovered Marduk-apal-iddina's record and removed it to his own residence, then at Kalakh (modern Nimrūd), substituting what has been described as an "improved" version that was more to his liking.

The extant texts reveal little about Sargon himself. With few exceptions, ancient Mesopotamian rulers have left no documents from which to write an actual biography.

No personal documents have survived from Sargon's reign, but it seems fair to assume that phraseologies uncommon in the inscriptions of other Assyrian kings, found in his texts, must have met with his approval, even though it is uncertain whether such phrases—sometimes turning into what is obviously poetry—were in fact conceived by Sargon himself or ascribed to him by his historiographers. The discovery, at Nimrūd, of a series of omens, the texts of which are written in cuneiform on beeswax encased in ivory and walnut boards and marked as being the property of the palace of Sargon, perhaps also throws some light on Sargon the man. Although he may not have introduced the method of recording cuneiform texts on wax, this novel method of committing texts to writing apparently took his fancy. This assumption tallies well with the interest he took in the engineering projects undertaken in cities he conquered. Sargon's palace at Khorsabad was dedicated in 706 BC, less than a year before he died.

An unparalleled record of Sargon's eighth campaign (714 BC)—in the form of a letter to the god Ashur—has been recovered. During the progress of this campaign, the author of the account visualized, or anticipated, the reactions of his adversary as, from a mountain, he watched the approach of the Assyrian armies. The passage, like many others in this unique text, constitutes an ingenious stylistic device unparalleled in Assyrian historical literature. The phraseology employed by the author is original by Mesopotamian standards as they are known today: inventive, resourceful, testifying to a fertile mind, and clearly deviating from the commonplace platitudes that mostly characterize the standard accounts of Assyrian kings. Whether or not Sargon himself is responsible for the wording of this narrative, it is to his credit that an account of this nature emerged from his chancery, with his approval and endorsement. Sargon is assumed to have died in battle in 705.

In 702 Sennacherib launched a raid into western Iran. In 701 there followed his most famous campaign, against Syria and Palestine, with the purpose of gaining control over the main road from Syria to Egypt in preparation for later campaigns against Egypt itself. When Sennacherib's army approached, Sidon immediately expelled its ruler, Luli, who was hostile to Assyria. The other allies either surrendered or were defeated. An Egyptian army was defeated at Eltekeh in Judah. Sennacherib laid siege to Jerusalem, and the king of Judah, Hezekiah, was called upon to surrender, but he did not comply. An Assyrian officer tried to incite the people of Jerusalem against Hezekiah, but his efforts failed. In view of the difficulty of surrounding a mountain stronghold such as Jerusalem, and of the minor importance of this town for the main purpose of the campaign, Sennacherib cut short the attack and left Palestine with his army, which according to the Bible (2 Kings chapter 19, verse 35) had been decimated by an epidemic. The number of Assyrian dead is reported to have risen to 185,000. Nevertheless, Hezekiah is reported to have paid tribute to Sennacherib on at least one occasion.

Bel-ibni of Babylonia seceded from the union with Assyria in 700. Sennacherib moved quickly, defeating Bel-ibni and replacing him with Sennacherib's oldest son, Ashur-nadin-shumi. The next few years were relatively peaceful. Sennacherib used this time to prepare a decisive attack against Elam, which time and again had supported Babylonian rebellions. The overland route to Elam had been cut off and fortified by the Elamites. Sennacherib had ships built in Syria and at Nineveh. The ships from Syria were moved on rollers from the Euphrates to the Tigris. The fleet sailed downstream and was quite successful in the lagoons of the Persian Gulf and along the southern coastline of Elam.

The Elamites launched a counteroffensive by land, occupying Babylonia and putting a man of their choice on the throne. Not until 693 were the Assyrians again able to fight their way through to the north. Finally, in 689, Sennacherib had his revenge. Babylon was conquered and completely destroyed, the temples plundered and leveled. The waters of the Arakhtu Canal were diverted over the ruins, and the inner city remained almost totally uninhabited for eight years. Even many Assyrians were indignant at this, believing that the Babylonian god Marduk must be grievously offended at the destruction of his temple and the carrying off of his image. Marduk was also an Assyrian deity, to whom many Assyrians turned in time of need. A political-theological propaganda campaign was launched to explain to the people that what had taken place was in accord with the wish of most of the gods. A story was written in which Marduk, because of a transgression, was captured and brought before a tribunal. Only a part of the commentary to this botched piece of literature is extant. Even the great poem of the creation of the world, the *Enuma elish*, was altered; the god Marduk was replaced by the god Ashur.

Sennacherib's boundless energies brought no gain to his empire, however, and probably weakened it. The tenacity of this king can be seen in his building projects; for example, when Nineveh needed water for irrigation, Sennacherib had his engineers divert the waters of a tributary of the Great Zab River. The canal had to cross a valley at Jerwan. An aqueduct was constructed, consisting of about two million blocks of limestone, with five huge, pointed archways over the brook in the valley. The bed of the canal on the aqueduct was sealed with cement containing magnesium. Parts of this aqueduct are still standing today. Sennacherib wrote of these and other technological accomplishments in minute detail, with illustrations.

Sennacherib built a huge palace in Nineveh, adorned with reliefs, some of them depicting the transport of colossal bull statues by water and by land. Many of the rooms were decorated with pictorial narratives in bas-relief telling of war and of building activities. Considerable advances can be noted in artistic execution, particularly in the portrayal of landscapes and animals. Outstanding are the depictions of the battles in the lagoons, the life in the military camps, and the deportations.

In 681 BC there was a rebellion. Sennacherib was assassinated by one or two of his sons in the temple of the god Ninurta at Kalakh. This god, along with the god Marduk, had been badly treated by Sennacherib, and the event was widely regarded as punishment of divine origin.

ESARHADDON

Ignoring the claims of his older brothers, an imperial council appointed Esarhaddon (Ashur-aha-iddina; 680–669) as Sennacherib's successor. The choice is all the more difficult to explain in that Esarhaddon, unlike his father, was friendly toward the Babylonians. It can be assumed that his energetic and designing mother, Zakutu (Naqia), who came from Syria or Judah, used all her influence on his behalf to override the national party of Assyria. The theory that he was a partner in plotting the murder of his father is rather improbable; at any rate, he was able to procure the loyalty of his father's army. His brothers had to flee to Urartu. In his inscriptions, Esarhaddon always mentions both his father and grandfather.

Defining the destruction of Babylon explicitly as punishment by the god Marduk, the new king soon ordered the reconstruction of the city. He referred to himself only as governor of Babylonia and through his policies obtained the support of the cities of Babylonia. At the beginning of his reign the Aramaean tribes were still allied with Elam against him, but Urtaku of Elam (675–664) signed a peace treaty and freed him for campaigning elsewhere. In 679 he stationed a garrison at the Egyptian border, because Egypt, under the Ethiopian king Taharqa, was planning to intervene in Syria. He put down with great severity a rebellion of the combined forces of Sidon, Tyre, and other Syrian cities. The time was ripe to attack Egypt, which was suffering under the rule of the Ethiopians and was by no means a united country. Esarhaddon's first attempt in 674–673 miscarried. In 671 BC, however, his forces took Memphis, the Egyptian capital. Assyrian consultants were assigned to assist the princes of the 22 provinces, their main duty being the collection of tribute.

Occasional threats came from the mountainous border regions of eastern Anatolia and Iran. Pushed forward by the Scythians, the Cimmerians in northern Iran and Transcaucasia tried to gain a foothold in Syria and western Iran. Esarhaddon allied himself with the Scythian king Partatua by giving him one of his daughters in marriage. In so doing he checked the movement of the Cimmerians. Nevertheless, the apprehensions of Esarhaddon can be seen in his many offerings, supplications, and requests to the sun god. These were concerned less with his own enterprises than with the plans of enemies and vassals and the reliability of civil servants. The priestesses of Ishtar had to reassure Esarhaddon constantly by calling out to him, "Do not be afraid." Previous kings, as far as is known, had never needed this kind of encouragement.

At home Esarhaddon was faced with serious difficulties from factions in the court. His oldest son had died early. The national party suspected his second son, Shamash-shum-ukin, of being too friendly with the Babylonians; he may also have been considered unequal to the task of kingship. His third son, Ashurbanipal, was given the succession in 672, Shamash-shum-ukin remaining crown prince of Babylonia. This arrangement caused much dissension, and some farsighted civil servants warned of disastrous effects. Nevertheless, the Assyrian nobles, priests, and city leaders were sworn to just such an adjustment of the royal line; even the vassal princes had to take very detailed oaths of allegiance to Ashurbanipal, with many curses against perjurers.

Another matter of deep concern for Esarhaddon was his failing health. He regarded eclipses of the moon as particularly alarming omens, and, in order to prevent a fatal illness from striking him at these times, he had substitute kings chosen who ruled during the three eclipses that occurred during his 12-year reign. The replacement kings died or were put to death after their brief term of office. During his off-terms Esarhaddon called himself "Mister Peasant." This practice implied that the gods could not distinguish between the real king and a false one—quite contrary to the usual assumptions of the religion.

Esarhaddon enlarged and improved the temples in both Assyria and Babylonia. He also constructed a palace in Kalakh, using many of the picture slabs of Tiglath-pileser III. The works that remain are not on the level of those of either his predecessors or of Ashurbanipal. He died while on an expedition to put down a revolt in Egypt.

ASHURBANIPAL (668–627) AND SHAMASH-SHUM-UKIN (668–648)

Although the death of his father occurred far from home, Ashurbanipal assumed the kingship as planned. He may have owed his fortunes to the intercession of his grandmother Zakutu, who had recognized his superior capacities. He tells of his diversified education by the priests and his training in armour-making as well as in other military arts. He may have been the only king in Assyria with a scholarly background. As crown prince he also had studied the administration of the vast empire. The record notes that the gods granted him a record harvest during the first year of his reign. There were also good crops in subsequent years. During these first years he also was successful in foreign policy, and his relationship with his brother in Babylonia was good.

In 668 he put down a rebellion in Egypt and drove out King Taharqa, but in 664 the nephew of Taharqa, Tanutamon, gathered forces for a new rebellion. Ashurbanipal went to Egypt, pursuing the Ethiopian prince far into the south. His decisive victory moved Tyre and other parts of the empire to resume regular payments of tribute. Ashurbanipal installed Psamtik (Greek: Psammetichos) as prince over the Egyptian region of Sais. In 656 Psamtik dislodged the Assyrian garrisons with the aid of Carian and Ionian mercenaries, making Egypt again independent. Ashurbanipal did not attempt to reconquer it. A former ally of Assyria, Gyges of Lydia, had aided Psamtik in his rebellion. In return, Assyria did not help Gyges when he was attacked by the Cimmerians. Gyges lost his throne and his life. His son Ardys decided that the payment of tribute to Assyria was a lesser evil than conquest by the Cimmerians.

Graver difficulties loomed in southern Babylonia, which was attacked by Elam in 664. Another attack came in 653, whereupon Ashurbanipal sent a large army that decisively defeated the Elamites. Their king was killed, and some of the Elamite states were encouraged to secede. Elam was no longer strong enough to assume an active part on the international scene. This victory had serious consequences for Babylonia. Shamash-shum-ukin had grown weary of being patronized by his domineering brother. He formed a secret alliance in 656 with the Iranians, Elamites, Aramaeans, Arabs, and Egyptians, directed against Ashurbanipal. The

withdrawal of defeated Elam from this alliance was probably the reason for a premature attack by Shamash-shum-ukin at the end of the year 652, without waiting for the promised assistance from Egypt. Ashurbanipal, taken by surprise, soon pulled his troops together. The Babylonian army was defeated, and Shamash-shum-ukin was surrounded in his fortified city of Babylon. His allies were not able to hold their own against the Assyrians. Reinforcements of Arabian camel troops also were defeated. The city of Babylon was under siege for three years. It fell in 648 amid scenes of horrible carnage, Shamash-shum-ukin dying in his burning palace.

After 648 the Assyrians made a few punitive attacks on the Arabs, breaking the forward thrust of the Arab tribes for a long time to come. The main objective of the Assyrians, however, was a final settlement of their relations with Elam. The refusal of Elam in 647 to extradite an Aramaean prince was used as pretext for a new attack that drove deep into its territory. The assault on the solidly fortified capital of Susa followed, probably in 646. The Assyrians destroyed the city, including its temples and palaces. Vast spoils were taken. As usual, the upper classes of the land were exiled to Assyria and other parts of the empire, and Elam became an Assyrian province. Assyria had now extended its domain to southwestern Iran. Cyrus I of Persia sent tribute and hostages to Nineveh, hoping perhaps to secure protection for his borders with Media. Little is known about the last years of Ashurbanipal's reign.

Ashurbanipal left more inscriptions than any of his predecessors. His campaigns were not always recorded in chronological order but clustered in groups according to their purpose. The accounts were highly subjective. One of his most remarkable accomplishments was the founding of the great palace library in Nineveh (modern Kuyunjik), which is today one of the most important sources for the study of ancient Mesopotamia. The king himself supervised its construction. Important works were kept in more than one copy, some intended for the king's personal use. The work of arranging and cataloging drew upon the experience of centuries in the management of collections in huge temple archives such as the one in Ashur. In his inscriptions Ashurbanipal tells of becoming an enthusiastic hunter of big game, acquiring a taste for it during a fight with marauding lions. In his palace at Nineveh the long rows of hunting scenes show what a masterful artist can accomplish in bas-relief; with these reliefs Assyrian art reached its peak. In the series depicting his wars, particularly the wars fought in Elam, the scenes are overloaded with human figures. Those portraying the battles with the Arabian camel troops are magnificent in execution.

One reason for the durability of the Assyrian empire was the practice of deporting large numbers of people from conquered areas and resettling others in their place. This kept many of the conquered nationalities from regaining their power. Equally important was the installation in conquered areas of a highly developed civil service under the leadership of trained officers. The highest-ranking civil servant carried the title of *tartān*, a Hurrian word. The *tartān*s also represented the king during his absence. In descending rank were the palace overseer, the main cupbearer, the palace administrator, and the governor of Assyria. The generals often held high official positions, particularly in the provinces. The civil service numbered about 100,000, many of them former inhabitants of subjugated provinces. Prisoners became slaves, but were later often freed.

No laws are known for the empire, although documents point to the existence of rules and standards for justice. Those who broke contracts were subject to severe penalties, even in cases of minor importance: the sacrifice of a son or the eating of a pound of wool and drinking of a great deal of water afterward, which led to a painful death. The position of women was inferior, except for the queen and some priestesses.

As yet there are no detailed studies of the economic situation during this period. The landed nobility still played an important role, in conjunction with the merchants in the cities. The large increase in the supply of precious metals—received as tribute or taken as spoils—did not disrupt economic stability in many regions.

Stimulated by the patronage of the kings and the great temples, the arts and crafts flourished during this period. The policy of resettling Aramaeans and other conquered peoples in Assyria brought many talented artists and artisans into Assyrian cities, where they introduced new styles and techniques. High-ranking provincial civil servants, who were often very powerful, saw to it that the provincial capitals also benefited from this economic and cultural growth.

Harran became the most important city in the western part of the empire; in the neighbouring settlement of Huzirina (modern Sultantepe, in northern Syria), the remains of an important library have been discovered. Very few Aramaic texts from this period have been found; the climate of Mesopotamia is not conducive to the preservation of the papyrus and parchment on which these texts were written. There is no evidence that a literary tradition existed in any of the other languages spoken within the borders of the Assyrian empire at this time, except in peripheral areas of Syria and Palestine.

Culturally and economically, Babylonia lagged behind Assyria in this period. The wars with Assyria—particularly the catastrophic defeats of 689 and 648—together with many smaller tribal wars disrupted trade and agricultural production. The great Babylonian temples fared best during this period, since they continued to enjoy the patronage of the Assyrian monarchs. Only a few documents from the temples have been preserved, however. There is evidence that the scribal schools continued to operate, and "Sumerian" inscriptions were even composed for Shamash-shum-ukin. In comparison with the Assyrian developments, the pictorial arts were neglected, and Babylonian artists may have found work in Assyria.

During this period people began to use the names of ancestors as a kind of family name. This increase in family consciousness is probably an indication that the number of old families was growing smaller. By this time the process of "Aramaicization" had reached even the oldest cities of Babylonia and Assyria.

Apparently this era was not very fruitful for literature either in Babylonia or in Assyria. In Assyria numerous royal inscriptions, some as long as 1,300 lines, were among the most important texts; some of them were diverse in content and well composed. Most of the hymns and prayers were written in the traditional style. Many oracles, often of unusual content, were proclaimed in the Assyrian dialect, most often by the priestesses of the goddess Ishtar of Arbela. In Assyria as in Babylonia, the beginnings of a real historical literature are observed; most of the authors have remained anonymous up to the present.

The many gods of the tradition were worshiped in Babylonia and Assyria in large and small temples, as in earlier times. Very detailed rituals regulated the sacrifices, and the interpretations of the ritual performances in the cultic

THE SIGNIFICANCE OF ASHURBANIPAL

Ashurbanipal carrying a basket in the rebuilding of the temple, stone bas-relief from the Esagila, Babylon, 650 BC; in the British Museum. Reproduced by courtesy of the trustees of the British Museum.

Ashurbanipal (also spelled Assurbanipal, or Asurbanipal), who reigned from 668 to 627 BC, was the last of the great kings of Assyria.

A person of religious zeal, he rebuilt or adorned most of the major shrines of Assyria and Babylonia, paying particular attention to the "House of Succession" and the Ishtar Temple at Nineveh. Many of his actions were guided by the omen reports, in which he took a personal and informed interest. He celebrated the New Year Festival, and one of his reliefs, showing him dining in a garden with his queen Ashur-sharrat, may illustrate this event. His younger brothers were priests in Harran and Ashur.

Ashurbanipal's outstanding contribution resulted from his academic interests. He assembled in Nineveh the first systematically collected and cataloged library in the ancient Middle East (of which approximately 20,720 Assyrian tablets and fragments have been preserved in the British Museum). At royal command, scribes searched out and collected or copied texts of every genre from temple libraries. These were added to the basic collection of tablets culled from Ashur, Calah, and Nineveh itself.

The major group includes omen texts based on observations of events; the behaviour and features of men, animals, and plants; and the motions of the Sun, Moon, planets, and stars. Lexicographical texts list in dictionary form Sumerian, Akkadian, and other words, all essential to the scribal educational system. Ashurbanipal also collected many incantations, prayers, rituals, fables, proverbs, and other "canonical" and "extracanonical" texts. The traditional Mesopotamian epics—such as the stories of Creation, Gilgamesh, Irra, Etana, and Anzu—have survived mainly due to their preservation in his library. The presence of handbooks, scientific texts, and some folk tales (The Poor Man of Nippur was a precursor of one of the Thousand and One Nights tales of Baghdad) show that this library, of which only a fraction of the clay tablets has survived, was more than a mere reference library geared to the needs of diviners and others responsible for the king's spiritual security; it covered the whole range of Ashurbanipal's personal literary interests, and many works bear the royal mark of ownership in their colophons.

The king was a patron of the arts; he adorned his new and restored palaces at Nineveh with sculptures depicting the main historical and ceremonial events of his long reign. The style shows a remarkable development over that of his predecessors, and many bas-reliefs have an epic quality unparalleled in the ancient world, which may well be because of the influence of this active and vigorous personality.

commentaries were rather different and sometimes very strange.

On some of the temple towers (ziggurats), astronomical observatories were installed. The earliest of these may have been the observatory of the Ninurta temple at Kalakh in Assyria, which dates back to the ninth century BC; it was destroyed with the city in 612. The most important observatory in Babylonia from about 580 was situated on the ziggurat Etemenanki, a temple of Marduk in Babylon. In Assyria the observation of the Sun, Moon, and stars had already reached a rather high level; the periodic recurrence of eclipses was established. After 600, astronomical observation and calculations developed steadily, and they reached their high point after 500, when Babylonian and Greek astronomers began their fruitful collaboration. Incomplete astronomical diaries, beginning in 652 and covering some 600 years, have been preserved.

DECLINE OF THE ASSYRIAN EMPIRE

Few historical sources remain for the last 30 years of the Assyrian empire. There are no extant inscriptions of Ashurbanipal after 640 BC, and the few surviving inscriptions of his successors contain only vague allusions to political matters. In Babylonia the silence is almost total until 625 BC, when the chronicles resume. The rapid downfall of the Assyrian empire was formerly attributed to military defeat, although it was never clear how the Medes and the Babylonians alone could have accomplished this. More recent work has established that after 635 a civil war occurred, weakening the empire so that it could no longer stand up against a foreign enemy. Ashurbanipal had twin sons. Ashur-etel-ilani was appointed successor to the throne, but his twin brother Sin-shar-ishkun did not recognize him. The fight between them and their supporters forced the old king to withdraw to Harran, in 632 at the latest, perhaps ruling from there over the western part of the empire until his death in 627. Ashur-etel-ilani governed in Assyria from about 633, but a general, Sin-shum-lisher, soon rebelled against him and proclaimed himself counter-king. Some years later (629?) Sin-shar-ishkun finally succeeded in obtaining the kingship. In Babylonian documents dates can be found for all three kings. To add to the confusion, until 626 there are also dates of Ashurbanipal and a king named Kandalanu. In 626 the Chaldean Nabopolassar (Nabu-apal-usur) revolted from Erech (Uruk) and occupied Babylon. There were several changes in government. King Ashur-etel-ilani was forced to withdraw to the west, where he died sometime after 625.

About the year 626 the Scythians laid waste to Syria and Palestine. In 625 the Medes became united under Cyaxares and began to conquer the Iranian provinces of Assyria. One chronicle relates of wars between Sin-shar-ishkun and Nabopolassar in Babylonia in 625–623. It was not long until the Assyrians were driven out of Babylonia. In 616 the Medes struck against Nineveh, but, according to the Greek historian Herodotus, were driven back by the Scythians. In 615, however, the Medes conquered Arrapkha (Kirkūk), and in 614 they took the old capital of Ashur, looting and destroying the city. Now Cyaxares and Nabopolassar made an alliance for the purpose of dividing Assyria. In 612 Kalakh and Nineveh succumbed to the superior strength of the allies. The revenge taken on the Assyrians was terrible: 200 years later Xenophon found the country still sparsely populated.

Sin-shar-ishkun, king of Assyria, found death in his burning palace. The commander of the Assyrian army in the west crowned himself king in the city of Harran, assuming the name of the founder of the empire, Ashur-uballiṭ II (611–609 BC). Ashur-uballiṭ had to face both the Babylonians and the Medes. They conquered Harran in 610, without, however, destroying the city completely. In 609 the remaining Assyrian troops had to capitulate. With this event Assyria disappeared from history. The great empires that succeeded it learned a great deal from the hated Assyrians, both in the arts and in the organization of their states.

THE NEO-BABYLONIAN EMPIRE

The Chaldeans, who inhabited the coastal area near the Persian Gulf, had never been entirely pacified by the Assyrians. About 630 Nabopolassar became king of the Chaldeans. In 626 he forced the Assyrians out of Erech (Uruk) and crowned himself king of Babylonia. He took part in the wars aimed at the destruction of Assyria. At the same time, he began to restore the dilapidated network of canals in the cities of Babylonia, particularly those in Babylon itself. He fought against the Assyrian Ashur-uballiṭ II and then against Egypt, his successes alternating with misfortunes. In 605 Nabopolassar died in Babylon.

NEBUCHADREZZAR II

Nabopolassar had named his oldest son, Nabu-kudurri-uṣur, after the famous king of the second dynasty of Isin, trained him carefully for his prospective kingship, and shared responsibility with him. When the father died in 605, Nebuchadrezzar was with his army in Syria; he had just crushed the Egyptians near Carchemish in a cruel, bloody battle and pursued them into the south. On receiving the news of his father's death, Nebuchadrezzar returned immediately to Babylon.

In his numerous building inscriptions he tells but rarely of his many wars; most of them end with prayers. The Babylonian chronicle is extant only for the years 605–594, and not much is known from other sources about the later years of this famous king. He went very often to Syria and Palestine, at first to drive out the Egyptians. In 604 he took the Philistine city of Ashkelon. In 601 he tried to push forward into Egypt but was forced to pull back after a bloody, undecided battle and to regroup his army in Babylonia. After smaller incursions against the Arabs of Syria, he attacked Palestine at the end of 598. King Jehoiakim of Judah had rebelled, counting on help from Egypt. According to the chronicle, Jerusalem was taken on March 16, 597. Jehoiakim had died during the siege, and his son, King Johoiachin, together with at least 3,000 Jews, was led into exile in Babylonia. They were treated well there, according to the documents. Zedekiah was appointed the new king. In 596, when danger threatened from the east, Nebuchadrezzar marched to the Tigris River and induced the enemy to withdraw. After a revolt in Babylonia had been crushed with much bloodshed, there were other campaigns in the west.

According to the Bible, Judah rebelled again in 589, and Jerusalem was placed under siege. The city fell in 587/586 and was completely destroyed. Many thousands of Jews were forced into the Babylonian Exile, and their country was reduced to a province of the Babylonian empire. The revolt had been caused by an Egyptian invasion that pushed as far as Sidon. Nebuchadrezzar laid siege to Tyre for 13 years without taking the city, because there was no fleet at his disposal. In 568/567 he attacked Egypt, again without much success, but from that time on the Egyptians refrained from further attacks on Palestine. Nebuchadrezzar lived at peace with Media throughout his reign and acted as a mediator after the Median-Lydian War of 590–585.

The Babylonian empire under Nebuchadrezzar extended to the Egyptian border. It had a well-functioning administrative system. Though he had to collect extremely high taxes and tributes in order to maintain his armies and carry out his building projects, Nebuchadrezzar made Babylonia one of the richest lands in western Asia—the more astonishing because it had been rather poor when it was ruled by the Assyrians. Babylon was the largest city of the "civilized world." Nebuchadrezzar maintained the existing canal systems and built many supplementary canals, making the land even more fertile. Trade and commerce flourished during his reign.

Nebuchadrezzar's building activities surpassed those of most of the Assyrian kings. He fortified the old double walls of

An artist's depiction of the biblical Tower of Babel as it may have appeared c. 1300 BC. This rendition was based on the Babylonian tower temple, built over the course of several centuries to twice the height of other temples. Hulton Archive/Getty Images

Babylon, adding another triple wall outside the old wall. In addition, he erected another wall, the Median Wall, north of the city between the Euphrates and the Tigris rivers. According to Greek estimates, the Median Wall may have been about 100 feet (30 metres) high. He enlarged the old palace and added many wings, so that hundreds of rooms with large inner courts were now at the disposal of the central offices of the empire. Colourful glazed-tile bas-reliefs decorated the walls. Terrace gardens, called the Hanging Gardens in

later accounts, were added. Hundreds of thousands of workers must have been required for these projects.

The temples were objects of special concern. Nebuchadrezzar devoted himself first and foremost to the completion of Etemenanki, the "Tower of Babel." Construction of this building began in the time of Nebuchadrezzar I, about 1110. It stood as a "building ruin" until the reign of Esarhaddon of Assyria, who resumed building about 680 but did not finish. Nebuchadrezzar II was able to complete the whole building. The mean dimensions of Etemenanki are to be found in the Esagila Tablet, which has been known since the late 19th century. Its base measured about 300 feet on each side, and it was 300 feet (91 metres) in height. There were five terracelike gradations surmounted by a temple, the whole tower being about twice the height of those of other temples. The wide street used for processions led along the eastern side by the inner city walls and crossed at the enormous Ishtar Gate with its world-renowned bas-relief tiles. Nebuchadrezzar also built many smaller temples throughout the country.

The Last Kings of Babylonia

Awil-Marduk (called Evil-Merodach in the Bible; 561–560), the son of Nebuchadrezzar, was unable to win the support of the priests of Marduk. His reign did not last long, and he was soon eliminated. His brother-in-law and successor, Nergal-shar-uṣur (called Neriglissar in classical sources; 559–556), was a general who undertook a campaign in 557 into the "rough" Cilician land, which may have been under the control of the Medes. His land forces were assisted by a fleet. His still-minor son Labashi-Marduk was murdered not long after that, allegedly because he was not suitable for his job.

The next king was the Aramaean Nabonidus (Nabu-naʿihd 556–539) from Harran, one of the most interesting and enigmatic figures of ancient times. His mother, Addagoppe, was a priestess of the god Sin in Harran. She came to Babylon and managed to secure responsible offices for her son at court. The god of the moon rewarded her piety with a long life—she lived to be 103—and she was buried in Harran with all the honours of a queen in 547. It is not clear which powerful faction in Babylon supported the kingship of Nabonidus. It may have been one opposing the priests of Marduk, who had become extremely powerful.

Nabonidus raided Cilicia in 555 and secured the surrender of Harran, which had been ruled by the Medes. He concluded a treaty of defense with Astyages of Media against the Persians, who had become a growing threat since 559 under their king Cyrus II. He also devoted himself to the renovation of many temples, taking an especially keen interest in old inscriptions. He gave preference to his god Sin and had powerful enemies in the priesthood of the Marduk temple. Modern excavators have found fragments of propaganda poems written against Nabonidus and also in support of him. Both traditions continued in Judaism.

Internal difficulties and the recognition that the narrow strip of land from the Persian Gulf to Syria could not be defended against a major attack from the east induced Nabonidus to leave Babylonia around 552 and to reside in Taima (Taymāʾ) in northern Arabia. There he organized an Arabian province with the assistance of Jewish mercenaries. His viceroy in Babylonia was his son Bel-shar-uṣur, the Belshazzar of the Book of Daniel in the Bible. Cyrus turned this to his own advantage by annexing Media in 550. Nabonidus, in turn, allied himself with Croesus of Lydia in order to fight Cyrus. Yet, when Cyrus attacked Lydia and annexed it in 546, Nabonidus was not able to help Croesus. Cyrus bode his time.

In 542 Nabonidus returned to Babylonia, where his son had been able to maintain good order in external matters but had not overcome a growing internal opposition to his father. Consequently, Nabonidus's career after his return was short-lived, though he tried hard to regain the support of the Babylonians. He appointed his daughter to be high priestess of the god Sin in Ur, thus returning to the Sumerian-Old Babylonian religious tradition. The priests of Marduk looked to Cyrus, hoping to have better relations with him than with Nabonidus. They promised Cyrus the surrender of Babylon without a fight if he would grant them their privileges in return. In 539 Cyrus attacked northern Babylonia with a large army, defeating Nabonidus, and entered the city of Babylon without a battle. The other cities did not offer any resistance either. Nabonidus surrendered, receiving a small territory in eastern Iran. Tradition has confused him with his great predecessor Nebuchadrezzar II. The Bible refers to him as Nebuchadrezzar in the Book of Daniel.

Babylonia's peaceful submission to Cyrus saved it from the fate of Assyria. It became a territory under the Persian crown but kept its cultural autonomy.

Even the racially mixed western part of the Babylonian empire submitted without resistance.

By 620 the Babylonians had grown tired of Assyrian rule. They were also weary of internal struggle. They were easily persuaded to submit to the order of the Chaldean kings. The result was a surprisingly rapid social and economic consolidation, helped along by the fact that after the fall of Assyria no external enemy threatened Babylonia for more than 60 years. In the cities the temples were an important part of the economy, having vast benefices at their disposal. The business class regained its strength, not only in the trades and commerce but also in the management of agriculture in the metropolitan areas. Livestock breeding—sheep, goats, beef cattle, and horses—flourished, as did poultry farming. The cultivation of corn, dates, and vegetables grew in importance. Much was done to improve communications, both by water and land, with the western provinces of the empire. The collapse of the Assyrian empire had the consequence that many trade arteries were rerouted through Babylonia. Another result of the collapse was that the city of Babylon became a world centre.

The immense amount of documentary material and correspondence that has survived has not yet been fully analyzed. No new system of law or administration seems to have developed during that time. The Babylonian dialect gradually became Aramaicized; it was still written primarily on clay tablets that often bore added material in Aramaic lettering. Parchment and papyrus documents have not survived. In contrast to advances in other fields, there is no evidence of much artistic creativity. Aside from some of the inscriptions of the kings, especially Nabonidus, which were not comparable from a literary standpoint with those of the Assyrians, the main efforts were devoted to the rewriting of old texts. In the fine arts, only a few monuments have any suggestion of new tendencies.

MESOPOTAMIA UNDER THE PERSIANS

Cyrus II, the founder of the Achaemenian Empire, united Babylonia with his country in a personal union, assuming the title of "King of Babylonia, King of the Lands." His son Cambyses was appointed vice-king and resided in Sippar. The Persians relied on the support of the priests and the business class in the cities. In a Babylonian inscription, Cyrus relates with pride his peaceful, bloodless conquest of the city of Babylon. At the same time, he speaks of Marduk as the king of gods. His moderation and restraint were rewarded. Babylonia became the richest province of his empire.

There is no indication of any national rebellion in Babylonia under Cyrus and Cambyses (529–522). That there must have been an accumulation of discontent became clear at the ascension to the throne of Darius I (522–486), when a usurper seized the throne of Babylonia under the name of Nebuchadrezzar (III) only to lose both the throne and his life after 10 weeks. Darius waived any punitive action. He had to take more drastic measures in 521, when a new Nebuchadrezzar incited another rebellion. This usurper's reign lasted two months. Executions and plundering followed; Darius ordered that the inner walls of Babylon be demolished, and he reformed the organization of the state. Babylon, however, remained the capital of the new satrapy and also became the administrative headquarters for the satrapies of Assyria and Syria. One result was that the palace had to be enlarged.

Babylonia remained a wealthy and prosperous land, in contrast to Assyria, which was still a poor country. At the same time, the administration of the kingdom was more and more in the hands of the Persians, and the tax burdens grew heavier. This produced discontent, centring especially on the large temples in Babylon. Xerxes (486–465) had his residence in Babylon while he was crown prince, and he knew the country very well. When he assumed his kingship, he immediately curtailed the autonomy of the satrapies. This, in turn, gave rise to many rebellions. In Babylonia there were two short interim governments of Babylonian pretenders during 484–482. Xerxes retaliated by desecrating and partially destroying the holy places of the god Marduk and the Tower of Babel in the city of Babylon. Priests were executed, and the statue of Marduk was melted down.

The members of the royal family still resided in the palaces of the city of Babylon, but Aramaic became more and more the language of the official administration. One source of information for this period are the clay-tablet archives of the commercial house of Murashu and Sons of Nippur for the years of 455–403, which tell much about the important role the Iranians played in the country. The state domains were largely in their hands. They controlled many minor feudal tenants, grouped into social classes according to ancestry and occupation. The business people were predominantly Babylonians and Aramaeans, but there were also Jews.

The documents become increasingly sparse after 400. The cultural life of Babylon became concentrated in a few central cities, particularly Babylon and Erech; Ur and Nippur were also important centres. The work of astronomers continued, as evidenced in records of observations. Nabu-rimanni, living and working around 500, and Kidinnu, fifth or fourth century BC, were known to the Greeks; both astronomers are famous for their methods of calculating the courses of the Moon and the planets. In the field of literature, religious poetic works as well as texts of omens and Sumero-Akkadian word lists were constantly copied, often with commentaries.

CHAPTER 5

MESOPOTAMIA FROM c. 320 BC TO c. AD 620

The political history of Mesopotamia between about 320 BC and AD 620 is divided among three periods of foreign rule—the Seleucids to 141 BC, the Parthians to AD 224, and the Sāsānians until the Arab invasions of the seventh century AD. Sources are scarce, consisting mainly of a few notices in the works of classical authors such as Strabo, Pliny, Polybius, and Ptolemy, while the cuneiform sources are mainly incantations, accounts of religious rites, and copies of ancient religious texts.

THE SELEUCID PERIOD

At the end of the Achaemenian Empire, Mesopotamia was partitioned into the satrapy of Babylonia in the south, while the northern part of Mesopotamia was joined with Syria in another satrapy. It is not known how long this division lasted, but, by the death of Alexander the Great in 323 BC, the north was removed from Syria and made a separate satrapy.

SELEUCUS

In the wars between the successors of Alexander, Mesopotamia suffered much from the passage and the pillaging of armies. When Alexander's empire was divided in 321 BC, one of his generals, Seleucus (later Seleucus I Nicator),

A silver coin (tetradrachma) minted with the image of Seleucus I. At first displaced as satrap of Babylonia, Seleucus fought his way back to rule over a wide swath of Mesopotamia. British Museum, London, UK/ The Bridgeman Art Library/Getty Images

received the satrapy of Babylonia to rule. From about 315 to about 312 BC, however, Antigonus I Monophthalmus (The "One-Eyed") took over the satrapy as ruler of all Mesopotamia, and Seleucus had to flee and accept refuge with Ptolemy of Egypt.

With the aid of Ptolemy, Seleucus was able to enter Babylon in 312 BC (311 by the Babylonian reckoning) and hold it for a short time against the forces of Antigonus before marching to the east, where he consolidated his power. It is uncertain when he returned to Babylonia and reestablished his rule there; it may have been in 308, but by 305 BC he had assumed the title of king. With the defeat and death of Antigonus at the Battle of Ipsus in 301, Seleucus became the ruler of a large empire stretching from modern Afghanistan to the Mediterranean Sea. He founded a number of cities, the most important of which were Seleucia, on the Tigris, and Antioch, on the Orontes River in Syria. The latter, named after his father or his son, both of whom were called Antiochus, became the principal capital, while Seleucia became the capital of the eastern provinces. The dates of the founding of these two cities are unknown, but presumably Seleucus founded Seleucia after he became king, while Antioch was built after the defeat of Antigonus.

Mesopotamia is scarcely mentioned in the Greek sources relating to the Seleucids, because the Seleucid rulers were occupied with Greece and Anatolia and with wars with the Ptolemies of Egypt in Palestine and Syria. Even the political division of Mesopotamia is uncertain, especially since Alexander, Seleucus, and Seleucus' son Antiochus I Soter all founded cities that were autonomous, like the Greek polis.

POLITICAL DIVISIONS

The political division of the land into 19 or 20 small satrapies, which is found later, under the Parthians, began under the Seleucids. Geographically, however, Mesopotamia can be divided into four areas: Characene, also called Mesene, in the south; Babylonia, later called Asūristān, in the middle; northern Mesopotamia, where there was later a series of small states such as Gordyene, Osroene, Adiabene, and Garamea; and finally the desert areas of the upper Euphrates, in Sāsānian times called Arabistān. These four areas had different histories down to the Arab conquest in the seventh century, although all of them were subject first to the Seleucids and then to the Parthians and Sāsānians. At times, however, several of the areas were fully independent, in theory as well as in fact, while the relations of certain cities with provincial governments and with the central government varied. From cuneiform sources it is known that traditional religious practices and forms of government as well as other customs continued in Mesopotamia; there were only a few Greek centres, such as Seleucia and the island of Ikaros (modern Faylakah, near Kuwait), where the practices of the Greek polis held sway. Otherwise, native cities had a few Greek officials or garrisons but continued to function as they had in the past.

Seleucia on the Tigris was not only the eastern capital, but also an autonomous city ruled by an elected senate, and it replaced Babylon as the administrative and commercial centre of the old province of Babylonia. In the south several cities, such as Furat and Charax, grew rich on the maritime trade with India;

Charax became the main entrepôt for trade after the fall of the Seleucids. In the north there was no principal city, but several towns, such as Arbela (modern Irbīl) and Nisibis (modern Nusaybin), later became important centres. In the desert region, "caravan cities" such as Hatra and Palmyra began their rise in the Seleucid period and had their heyday under the Parthians.

The only time that the Seleucid kings lost control of Mesopotamia was from 222 to 220 BC, when Molon, the governor of Media, revolted and marched to the west. When the new Seleucid king, Antiochus III, moved against him from Syria, however, Molon's forces deserted him, and the revolt ended. The Parthians, under their able king Mithradates I, conquered Seleucid territory in Iran and entered Seleucia in 141 BC. After the death of Mithradates I in 138 BC, Antiochus VII began a campaign to recover the Seleucid domains in the east. This campaign was successful until Antiochus VII lost his life in Iran in 129 BC. His death ended Seleucid rule in Mesopotamia and marked the beginning of small principalities in both the south and north of Mesopotamia.

GREEK INFLUENCE

Seleucid rule brought changes to Mesopotamia, especially in the cities where Greeks and Macedonians were settled. In these cities the king usually made separate agreements with the Greek officials of the city regarding civil and military authority, immunity from taxes or corvée, or the like. Native cities continued with their old systems of local government, much as they had under the Achaemenians. Greek gods were worshiped in temples dedicated to them in the Greek cities, and native Mesopotamian gods had temples dedicated to them in the native cities. In time, however, syncretism and identification of the foreign and local deities developed. Although the policy of Hellenization was not enforced upon the population, Greek ideas did influence the local educated classes, just as local practices were gradually adopted by the Greeks. As in Greece and the lands of the eastern Mediterranean, in Mesopotamia the philosophies of the Stoics and other schools probably had an impact, as did mystery religions. Both were hallmarks of the Hellenistic Age. Unfortunately there is no evidence from the east on the popularity of Greek beliefs among the local population, and scholars can only speculate on the basis of the fragmentary notices in authors such as Strabo. The Seleucid rulers respected the native priesthoods of Mesopotamia, and there is no record of any persecutions. On the contrary, the rulers seem to have favoured local religious practices, and ancient forms of worship continued. Cuneiform writing by priests, who copied incantations and old religious texts, continued into the Parthian period.

The administrative institutions of the countryside of Mesopotamia remained even more traditional than those of the cities; the old taxes were simply paid to new masters. The satrapy, much reduced in size from Achaemenian times, was the basis for Seleucid control of the countryside. A satrap or strategus (a military title) headed each satrapy, and the satrapies were divided into hyparchies or eparchies. The sources that use these and other words, such as toparchy, are unclear about the subdivisions of the satrapy. There was a great variety of smaller units of administration. In the capital and in the provincial centres, both Greek and Aramaic were used as the written languages of the government. The use of cuneiform in government documents ceased sometime during the Achaemenian period, but it continued in religious texts until the first century of the Common Era. The archives were managed both in the capital and in provincial cities by an official called a *bibliophylax*. There were many financial officials (*oikonomoi*); some of them oversaw royal possessions, and others managed local taxes and other economic matters. The legal system in the Seleucid empire is not well understood, but presumably both local Mesopotamian laws and Greek laws, which had absorbed or replaced old Achaemenian imperial laws, were in force. Excavations at Seleucia have uncovered thousands of seal impressions on clay, evidence of a developed system of controls and taxes on commodities of trade. Many of the sealings are records of payment of a salt tax. Most of the tolls and tariffs, however, were local assessments rather than royal taxes.

Artistic remains from the Seleucid period are exceedingly scarce, and, in contrast to Achaemenian art, no royal or monumental art has been recovered. One might characterize the objects that can be dated to the Seleucid era as popular or private art, such as seals, statuettes, and clay figurines. Both Greek and local styles are found, with an amalgam of styles prevalent at the end of Seleucid rule, evidence of a syncretism in cultures. The numerous statues and statuettes of Heracles found in the east testify to the great popularity of the Greek deity, in Mesopotamia identified with the local god Nergal.

Aramaic was the "official" written language of the Achaemenian Empire. After the conquests of Alexander the Great, Greek, the language of the conquerors, replaced Aramaic. Under the Seleucids, however, both Greek and Aramaic were used throughout the empire, although Greek was the principal language of government. Gradually Aramaic underwent changes in different parts of the empire, and in Mesopotamia in the time of the Parthians it evolved into Syriac, with dialectical differences from western Syriac, used in Syria and Palestine. In southern Mesopotamia, other dialects evolved, one of which was Mandaic, the scriptural language of the Mandaean religion.

Literature in local languages is nonexistent, except for copies of ancient religious texts in cuneiform writing and fragments of Aramaic writing. There were authors who wrote in Greek, but little of their work has survived and that only as excerpts in later works. The most important of these authors was Berosus, a Babylonian priest who wrote about the history of his country, probably under Antiochus I (reigned 281–261 BC). Although the excerpts of his work that are preserved deal with the ancient, mythological past and with astrology and astronomy, the fact that they are in Greek is indicative of interest among local Greek colonists in the culture of their neighbours. Another popular author was Apollodorus of Artemita (a town near Seleucia), who wrote under the Parthians a history of Parthia in Greek as well as other works on geography. Greek continued to be a lingua franca used by educated people in Mesopotamia well into the Parthian period.

Under the Seleucid system of dating, as far as is known, a fixed year became the basis for continuous dating for the first time in the Middle East. The year chosen was the year of entry of Seleucus into Babylon, 311 BC according to the Mesopotamian reckoning and 312 BC according to the Syrians. Before this time, dating had been only according to the regnal years of the ruling monarch (e.g., "fourth year of Darius"). The Parthians, following the Seleucids, sought to institute their own system of reckoning based on some event in their past that scholars can only surmise—possibly the assumption of the title of king by the first ruler of the Parthians, Arsaces.

Since Greece was overpopulated at the beginning of Seleucid rule, it was not difficult to persuade colonists to come to the east, especially when they were given plots of land (*cleroi*) from royal domains that they could pass on to their descendants; if they had no descendants, the land would revert to the king. Theoretically all land belonged to the ruler, but actually local interests prevailed. As time passed, however, the influx of Greek colonists diminished and then ended when the wars of the Hellenistic kings interrupted this movement. Nonetheless, Greek influences continued, and it is fascinating to find in cuneiform documents records of families where the father has a local name and his son a Greek one, and vice versa. Inasmuch as Mesopotamia was peaceful under the Seleucids, the processes of accommodation and assimilation among the people appear to have flourished.

THE PARTHIAN PERIOD

MITHRADATES II AND HIS SUCCESSORS

The coming of the Parthians changed Mesopotamia even less than the establishment of the Seleucid kingdom had, for as early as the middle of the second century BC local dynasts had proclaimed their independence. There is no evidence indicating whether the cities of Mesopotamia surrendered piecemeal or all at once or whether they submitted voluntarily or after fighting.

In any case, Seleucia was treated better by the Parthians than it had been by the Seleucids, and the local government retained its autonomy. Parthian troops did not occupy Seleucia but remained in a garrison site called Ctesiphon near Seleucia; it later grew into a city and replaced Seleucia as the capital. In Characene in southern Mesopotamia a Seleucid satrap with an Iranian name, Hyspaosines, issued coins about 125 BC, a sign of his independence; the actual date for this may have been earlier. He changed the name of the city Antiochia on the lower Tigris to Spasinou Charax, meaning "The Fort of Hyspaosines," and made it his capital. All the coins issued from his capital have Greek legends. His troops moved north and occupied Babylon and Seleucia probably sometime in 127 BC, when the Parthians were fighting nomadic invaders in the eastern part of their territory.

His rule there must have been short, however, for the Parthian governor of Babylon and the north, Himerus, was back in Seleucia and Babylon by 126. Himerus could not have been a rebel, since he struck coins in the name of the Parthian rulers Phraates II and Artabanus II, both of whom were killed in fighting in eastern Iran. Himerus abused his power and is said to have oppressed the cities of Mesopotamia, plundering them and killing their inhabitants. Cuneiform documents from Babylon stop after this date, indicating that the city did not survive the depredations of Himerus, who vanished.

Parthian sovereignty was restored by the ninth Arsacid king, Mithradates II, who came to the throne about 124 BC. The son of Artabanus II, Mithradates II

recovered all Mesopotamia and conquered Characene, overstriking coins of Hyspaosines and driving him from his capital in 122 or 121 BC. By 113, if not earlier, Dura-Europus on the Euphrates was in Parthian hands. In 95 BC the Armenian Tigranes II, a hostage at the court of Mithradates, was placed on the throne of Armenia by his Parthian overlord, and the small kingdoms of northern Mesopotamia—Adiabene, Gordyene, and Osroene—gave allegiance to Mithradates. Mithradates II died about 87 BC, although he may have died earlier, since the period after 90 BC is dark and a usurper named Gotarzes may have ruled for a few years in Mesopotamia.

During the reign of Mithradates II the first contacts with Rome, under Lucius Cornelius Sulla, were made, and portents of future struggles were evident in the lack of any agreement between the two powers. Sulla was sent to the east by the Roman Senate to govern Cilicia in Anatolia. In 92 BC Orobazes, an ambassador from Mithradates II, came to him seeking a treaty, but nothing was concluded, since instructions from Rome did not include negotiations with the Parthian power.

Tigranes II took advantage of struggles between several claimants to the Parthian throne to expand Armenian territory into Mesopotamia, and the small states in the north gave him their allegiance. It was not until 69 BC, when the Roman general Lucius Licinius Lucullus captured Tigranokerta, Tigranes' capital, that Mesopotamia returned to Parthian rule. Thereafter wars between the Romans and the Parthians were to dominate the political history of Mesopotamia.

The Parthians left the local administrations and rulers intact when they conquered Mesopotamia. According to Pliny the Elder (*Natural History* VI. 112) the Parthian empire consisted of 18 kingdoms, 11 of which were called the upper kingdoms (or satrapies), while seven were called lower kingdoms, meaning that they were located on the plains of Mesopotamia. The centre of the lower kingdoms was ancient Babylonia, called Beth Aramaye in Aramaic, and it was governed directly by the Parthian ruler. In the south was Characene, while to the northeast of Ctesiphon, which had supplanted Seleucia as the Parthian capital, was Garamea, with its capital at modern Kirkūk. Adiabene had Arbela as its capital, and farther north was a province called Beth Nuhadra in Aramaic, which seems to have been governed by a general who was directly responsible to the Parthian king, because this province bore the brunt of Roman invasions. Nisibis was the main city of the desert area of Arabistān, but at the end of the Parthian period the desert caravan city of Hatra claimed hegemony over this area. There were other principalities in the northwest: Sophene, where Tigranes' capital was located; Gordyene and Zabdicene (near modern Çölemerik in eastern Turkey), located to the east of Sophene; and Osroene, with its capital Edessa (modern Urfa, Tur.), which lay inside the Roman sphere of influence. Rule over so many small kingdoms gave Mithradates II the title "King of Kings," also borne by later Parthian rulers.

CONFLICT WITH ROME

The defeat of the Roman legions under Marcus Licinius Crassus by the Parthians at the Battle of Carrhae (Carrhae is the Roman name for Harran) in 53 BC heralded a period of Parthian power and expansion in the Middle East, but the tide turned under Mark Antony in 36–34 BC, and thereafter the power structure in the east remained volatile, with the two great states, Rome and Parthia, contending for predominance in the region. Armenia was a perennial bone of contention between the two powers, each of which sought to put its candidate on the throne.

Parthian rule was not firm over all Mesopotamia. Thus, for example, during the reign of Artabanus III (AD 12–38), the Jewish brigands Asinaeus and Anilaeus set up a free state north of Ctesiphon that lasted 15 years before it was overcome by the Parthians. With the end of cuneiform records and with the attention of classical sources turned to the wars between the Romans and the Parthians, information about internal affairs in Mesopotamia becomes almost nonexistent. Hellenism continued to flourish, for many Parthian kings had the epithet "Philhellene" placed on their coins, but during the last two centuries of Parthian rule Greek influences declined in favour of Iranian ones, while central authority suffered from the usurpations of powerful nobles and local kings. From coinage it is known that the city of Seleucia revolted against central control at the end of Artabanus' reign and maintained its independence for a number of years.

Peace was broken by the Roman emperor Nero, who sought to put his client on the throne of Armenia, but, after several years of conflict, peace was arranged in 63. Vologeses I (c. AD 51–80) founded the city Vologesias, near Seleucia, as his capital, but the whole area (including Ctesiphon and Seleucia) became an urban complex called Māhōzē in Aramaic and Al-Madā'in in Arabic; both names mean "The Cities."

Internal rivalries in the Parthian state gave the Romans an opportunity to attack, and control over Armenia was the casus belli for the Roman emperor Trajan's advance into Mesopotamia in 116. Adiabene, as well as the entire Tigris-Euphrates basin of northern Mesopotamia, was incorporated as a province into the Roman Empire. Trajan advanced to the Persian Gulf, but he died of illness and his successor Hadrian made peace, abandoning the conquests in Mesopotamia, although client states remained.

The second century of the Common Era was a dark period in Parthian history, but it was a time of growth in wealth and influence of the caravan cities of Palmyra, Hatra, and Mesene (formerly Characene). Armenia continued to be a bone of contention between the two great powers, and hostilities occasionally flared up. In 164–165 the Roman general Gaius Avidius Cassius captured the capital cities Ctesiphon and Seleucia, but an epidemic forced the Romans to retreat and peace was restored. Returning soldiers spread the disease throughout the Roman Empire, with devastating consequences. The terms of peace favoured the Romans, who secured control of Nisibis and the Khābūr River valley.

The next great war was the invasion of the Roman emperor Septimius Severus to punish the Parthians, who had supported his rival Pescennius Niger and had annexed some territory in Mesopotamia in return for their support. Severus took and sacked Ctesiphon in 198. Because the devastated countryside contained no supplies for the Romans, they were soon compelled to retreat. A siege of Hatra in 199 by Severus failed, and peace was made. Conflict between two claimants to the Parthian throne, Vologeses IV or V and Artabanus V, gave the Roman emperor Caracalla an excuse to invade Adiabene, but in 217 he was assassinated on the road from Edessa to Carrhae, and the Romans made peace. The end of the Parthian kingdom was near, and the advent of the Sāsānians brought a new phase in the history of Mesopotamia.

DEMOGRAPHIC CHANGES

Parthian rule brought little change in the administration and institutions of Mesopotamia as it had existed under the Seleucids, except for a general weakening of central authority under the feudal

Tablet dedicated to Shamash Utu, the Mesopotamian sun god. Citizens continued to worship Shamash even as Parthian rule brought about a move toward a more universalist form of religion. Erich Lessing/Art Resource, NY

Parthians. The Parthians instituted a new era, beginning in 247 BC, but it paralleled rather than replaced the Seleucid era of reckoning, and the Parthian vanished at the end of the dynasty. As far as can be determined, Hellenism was never proscribed under the Parthians, although it grew weaker toward the end of Parthian rule. From archaeological surveys around Susa, located in the kingdom of Elymais in modern Khūzestān, and from the Diyālā plain northeast of Ctesiphon, it seems that the population of the land increased greatly under the Parthians, as did trade and commerce. The coinage of the later Parthian rulers became more and more debased, probably as a result of the many internecine wars and the lack of control by the central authority. Local rulers also issued their own coinages in Persis, Elymais, Mesene, and elsewhere.

Changes took place in the demography of Mesopotamia under the Parthians, and perhaps the most striking development among the population was the increase of Arab infiltration from the desert, which resulted in Arab dynasties in the oasis settlements of Palmyra and

Hatra. Similarly, an influx of Armenian settlers in the north changed the composition of the local population. After the fall of the Temple of Jerusalem to the Romans in 70, many Jews fled to Mesopotamia, where they joined their coreligionists. Nehardea, north of Ctesiphon, became a centre of Jewish population. Naturally, many migrants from the east also came to Mesopotamia in the wake of the Parthian occupation. With many merchants from east and west passing through or remaining in Mesopotamia, the population became more diverse than it had previously been.

During the Parthian occupation the ancient religion and cults of Mesopotamia came to an end and were replaced by mixed Hellenic and Asian mystery religions and Iranian cults. Local Semitic cults of Bel, Allat, and other deities flourished alongside temples dedicated to Greek gods such as Apollo. The sun deity Shamash was worshiped at Hatra and elsewhere, but the henotheism (belief in the worship of one god, though the existence of other gods is granted) of the ancient Middle East was giving way to acceptance of universalist religions, if the prevalent view cannot yet be called one of monotheism. In Mesopotamia, in particular, the influence of Jewish monotheism, with the beginning of rabbinic schools and the organization of the community under a leader, the exilarch (*resh galuta* in Aramaic), must have had a significant influence on the local population. Toward the end of the reign of Artabanus

III, the royal family of Adiabene converted to Judaism.

In the first two centuries of the Common Era, Christianity and various baptismal sects also began to expand into Mesopotamia. So far no Mithraeums (underground temples for the worship of the god Mithra), such as existed in the Roman Empire, have been found in Mesopotamia, except at Dura-Europus, where Roman troops were stationed. Many local cults and shrines, such as that of the Sabians and their moon deity at Harran, however, continued to exist until the Islamic conquest. Parthian Zoroastrianism reinforced local Zoroastrian communities in Mesopotamia left from the time of the Achaemenians, and one of the Gnostic baptismal religions, Mandaeanism, which is still in existence, had its beginning at this time. Although Christian missionaries were active in Mesopotamia in the Parthian period, no centres, such as the one established later at Nisibis, have been reported, and it may be supposed that their activity at first was mainly confined to Jewish communities.

PARTHIAN ARTS

Archaeological evidence indicates that the Parthians had a more marked influence on art and architecture. Local schools of art flourished, and at first Greek ideals predominated, but in the last two centuries of Parthian rule a "Parthian style" is evident in the art recovered from Mesopotamia and other regions. Whereas Achaemenian and Sāsānian art are royal or imperial and monumental, Parthian art, like Seleucid art, can be characterized as "popular." Parthian works of art reflect the many currents of culture among the populace, and one may say that it is expressionist and stylized, in contrast with Greek and Roman naturalistic or realistic art.

The characteristics of Parthian art in Mesopotamia are total frontality (i.e., the representation of figures in full face) in portraits, along with an otherworldly quality. In Middle Eastern art from previous periods, figures were almost always shown in profile. Another new feature of Parthian art is the frequent portrayal of the "flying gallop" in sculpture and painting, not unexpected in view of the importance of cavalry and mounted archers in the Parthian armies. Likewise, Parthian costume, with baggy trousers, became the mode over much of the Middle East and is portrayed in painting and sculpture. In architecture the use of *eyvan*s (arches in porticoes) and domed vaults is attributed to the Parthian period; they may have originated in Mesopotamia. Parthian art influenced that of the Nabataeans in Roman territory, as it did others throughout the Middle East.

Parthian was an Iranian language written in the Aramaic alphabet. It had an enormous number of words and even phrases that were borrowed from Aramaic, and scribal training was necessary to learn these. Syriac, being a Semitic language with emphasis on consonants, evolved several alphabets based on the Aramaic alphabet. The Aramaic alphabet was better suited to Syriac than to Parthian phonology. Parthian was therefore difficult to read and was mainly used by scribes or priests for official or religious writings.

The largest lacuna is in literature from the Parthian period. The largely oral literature of the Parthians, famous for their minstrels and poetry, does not seem to have found many echoes in Mesopotamia, where the settled society contrasted with the heroic, chivalric, and feudal society of the Iranian nomads that continued to dominate Parthian mores even after they had settled in Mesopotamia. Nonetheless, the end of the Parthian period saw the beginning of Syriac literature, which is Christian Aramaic, and some of early Syriac literature, such as the "Song of the Pearl," contains Parthian elements.

In the realm of language, rather than literature, the writing of Aramaic changes to Parthian in the second century AD, as can be seen from a bilingual (Greek and Parthian) inscription on a bronze statue from Seleucia dated AD 150–151. It tells how Vologeses III defeated the king of Mesene and took over the entire country. After this period one no longer speaks of Aramaic, but of Parthian and Syriac written in a new cursive alphabet.

THE SĀSĀNIAN PERIOD

The Sāsānian period marks the end of the ancient and the beginning of the

Depiction of the Roman Emperor Valerian being captured by the Persian King Shāpūr. Mansell/ Time & Life Pictures/Getty Images

medieval era in the history of the Middle East. Universalist religions such as Christianity, Manichaeism, and even Zoroastrianism and Judaism absorbed local religions and cults at the beginning of the third century. Both the Sāsānian and the Roman empires ended by adopting an official state religion, Zoroastrianism for the former and Christianity for the latter. In Mesopotamia, however, older cults such as that of the Mandaeans, the moon cult of Harran, and others continued alongside the great religions. The new rulers were not as tolerant as the Seleucids and Parthians

had been, and persecutions occurred under Sāsānian rule.

ARDASHĪR I AND HIS SUCCESSORS

After Ardashīr I, the first of the Sāsānians, consolidated his position in Persis (modern Fārs province), he moved into southern Mesopotamia, and Mesene submitted. In 224 he defeated and killed the last Parthian ruler, Artabanus V, after which Mesopotamia quickly fell before him and Ctesiphon became the main capital of the Sāsānian empire. In 230

Ardashīr besieged Hatra but failed to take it. Hatra called on Roman aid, and in 232 the Roman emperor Severus Alexander launched a campaign that halted Ardashīr's progress. At the death of Severus Alexander in 235, the Sāsānians took the offensive, and probably in 238 Nisibis and Harran came under their control. Hatra was probably captured in early 240, after which Ardashīr's son Shāpūr was made coregent. Ardashīr himself died soon afterward.

The Roman emperor Gordian III led a large army against Shāpūr I in 243. The Romans retook Harran and Nisibis and defeated the Sāsānians at a battle near Resaina, but at Anbār, renamed Pērōz-Shāpūr ("Victorious Is Shāpūr"), the Sāsānians inflicted a defeat on the Romans, who lost their emperor. His successor, Philip the Arabian, made peace, giving up Roman conquests in northern Mesopotamia. Osroene, however, which had been returned to the local ruling family of Abgar by Gordian, remained a vassal state of the Romans. Shāpūr renewed his attacks and took many towns, including Dura-Europus, in 256 and later moved into northern Syria and Anatolia. The defeat and capture of the Roman emperor Valerian at the gates of Edessa, probably in 259, was the high point of his conquests in the west.

On Shāpūr's return to Ctesiphon the ruler of Palmyra, Septimius Odaenathus (also called Odainath), attacked and defeated his army, seizing booty. Odeanathus took the title of emperor, conquered Harran and Nisibis, and threatened Ctesiphon in 264–266. His murder relieved the Sāsānians, and in 273 the Roman emperor Aurelian sacked Palmyra and restored Roman authority in northern Mesopotamia. Peace between the two empires lasted until 283, when the Roman emperor Carus invaded Mesopotamia and advanced on Ctesiphon, but the Roman army was forced to withdraw after Carus's sudden death.

In 296 Narseh I, the seventh Sāsānian king, took the field and defeated a Roman force near Harran, but in the following year he was defeated and his family was taken captive. As a result, the Romans secured Nisibis and made it their strongest fortress against the Sāsānians. The Roman province of Mesopotamia, which was the land between the Euphrates and Tigris in the northern foothills, became in effect a military area with *limes* (the fortified frontiers of the Roman Empire) and highly fortified towns.

WARS WITH THE BYZANTINE EMPIRE

Under Shāpūr II the Sāsānians again took the offensive, and the first war lasted from 337 to 350. It ended with no result as Nisibis was successfully defended by the Romans. In 359 Shāpūr again invaded Roman territory and captured the Roman fortress Amida after a long and costly siege. In 363 the emperor Julian advanced almost to Ctesiphon, where he died, and

THE LEGACY OF KHOSROW II

Khosrow II, coin, AD 590–628; in the collection of the American Numismatic Society. Courtesy of the American Numismatic Society

Under Khosrow II (whose byname was Khosrow Parvīz, or Khosrow the Victorious), the Sāsānian empire achieved its greatest expansion. After his defeat (628 AD) at the hands of the Byzantines, he was deposed in a palace revolution and executed. His influence nonetheless was vast.

Khosrow was a serious patron of the arts; silverworking and carpet weaving reached their peak during his reign. Sources tell of the enormous *Spring of Khosrow*, a carpet whose design was a garden. A splendid silver dish in the Bibliothèque Nationale is thought to depict him in the traditional Sāsānian royal hunt. Most authorities attribute to Khosrow II the grottoes at Taq-e Bostan (Kermanshah), taking them as evidence of a renaissance of rock sculpture in his reign. The reliefs depict the king in hunting scenes and standing motionless listening to a group of harpists—a reminder of the famous musicians Bārbad and Sarkash, who were kept at Khosrow's court. Khosrow's architectural work is chiefly known from the ruins of the enormous palace Imirat-e Khosrow near Qasr-e Shīrīn (near Khānaqīn) and at nearby Hawsk-Kuri. A provincial palace exists at Qasr al-Mushattā, Jordan.

Booty and taxes brought Khosrow enormous wealth, including thousands of elephants, camels, horses, and women. The ninth-century Arab historian al-Ṭabarī describes his golden throne supported by legs of rubies, as well as such curios as a piece of malleable gold and an asbestos napkin. But, despite widespread trade connections and the amassing of individual fortunes, there is no evidence that the economy flourished. High taxation and the uncertainties of war did nothing for the merchant class. By creating a military aristocracy, Khosrow II had weakened the authority of the king, while his administrative reforms and bureaucratic centralization removed the power of regional dynasties and their feudal armies, which might otherwise have resisted the invasion of the Arabs 12 years after Khosrow's death. Already in 611 the Arabs had inflicted a defeat on the Sāsānian army at Dhu-Qar. The destruction by Khosrow II of the Christian Arab states of the Lakhmids and Ghassānids in Syria and western Iraq was a further factor exposing Iran to Arab attack.

The love of Khosrow for his Christian wife Shīrīn was celebrated by the poets, especially by the 12th-century poet Neẓāmī in Khosrow-va-Shīrīn.

his successor Jovian had to give up Nisibis and other territories in the north to the Sāsānians. The next war lasted from 502 to 506 and ended with no change. War broke out again in 527, lasting until 531, and even the Byzantine general Belisarius was not able to prevail. As usual, the boundaries remained unchanged. In 540 the Sāsānian king Khosrow (Chosroes) I invaded Syria and even took Antioch, although many fortresses behind him in northern Mesopotamia remained in Byzantine hands. After much back-and-forth fighting, peace was made in 562. War with the Byzantine Empire resumed 10 years later, and it continued under Khosrow's successor, Hormizd IV.

Only in 591, in return for their assistance in the restoration to the Sāsānian throne of Khosrow II, who had been deposed and had fled to Byzantine territory, did the Byzantines regain territory in northern Mesopotamia. With the murder in 602 of the Byzantine emperor Maurice, who had been Khosrow's benefactor, and the usurpation of Phocas, Khosrow II saw a golden opportunity to enlarge Sāsānian domains and to take revenge for Maurice. Persian armies took all northern Mesopotamia, Syria, Palestine, Egypt, and Anatolia. By 615, Sāsānian forces were in Chalcedon, opposite Constantinople. The situation changed completely with the new Byzantine emperor Heraclius, who, in a daring expedition into the heart of enemy territory in 623–624, defeated the Sāsānians in Media. In 627–628 he advanced toward Ctesiphon, but, after sacking the royal palaces at Dastagird, northeast of Ctesiphon, he retreated.

After the death of Khosrow II, Mesopotamia was devastated not only by the fighting but also by the flooding of the Tigris and Euphrates, by a widespread plague, and by the swift succession of Sāsānian rulers, which caused chaos. Finally in 632 order was restored by the last king, Yazdegerd III, but in the following year the expansion of the Muslim Arabs began and the end of the Sāsānian empire followed a few years afterward.

Unlike the Parthians, the Sāsānians established their own princes as rulers of the small kingdoms they conquered, except on the frontiers, where they accepted vassals or allies because their hold over the frontier regions was insecure. By placing Sāsānian princes over the various parts of the empire, the Sāsānians maintained more control than the Parthians had. The provincial divisions were more systematized, and there was a hierarchy of four units—the satrapy (*shahr* in Middle Persian), under which came the province (*ōstan*), then a district (*tassug*), and finally the village (*deh*). In Mesopotamia these divisions were changed throughout Sāsānian history, frequently because of Roman invasions.

POLITICAL DIVISIONS AND TAXATION

Many native tax collectors were replaced by Persians, who were more trusted by the rulers. In addition to the many tolls and tariffs, corvée, and the like, the two basic taxes were the land and poll taxes. The latter were not paid by the nobility, soldiers, civil servants, and the priests of the Zoroastrian religion. The land tax was a percentage of the harvest, but it was determined before the collection of the crops, which naturally caused many problems.

Khosrow I undertook a new survey of the land and imposed the tax in a prearranged sum based on the amount of cultivable land, the quantity of date palms and olive trees, and the number of people working on the land. Taxes were to be paid three times a year. Abuses were still rampant, but this was better than the old system; at least, if a drought or some other calamity occurred, taxes could be reduced or remitted. Although information is contradictory, it appears that religious communities other than the Zoroastrian one had extra taxes imposed on them from time to time. This was especially true of the growing Christian community, particularly in the time of Shāpūr II, after Christianity became the official religion of the Roman Empire.

Religious communities became fixed under the Sāsānians, and Mesopotamia with its large Jewish and Christian populations experienced changes because of the shift in primary allegiance from the ruler to the head of the religious group. The exilarch of the Jews had legal and tax-collecting authority over the Jews of the Sāsānian empire. Mani, the founder of the Manichaean religion, was born in lower Mesopotamia, and his religion spread quickly both to the east and west, even before his death. In its homeland, Mesopotamia, it came under severe persecution by the priests of the Zoroastrian religion, who viewed Manichaeism as a dangerous heresy. Christianity, however, was viewed not as a heresy but as a separate religion, tolerated until it became the official religion of the enemy Roman Empire; Christians were then regarded as potential traitors to the Sāsānian state. The first large growth of Christianity in Mesopotamia came with the deportation and resettlement of Christians, especially from Antioch with its patriarch, during Shāpūr I's wars with the Romans. In a synod convened in 325, the metropolitan see of Ctesiphon was made supreme over other sees in the Sāsānian empire, and the first patriarch or catholicos was Papa. In 344 the first persecutions of Christians began; they lasted with varying degrees of severity until 422, when a treaty with the government ended the persecutions.

The earliest contemporary mention of Christians in Mesopotamia is in the inscriptions of Kartēr, the chief Zoroastrian priest after the reign of Shāpūr I. He mentions both Christians and Nazareans, possibly two kinds of Christians, Greek-speaking and Syriac-speaking, or two sects. It is not known which groups are meant, but it is known that followers of the Gnostic Christian leaders Bardesanes (Bar Daiṣān) and Marcion were active in Mesopotamia. Later, after the Nestorian church separated from the Monophysites, whose centre was in Antioch, the Nestorian church dominated Mesopotamia until the end of the Sāsānian dynasty, when the Monophysites were growing in numbers. After about 485 the Sāsānian government was satisfied that the Nestorian church in their domains was not loyal to Byzantium, and further persecutions were not state-inspired but rather prosecuted by the Zoroastrian clergy. At the end of the Sāsānian period, the Nestorians were fighting the Monophysites, now called Jacobites, more than the Zoroastrians. The Jacobites established many monasteries, especially in northern Mesopotamia, whereas the Nestorians were cool toward monasticism.

Ethnicity became less important than religious affiliation under the Sāsānians, who thus changed the social structure of Mesopotamia. The Arabs continued to grow in numbers, both as nomads and as settled folk, and Arabic became widely spoken. King Nu'mān III of the Arab client kingdom of the Lakhmids of Al-Ḥīrah in southern Mesopotamia became a Christian in 580, but in 602 he was deposed by Khosrow II, who made the kingdom a province of the empire. This act removed a barrier against inroads by Arab tribesmen from the desert, and, after the union of Arabs in the peninsula under the banner of Islam, the fate of the Sāsānian empire was sealed. The Muslims, on the whole, were welcomed in Mesopotamia as deliverers from the foreign yoke of the Persians, but the conversion of the mass of the population to Islam did not proceed rapidly, mainly because of the well-organized Christian and Jewish communities. The arrival of Islam, of course, changed the history of Mesopotamia more than any other event in its history.

CHAPTER 6

MESOPOTAMIAN ART AND ARCHITECTURE

The name "Mesopotamia" was used with varying connotations by ancient writers. If, for convenience, it is to be considered synonymous with the modern state of Iraq, it can be seen in terms of two fairly well-defined provinces: a flat alluvial plain in the south and, in the north, the uplands through which the country's twin rivers flow in their middle courses. This geographic division of the area is reflected in the history of its cultural development from the earliest times.

The first traces of settled communities date from the mid-sixth millennium BC, a period that archaeologists associate with the transition from a Neolithic to a Chalcolithic age. It is of some importance that this period also corresponds to the earliest use of painted ornament on pottery vessels, since the designs used for this purpose are the most reliable criteria by which ethnological groupings and migratory movements can be distinguished. Archaeologically, such groupings are, for the most part, arbitrarily named after the site at which traces of them were first found, and the same names are sometimes attributed to the prehistoric periods during which they were predominant. Hence, Hassuna, Hassuna-Sāmarrā', and Halaf in northern Iraq are the names given to the first three periods during which known early settlements were successively occupied by peoples whose relations were apparently with Syria and Anatolia.

The designs on their pottery, sometimes in more than one colour, usually consist of zones filled with "geometric" ornament in patterns reminiscent of woven fabrics. These designs are often adapted to the shape of the vessels with creditable artifice. Only in Hassuna-Sāmarrā' pottery do devices occasionally appear that consist of animal, bird, or even human figures, ingeniously stylized and aesthetically attractive. Such motifs, however, appear to be adopted from contemporary Iranian ceramics. The only other notable art form popular at this time is that of hominoid figurines of stone or clay, associated with primitive religious cults; however, their formal idiosyncrasies vary greatly from group to group, and the meaning of their symbolism is unknown. Nor can they—or the pottery designs—be considered as ancestral to Mesopotamian art of historical times, the antecedents of which must be sought in southern Iraq.

Here, in the delta, the earliest phase of prehistory is associated with the name Ubaid I. Since this phase has a parallel in Susiana, north of the Iranian frontier, the first settlers in both areas may have a common origin. Among these settlers, according to some scholars, was the germ of Sumerian genius, but this is not indisputably authenticated until the end of the fourth millennium. By 3100 BC, however, the presence of the Sumerians is finally proved by the invention of writing as a vehicle for their own language. From then onward, successive phases in the evolution of Sumerian art can satisfactorily be studied.

Three factors may be recognized as contributing to the character of Mesopotamian art and architecture. One is the sociopolitical organization of the Sumerian city-states and of the kingdoms and empires that succeeded them. From the earliest times, cities were fortified by and adorned with public buildings; irrigation systems were organized and jealously protected; armies were efficiently equipped and troops trained in concerted action; victories were celebrated and treaties ratified. Because interstate warfare or foreign conquests were primary preoccupations of Mesopotamian rulers, it is understandable that in most periods a certain class of artworks was dedicated simply to the glorification of their military prowess.

A second and even more important factor, however, is the major role played by organized religion in Mesopotamian affairs of state. Particularly in Sumerian times, the municipal and economic organization of a city was the responsibility of the temple, with its hierarchical priesthood in which was vested an authority almost equal to that of the ruler and his advisory council of elders. Accordingly, in the early days of Sumer and Babylonia, architectural attention was paid primarily to religious buildings, and all sculpture served religious purposes. The elaboration and adornment of palaces was an innovation of Assyrian times.

The third factor that contributed to the character of Mesopotamian art is the influence of the natural environment. The practical limitations imposed upon both artist and architect by the geology and climate of southern Iraq are immediately apparent. Since no stone or wood was available in the alluvial plain, sculptors were dependent on scarce imported material or compelled to use such substitutes as terra-cotta (baked clay). Architecture also was profoundly affected, first, by the restriction of building material to brickwork and, second, by problems of roof construction, only partially solved by the contrivance of brick vaulting, in the second millennium BC. For the Assyrians, in the north, good-quality stone was plentiful, but the cost of quarrying and transport, combined with an obstinate conservatism, caused it to be regarded as a luxury material and its use to be confined to sculptured ornament and conspicuous architectural features.

An equally apparent, if more abstract, association between Mesopotamian art and environment can be detected when the intellectual climate engendered by the latter is understood. In a country where summer and winter temperatures reach thermometric extremes, where agriculture depends exclusively on the artificial distribution of river water and contends precariously with the timing of seasonal floods, where the herdsman is afflicted by the depredations of wild beasts and the cultivator by the menace of poisonous insects—in such a country, the inhabitants must have felt themselves in perpetual conflict with hostile and potentially destructive elements in nature. All this confrontation and frustration is reflected in the melancholy undertones of their religious beliefs, particularly those of the Sumerians, for whom success and prosperity came to be identified with the principle of fertility and thus could only be attained by the appeasement of capricious deities. Such convictions are inherent in the fabric of their complicated mythology, which lends itself easily to expression in pictorial form and provides the predominant subject of almost all Sumerian art. Furthermore, since their mythical traditions and religious beliefs persisted for many centuries after the demise of the Sumerians themselves, they provided the basic imagery of almost all Mesopotamian art.

SUMERIAN PERIOD

The beginnings of monumental architecture in Mesopotamia are usually considered to have been contemporary with the founding of the Sumerian cities and the invention of writing, in about 3100 BC.

ARCHITECTURE

Conscious attempts at architectural design during this so-called Protoliterate period (c. 3400–c. 2900 BC) are recognizable in the construction of religious buildings. There is, however, one temple, at Eridu (modern Abū Shahrayn), that is no more than a final rebuilding of a shrine the original foundation of which dates back to the beginning of the fourth millennium; the continuity of design has been thought by some to confirm the presence of the Sumerians throughout the temple's history. Already, in the Ubaid period (c. 5200–c. 3500 BC), this temple anticipated most of the architectural characteristics of the typical Protoliterate Sumerian platform temple. It is built of mud brick on a raised plinth (platform base) of the same material, and its walls are ornamented on their outside surfaces with alternating buttresses (supports) and recesses. Tripartite in form, its long central sanctuary is flanked on two sides by subsidiary chambers, provided with an altar at one end and a freestanding offering table at the other.

Typical temples of the Protoliterate period—both the platform type and the type built at ground level—are, however, much more elaborate both in planning and ornament. Interior wall ornament often consists of a patterned mosaic of terra-cotta cones sunk into the wall, their exposed ends dipped in bright colours or sheathed in bronze. An open hall at the Sumerian city of Erech (modern Tall al-Warkā', Iraq) contains freestanding and attached brick columns that have been brilliantly decorated in this way. Alternatively, the internal-wall faces of a platform temple could be ornamented with mural paintings depicting mythical scenes, such as at 'Uqair.

The two forms of temple—the platform variety and that built at ground level—persisted throughout the early dynasties of Sumerian history (c. 2900–c. 2400 BC). It is known that two of the platform temples originally stood within walled enclosures, oval in shape and containing, in addition to the temple, accommodation for priests. But the raised shrines themselves are lost, and their appearance can be judged only from facade ornaments discovered at Tall al-'Ubayd. These devices, which were intended to relieve the monotony of sun-dried brick or mud plaster, include a huge copper-sheathed lintel, with animal figures modeled partly in the round; wooden columns sheathed in a patterned mosaic of coloured stone or shell; and bands of copper-sheathed bulls and lions, modeled in relief but with projecting heads. The planning of ground-level temples continued to elaborate on a single theme: a rectangular sanctuary, entered on the cross axis, with altar, offering table, and pedestals for votive statuary (statues used for vicarious worship or intercession).

Considerably less is known about palaces or other secular buildings at this time. Circular brick columns and austerely simplified facades have been found at Kish (modern Tall al-Uhaimer, Iraq). Flat roofs, supported on palm trunks, must be assumed, although some knowledge of corbeled vaulting (a technique of spanning an opening like an arch by having successive cones of masonry project farther inward as they rise on each side off the gap)—and even of dome construction—is suggested by tombs at Ur, where a little stone was available.

SCULPTURE

Practically all Sumerian sculpture served as adornment or ritual equipment for the temples. No clearly identifiable cult statues of gods or goddesses have yet been found. Many of the extant figures in stone are votive statues, as indicated by the phrases used in the inscriptions that they often bear: "It offers prayers," or "Statue, say to my king (god)... ." Male statues stand or sit with hands clasped in an attitude of prayer. They are often naked above the waist and wear a woolen skirt curiously woven in a pattern that suggests overlapping petals (commonly described by the Greek word *kaunakes*, meaning "thick cloak"). A togalike garment sometimes covers one shoulder. Men generally wear long hair and a heavy beard, both often trimmed in corrugations and painted black. The eyes and eyebrows are emphasized with coloured inlay. The female coiffure varies considerably but predominantly consists of a heavy coil arranged vertically from ear to ear and a chignon behind. The hair is sometimes concealed by a headdress of folded linen. Ritual nakedness is confined to priests.

It has been thought that the rarity of stone in Mesopotamia contributed to the primary stylistic distinction between Sumerian and Egyptian sculpture. The Egyptians quarried their own stone in prismatic blocks, and one can see that, even in their freestanding statues, strength of design is attained by the retention of geometric unity. By contrast, in Sumer, stone must have been imported from remote sources, often in the form of miscellaneous boulders, the amorphous character of which seems to have been retained by the statues into which they were transformed.

Beyond this general characteristic of Sumerian sculpture, two successive styles have been distinguished in the middle and late subdivisions of the early dynastic period. One very notable group of figures, from Tall al-Asmar, Iraq (ancient Eshnunna), dating from the first of these phases, shows a geometric simplification of forms that, to modern taste, is ingenious and aesthetically acceptable. Statues characteristic of the second phase, on the other hand, though technically more competently carved, show aspirations to naturalism that are sometimes overly ambitious. In this second style, some scholars see evidence of occasional attempts at portraiture. Yet, in spite of minor variations, all these figures adhere to the single formula of presenting the conventional characteristics of Sumerian physiognomy. Their provenance is not confined to the Sumerian cities in the south. An important group of statues is derived from the ancient capital of Mari, on the middle Euphrates, where the population is known to have been racially different from the Sumerians. In the Mari statues there also appears to have been no deviation from the sculptural formula. They are distinguished only by technical peculiarities in the carving.

Peace side of the "Standard of Ur," mosaic of lapis lazuli, shell, coloured stone, and mother-of-pearl, from the Royal Cemetery, Ur, Early Dynastic period, c. 2500 BC. In the British Museum. Length 47 cm. Courtesy of the trustees of the British Museum

Deprived of stone, Sumerian sculptors exploited alternative materials. Fine examples of metal casting have been found, some of them suggesting knowledge of the cire perdue (lost-wax) process, and copper statues more than half life-size are known to have existed. In metalwork, however, the ingenuity of Sumerian artists is perhaps best judged from their contrivance of composite figures. The earliest and one of the finest examples of such figures—and of Sumerian sculpture as a whole—comes from a Protoliterate level of excavation at Tall al-Warkā'. It is the limestone face of a life-size statue (Iraqi Museum, Baghdad), the remainder of which must have been composed of other materials. The method of attachment is visible on the surviving face.

Devices of this sort were brought to perfection by craftsmen of the early dynastic period, the finest examples of whose work are to be seen among the treasures from the royal tombs at Ur: a bull's head decorating a harp, composed of wood or bitumen covered with gold and wearing a lapis lazuli beard (British

Museum); a rampant he-goat in gold and lapis, supported by a golden tree (University Museum, Philadelphia); the composite headdresses of court ladies (British Museum, Iraqi Museum, and University Museum); or, more simply, the miniature figure of a wild ass, cast in electrum (a natural yellow alloy of gold and silver) and mounted on a bronze rein ring (British Museum). The inlay and enrichment of wooden objects reaches its peak in this period, as may be seen in the so-called standard or double-sided panel from Ur (British Museum), on which elaborate scenes of peace and war are depicted in a delicate inlay of shell and semiprecious stones. The refinement of craftsmanship in metal is also apparent in the famous wig-helmet of gold (Iraqi Museum), belonging to a Sumerian prince, and in weapons, implements, and utensils.

Relief carving in stone was a medium of expression popular with the Sumerians and first appears in a rather crude form in Protoliterate times. In the final phase of the early dynastic period, its style became conventional. The most common form of relief sculpture was that of stone plaques, 1 foot (30 centimetres) or more square, pierced in the centre for attachment to the walls of a temple, with scenes depicted in several registers (horizontal rows). The subjects usually seem to be commemorative of specific events, such as feasts or building activities, but representation is highly standardized, so that almost identical plaques have been found at sites as much as 500 miles (800 kilometres) apart. Fragments of more ambitious commemorative stelae have also been recovered; the Stele of Vultures (Louvre Museum) from Telloh, Iraq

Feeding the sacred herd, cylinder seal impression from Tall al-Warkā', Iraq, Protoliterate period (before c. 2900 BC); in the National Museums of Berlin. Courtesy of the Vorderasiatisches Museum, Staatliche Museen zu Berlin

(ancient Lagash), is one example. Although it commemorates a military victory, it has a religious content. The most important figure is that of a patron deity, emphasized by its size, rather than that of the king. The formal massing of figures suggests the beginnings of mastery in design, and a formula has been devised for mutiplying identical figures, such as chariot horses.

In a somewhat different category are the cylinder seals so widely utilized at this time. Used for the same purposes as the more familiar stamp seal and likewise engraved in negative (intaglio), the cylinder-shaped seal was rolled over wet clay on which it left an impression in relief. Delicately carved with miniature designs on a variety of stones or shell, cylinder seals rank as one of the higher forms of Sumerian art.

Prominent among their subjects is the complicated imagery of Sumerian mythology and religious ritual. Still only partially understood, their skillful adaptation to linear designs can at least be easily appreciated. Some of the finest cylinder seals date from the Protoliterate period. After a slight deterioration in the first early dynastic period, when brocade patterns or files of running animals were preferred, mythical scenes returned. Conflicts are depicted between wild beasts and protecting demigods or hybrid figures, associated by some scholars with the Sumerian epic of Gilgamesh. The monotony of animated motifs is occasionally relieved by the introduction of an inscription.

AKKADIAN PERIOD

Sargon of Akkad's (reigned c. 2334–c. 2279 BC) unification of the Sumerian city-states and creation of a first Mesopotamian empire profoundly affected the art of his people, as well as their language and political thought. The increasingly large proportion of Semitic elements in the population were in the ascendancy, and their personal loyalty to Sargon and his successors replaced the regional patriotism of the old cities. The new conception of kingship thus engendered is reflected in artworks of secular grandeur, unprecedented in the god-fearing world of the Sumerians.

ARCHITECTURE

One would indeed expect a similar change to be apparent in the character of contemporary architecture, and the fact that this is not so may be due to the paucity of excavated examples. It is known that the Sargonid dynasty had a hand in the reconstruction and extension of many Sumerian temples (for example, at Nippur) and that they built palaces with practical amenities (Tall al-Asmar) and powerful fortresses on their lines of imperial communication (Tell Brak, or Tall Birāk al-Taḥtānī, Syria). The ruins of their buildings, however, are insufficient to suggest either changes in architectural style or structural innovations.

SCULPTURE

Two notable heads of Akkadian statues have survived: one in bronze and the other of stone. The bronze head of a king, wearing the wig-helmet of the old Sumerian rulers, is probably Sargon himself (Iraqi Museum). Though lacking its inlaid eyes and slightly damaged elsewhere, this head is rightly considered one of the great masterpieces of ancient art. The Akkadian head (Iraqi Museum) in stone, from Bismāyah, Iraq (ancient Adab), suggests that portraiture in materials other than bronze had also progressed.

Where relief sculpture is concerned, an even greater accomplishment is evident in the famous Naram-Sin (Sargon's grandson) stela (Louvre), on which a pattern of figures is ingeniously designed to express the abstract idea of conquest. Other stelae and the rock reliefs (which by their geographic situation bear witness to the extent of Akkadian conquest) show the carving of the period to be in the hands of less competent artists. Yet two striking fragments in the Iraqi Museum, which were found in the region of Al-Nāṣiriyyah, Iraq, once more provide evidence of the improvement in design and craftsmanship that had taken place since the days of the Sumerian dynasties. One of the fragments shows a procession of naked war prisoners, in which the anatomic details are well observed but skillfully subordinated to the rhythmical pattern required by the subject.

Bronze head of a king, perhaps Sargon of Akkad, from Nineveh (now in Iraq), Akkadian period, c. 2300 BC. In the Iraqi Museum, Baghdad. Courtesy of the Directorate General of Antiquities, Baghdad, Iraq

Some compensation for the paucity of surviving Akkadian sculptures is to be found in the varied and plentiful repertoire of contemporary cylinder seals. The Akkadian seal cutter's craft reached a standard of perfection virtually unrivaled in later times. Where the aim of his Sumerian predecessor had been to produce an uninterrupted, closely woven design, the Akkadian seal cutter's own preference was for clarity in the arrangement of a number of carefully spaced figures.

The Akkadian dynasty ended in disaster when the river valley was overrun by the mountain tribes of northern Iran. Of all the Mesopotamian cities, only Lagash appears somehow to have remained aloof from the conflict and, under its famous governor Gudea, to have successfully maintained the continuity of the Mesopotamian cultural tradition. In particular, the sculpture dating from this short interregnum (c. 2100 BC) seems to represent some sort of posthumous flowering of Sumerian genius. The well-known group of statues of the governor and other notables, discovered at the end of the 19th century, long remained the only criterion by which Sumerian art could be judged, and examples in the Louvre and British Museum are still greatly admired. The hard stone, usually diorite, is carved with obvious mastery and brought to a fine finish. Details are cleverly stylized, but the musculature is carefully studied, and the high quality of the carving makes the use of inlay unnecessary. The powerful impression of serene authority that these statues convey justifies their inclusion among the finest products of ancient Middle Eastern art.

SUMERIAN REVIVAL

The short historical interlude represented by the Gudea sculptures was followed by a full-scale Sumerian revival, one that lasted for four centuries and culminated in the unification of the whole country under the rule of Hammurabi in the early 18th century BC. Dominated first by the powerful third dynasty of Ur and later by the rival states of Isin and Larsa, the peoples of ancient Sumer reverted to their pre-Akkadian cultural traditions. On their northern frontiers the Sumerian culture was extended to increasingly prosperous younger city-states, such as Mari, Ashur, and Eshnunna, located on the middle courses of the Tigris and Euphrates rivers.

In all these cities, both old and new, the period is notable for the advances made in architectural planning and the large-scale reconstruction of ancient buildings. In the south the early promise of Sumerian architecture had reached fulfillment, first in the great ziggurats, or stepped towers, rising above their walled temple enclosures at such cities as Ur, Eridu, Kish, Erech, and Nippur. These huge structures, with their summit sanctuaries, the appearance of which can only be guessed at, were faced with kiln-baked brick, paneled and recessed to break the monotony of their colossal facades, and were strengthened with bitumen and reinforced with twisted reeds. Tradition associates the ziggurat at Borsippa (modern Birs Nimrūd, Iraq), near Babylon,

ZIGGURATS

Ziggurat at Choghā Zanbīl near Susa, Iran. Robert Harding Picture Library/Sybil Sassoon

A ziggurat is a pyramidal, stepped temple tower, at once both an architectural and a religious structure. It was a characteristic structure of the major cities of Mesopotamia from approximately 2200 until 500 BC. The ziggurat was always built with a core of mud brick and an exterior covered with baked brick. It had no internal chambers and was usually square or rectangular, averaging either 170 feet (50 metres) square or 125 × 170 feet (40 × 50 metres) at the base. Approximately 25 ziggurats are known, being equally divided among Sumer, Babylonia, and Assyria.

No ziggurat is preserved to its original height. Ascent was by an exterior triple stairway or by a spiral ramp, but for almost half of the known ziggurats, no means of ascent has been discovered. The sloping sides and terraces were often landscaped with trees and shrubs (hence the Hanging Gardens of Babylon). The best-preserved ziggurat is at Ur (modern Tall al-Muqayyar, Iraq). The largest, at Choghā Zanbīl in Elam (in what is now southwestern Iran), is 335 feet (102 metres) square and 80 feet (24 metres) high and stands at less than half its estimated original height. A ziggurat, apparently of great antiquity, is located at Tepe Sialk in modern Kāshān, Iran. The legendary Tower of Babel has been popularly associated with the ziggurat of the great temple of Marduk in Babylon.

An artist's re-creation of the Hanging Gardens of Babylon. One of the Seven Wonders of the Ancient World, the Hanging Gardens consisted of roof gardens laid out on a series of ziggurat terraces. Brown Brothers

with the biblical Tower of Babel. Surrounding temples at ground level were also much elaborated. The basic plan consisted of a tower-flanked entry, central court, antecella (or inner vestibule), and sanctuary, all arranged on a single axis; however, in the larger examples this plan could be expanded by means of communicating courtyards. Facades were often elaborately decorated with panels of pilasters (recessed columns) or engaged half columns, skillfully modeled in mud-brick. At Ur, kiln-baked brick was again used to construct corbeled vaulting over huge subterranean tomb chambers, entered through funerary chapels at ground level. Here, too, there are temple-palaces, the complicated planning of which is seldom self-explanatory.

Better examples of residential palaces are found in the newer cities of the north, especially Mari, where a vast building with more than 200 rooms was constructed by a ruler named Zimrilim (c. 1779–c. 1761). In this palace is found the standard reception unit common to all Babylonian palaces: a rectangular throne room that is entered by a central doorway from a square court of honour; and behind it a great hall, in this case apparently serving some religious purpose. There also is an immense outer courtyard, overlooked by a raised audience chamber, and, in the remotest corner of the building, a heavily protected residential suite. In some of the main chambers, mural paintings depicting ritual scenes and processions have been preserved.

The sculpture of this period is perhaps best represented by some well-preserved statues, also from the Mari palace. Their style owes much to the preceding Gudea period in the south, but they lack the authentic stamp of Sumerian design and workmanship. The same may be said of the few surviving pieces from the reign of Hammurabi (c. 1792–c. 1750), whose conquests ended the epoch—for example, the relief at the head of the stela in the Louvre on which his law code is inscribed.

ASSYRIAN PERIOD

Ashur, a small Sumerian city-state on the middle Euphrates, began to gain political prominence during the pre-Hammurabi period. During the latter half of the second millennium BC, the frontiers of Assyria were extended to include the greater part of northern Mesopotamia, and, in the city of Ashur itself, excavations have revealed the fortifications and public buildings constructed or rebuilt by a long line of Assyrian kings.

ARCHITECTURE

The character of these buildings suggests a logical development of Old Babylonian architecture. There are certain innovations, such as the incorporation of small twin ziggurats in the design of a single temple, while in the temples themselves the sanctuary was lengthened on its main axis, and the altar itself was withdrawn into a deep

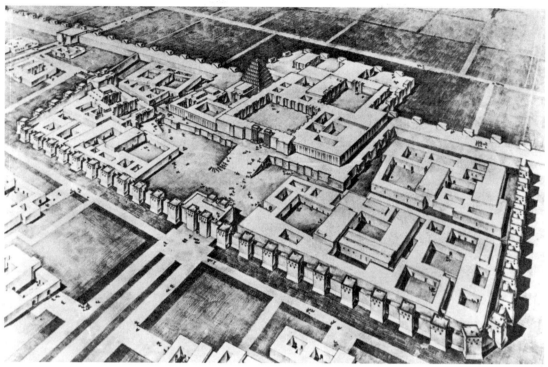

A reconstruction drawing of the citadel of Khorsabad, now in Iraq, as it may have appeared in the time of Sargon II (721–705 BC). Drawing by Charles Altman. Courtesy of the Oriental Institute, the University of Chicago

recess. For the rest, the absence of ornament and the multiplication of buttressed facades with crenellated battlements tend to monotony.

Other forms of art are inconspicuous, except perhaps the contemporary cylinder seals, which show an interest in animal forms that anticipates the relief carving of a later phase of Mesopotamian civilization. Sometimes known as Middle Assyrian, this later period corresponds to the occupation of southern Mesopotamia by the Kassites and to the Mitanni kingdom on the north Syrian frontier, neither of which contributed greatly to the total development of ancient Middle Eastern art.

The fuller manifestation of Assyrian art and architecture is not seen until the ninth century BC, when Ashurnasirpal II transferred his capital from Ashur to Nimrūd (ancient Kalakh; biblical Calah). The rise of Assyria to imperial power during this century and those that followed gave increased vitality to Mesopotamian architecture. The vast palaces brought to light in the 19th century emphasize the new interest in secular building and reflect the ostentatious grandeur of the Assyrian kings. Like the temples of earlier days, they are usually artificially raised up on a platform level with the tops of the city walls, astride which they often stand. Their gates are flanked by colossal portal sculptures in stone, and their internal chambers are decorated with pictorial reliefs carved on upright stone slabs, or orthostats. In addition to the ninth-century structure at Nimrūd, palace platforms have been exposed at Khorsabad (ancient Dur-Sharrukin), where Sargon II established a short-lived capital of his own in the late eighth century BC, and at Nineveh, which was rebuilt in the seventh century, first by Sargon's son Sennacherib and then by his grandson Esarhaddon. On the platforms at both Nineveh and Nimrūd, palaces and temples were multiplied by successive kings.

The platform at Khorsabad is occupied by a single royal residence, associated with a group of three modest temples and a small ziggurat. Similar buildings occupy a walled citadel at the foot of the platform, thus completing a complex that has been thoroughly excavated and provides the most informative example of typical contemporary architecture. Sargon's palace itself, like that of Zimrilim 1,000 years earlier, is planned, first, around a gigantic open courtyard accessible to the public and, second, around an inner court of honour. From the latter the great throne room is entered through triple doorways, around which, in common with the main outer entrance to the palace, are concentrated a fine array of portal sculptures. The throne room has an adjoining stairway leading to a flat roof and a suite of living apartments behind. Other state rooms, conventionally planned, open onto an open terrace facing the mountains beyond. All the principal internal chambers are decorated with reliefs, except for the throne room itself, where mural painting seems to have been preferred. The individual purpose and function of the innumerable administrative and domestic offices must remain largely conjectural.

SCULPTURE

Any history of late Assyrian art must be concerned primarily with relief carving. Some statues in the round have been found, but the comparative ineptitude of the majority of them suggests that this form of expression did not come naturally to Assyrian sculptors. Portal sculptures, which many would consider the most characteristic Assyrian art form, are not statues in the round but "double-aspect" reliefs (that is, they are meant to be seen from either the front or the side), apparently derived from a Hittite invention of the 14th century BC. These impressive guardian figures, usually human-headed bulls or lions, decorate the arched gateways and are sometimes supplemented by others set at right angles on the adjoining facades, their heads facing sideways. Each is composed from a single block of stone weighing up to 30 tons, roughly shaped in the quarry and then carved in situ.

Less spectacular orthostat reliefs form a continuous frieze of ornament around the bases of interior wall faces. There is evidence that they were placed in position before the walls that they decorate had been completed. Their carving in situ could thus be executed in full daylight. This form of architectural ornament dates from the first quarter of the ninth century BC and seems to have been a genuine Assyrian innovation. The earliest slabs, from the ninth-century palaces of Ashurnasirpal II and his son Shalmaneser III at Nimrūd, are about 7 feet (2 metres) high, with the design arranged in two superimposed registers separated by a band of cuneiform inscription. In those from later buildings, such as Sargon II's palace at Khorsabad, the individual sculptured figures reach a height of 9 feet (3 metres).

The subjects of the designs on these reliefs are rarely related in any way to religion. Superstitious symbols do occasionally appear in the form of benevolent winged beings, or genies, but the primary purpose of the picture is the glorification of the king himself, either by scenes of ceremonial homage or by extended pictorial narratives of his achievements. The most popular theme, giving rise to numerous variations, involves detailed scenes of military conquest and the ruthless suppression of revolt. These are often arranged episodically to represent successive events in the progress of a single campaign: the Assyrian army prepares for war; led by the king, it crosses difficult country on the way to attack a walled city; the city is taken, burnt, and demolished; the enemy leaders are punished with conspicuous brutality; and, finally, the victory is celebrated. Scenes such as these are distinguished above all by their stylistic vitality and fanciful detail. Animals as well as men are carefully observed and beautifully drawn. The principles of perspective as later defined by the Greeks are unknown, but attention is given to the relationship of figures in space and to devices for suggesting comparative distance.

At Khorsabad, late in the eighth century BC, some notable stylistic changes are perceptible. The lively carving of narrative and historical subjects has been replaced by more tedious symbols of pomp and ceremony. In keeping with the winged bulls and genies of the portal sculptures, stiffly arranged files of courtiers, officials, and servants stand immobilized in the routine of ceremonial homage. The monotony of the figures is occasionally relieved by the sparing use of coloured pigment on the stone.

In the seventh-century palaces of Sennacherib and Ashurbanipal at Nineveh, the reliefs suggest a reaction in favour of narrative and violent activity. The slabs are covered to their full height by complicated battle scenes in which the progress of the fighting is suggested by episodic repetition. Types of landscape are depicted schematically, and significant episodes or individuals are identified by a short inscription, without impairing the overall rhythm of the design.

In the intervals between their military campaigns, Assyrian kings appear to have been much preoccupied with hunting, and scenes from the chase provided an alternative subject for the reliefs. Lions hunted with spears from a light chariot and herds of wild asses (onagers) or gazelles are subjects that stimulated the imagination and sensibility of the Assyrian artist.

A contrast to these descriptive carvings is provided by the formal monumentality of the Assyrian rock reliefs, secular or religious devices carved on vertical rock faces in localities such as Bavian and Maltai to commemorate historical events that took place there.

The Assyrian talent for relief ornament was not confined to sculpture in stone. First seen during the reign of Shalmaneser III (858–824 BC) are striking examples of relief modeling in bronze. The huge wooden gates of a minor palace at Imgur-Enlil (Balawat), near Nimrūd, were decorated with horizontal bands of metal, 11 inches (28 centimetres) high, each modeled by a repoussé process (relief hammered out from behind), with a double register of narrative scenes. Their subjects are much the same as the stone reliefs, but even greater ingenuity has been used in adapting the designs to so confined a space.

PAINTING AND DECORATIVE ARTS

When greater economy of labour and material was necessary, mural paintings were substituted for slab reliefs. At the time of Tiglath-pileser III (744–727 BC), a country palace at Til Barsip (modern Tall al-Ahmar) was decorated in this way, with the conventional motifs of relief designs rather clumsily adapted to this very different medium. A few years later, such paintings were extensively used to decorate both wall faces and ceilings in Sargon II's palace buildings at Khorsabad. One magnificent panel of formalized ornament has been reconstructed. It is painted in primary colours on a white ground.

There is evidence that the Assyrian palaces were well equipped with furniture. The wooden components have perished, but the ivory ornaments with which the furniture was enriched have survived in great quantities. Of these "Assyrian ivories"—relief panels, inlays, and other forms of ornament—only a small proportion can be attributed to indigenous workmanship. The remainder represent either loot from the cities of Syria and Phoenicia or the work of craftsmen imported from those regions. The carving is often technically superb, and the enrichment of the ivory with gold, semiprecious stones, or coloured paste by cloisonné or champlevé processes (whereby the applied decoration is outlined by raised metal strips or fills depressed areas of the surface that have been cut out to receive it) gives increased elegance. The designs, however, are for the most part a pastiche of misunderstood Egyptian symbolism and are often less attractive than the purely Assyrian devices.

NEO-BABYLONIAN PERIOD

During the half century following the fall of Nineveh, in 612 BC, there was a final flowering of Mesopotamian culture in southern Iraq under the last dynasty of Babylonian kings. During the reigns of Nabopolassar (625–605 BC) and his son Nebuchadrezzar II (604–562 BC), there was widespread building activity. Temples and ziggurats were repaired or rebuilt in almost all the old dynastic cities, while Babylon itself was enormously enlarged and surrounded by a double enceinte, or line of fortification, consisting of towered and moated fortress walls.

Inside the city the most grandiose effect was obtained by the disposal of public buildings along a wide processional way, leading through the centre of the town to the temple and ziggurat of its patron god, Marduk. Where the street passed through the inner-city wall, the facades of the famous Ishtar Gate (Pergamon Museum, Berlin) and those facing the adjoining street were ornamented in brightly glazed brickwork, with huge figures of bulls, lions, and dragons modeled in relief. This form of decoration—a costly process, since each of the bricks composing the figures had to be separately cast—provided a solution for the problem of embellishing mud-brick facades. It appears again in the court of honour of Nebuchadrezzar's palace, using a more sophisticated design that suggests familiarity with Greek ornament. For the rest, there are few innovations in the planning of either palaces or temples during the neo-Babylonian period. Also (strangely enough, in view of the prolonged excavations that took place at this site), examples of contemporary art are limited almost exclusively to cylinder seals and terracotta figurines of unpretentious design.

CHAPTER 7

MESOPOTAMIAN RELIGION

T he religious beliefs and practices of the Sumerians and Akkadians and their successors, the Babylonians and Assyrians, form a single stream of tradition. Sumerian in origin, Mesopotamian religion was added to and subtly modified by the Akkadians, whose own beliefs were in large measure assimilated to, and integrated with, those of their new environment.

As the only available intellectual framework that could provide a comprehensive understanding of the forces governing existence and also guidance for right conduct in life, religion ineluctably conditioned all aspects of ancient Mesopotamian civilization. It yielded the forms in which that civilization's social, economic, legal, political, and military institutions were, and are, to be understood, and it provided the significant symbols for poetry and art. In many ways it even influenced peoples and cultures outside Mesopotamia, such as the Elamites to the east, the Hurrians and Hittites to the north, and the Aramaeans and Israelites to the west.

STAGES OF RELIGIOUS DEVELOPMENT

The religious development—as indeed that of the Mesopotamian culture generally—was not significantly influenced by the movements of the various peoples into and within the area—the Sumerians, Akkadians, Gutians, Kassites, Hurrians, Aramaeans, and Chaldeans. Rather, it forms a uniform, consistent, and coherent Mesopotamian tradition changing in response to its own internal needs of insights and expression. It is possible to discern a basic substratum involving worship of the forces in nature—often visualized in nonhuman forms—especially those that were of immediate import to basic economic pursuits. Many of these figures belong to the type of the "dying god" (a fertility deity displaying death and regeneration characteristics) but show variant traits according to whether they are powers of fertility worshiped by marsh dwellers, orchard growers, herders, or farmers. This stage may be tentatively dated back to the fourth millennium BC and even earlier.

A second stage was characterized by a visualization of the gods as human in shape and organized in a polity of a primitive democratic cast in which each deity had his or her special offices and functions,. This stage overlaid and conditioned the religious forms and characteristics of the earlier stage during the third millennium BC.

Lastly, a third stage evolved during the second and first millennia BC. It was characterized by a growing emphasis on personal religion involving concepts of sin and forgiveness and by a change of the earlier democratic divine polity into an absolute monarchical structure, dominated by the god of the national state—to the point that the pious abstained from all human initiative, in absolute faith and reliance on divine intervention. As a result of this development, since the ancient Mesopotamians were intensely conservative in religious matters and unwilling to discard anything of a hallowed past, the religious data of any period, and particularly that of the later periods, is a condensed version of earlier millennia that must be carefully analyzed and placed in proper perspective before it can be evaluated.

THE LITERARY LEGACY: MYTH AND EPIC

Present knowledge of ancient Mesopotamian religion rests almost exclusively on archaeological evidence recovered from the ruined city-mounds of Mesopotamia during the 19th and 20th centuries. Of greatest significance is the literary evidence, texts written in cuneiform (wedge-shaped) script on tablets made of clay or, for monumental purposes, on stone. Central, of course, are the specifically religious texts comprising god lists, myths, hymns, laments, prayers, rituals, omen texts, incantations, and other forms. However, since religion permeated the culture, giving form and meaning to all aspects of it, any written text, any work of art, or any of its material remains are directly or indirectly related to the religion and may further scholarly knowledge of it.

Among the archaeological finds that have particularly helped to throw light on religion are the important discoveries of inscribed tablets with Sumerian texts in copies of Old Babylonian date (c. 1800–c. 1600 BC) at Nippur and Ur, the Sumerian

Detail of the stela inscribed with Hammurabi's code, showing the king before the god Shamash Utu; bas-relief from Susa, 18th century BC; in the Louvre, Paris. Courtesy of the trustees of the British Museum; photograph, J.R. Freeman & Co. Ltd.

and Akkadian texts of the second and first millennia from Ashur and Sultantepe, and particularly the all-important library of the Assyrian king Ashurbanipal (reigned 668–627 BC) from Nineveh. Of nonliterary remains, the great temples and temple towers (ziggurats) excavated at almost all major sites—e.g., Eridu, Ur, Nippur, Babylon, Ashur, Kalakh (biblical Calah), Nineveh—as well as numerous works of art from various periods, are

important sources of information. The Erech Vase, with its representation of the rite of the sacred marriage, the Naram-Sin stela (inscribed commemorative pillar), the Ur-Nammu stela, and the stela with the Code of Hammurabi (Babylonian king, 18th century BC), which shows at its top the royal lawgiver before the sun god Shamash, the divine guardian of justice, are important works of art that may be singled out. Other important sources are the representations on cylinder seals and on boundary stones (*kudurru*s), both of which provide rich materials for religious iconography in certain periods.

In working with, and seeking to interpret, these varied sources two difficulties stand out: the incompleteness of the data and the remoteness of the ancients from modern man, not only in time but also in experience and in ways of thought. Thus, for all periods before the third millennium, scholars must rely on scarce, nonliterary data only, and, even though writing appears shortly before that millennium, it is only in its latter half that written data become numerous enough and readily understandable enough to be of significant help. It is generally necessary, therefore, to interpret the scarce data of the older periods in the light of survivals and of what is known from later periods, an undertaking that calls for critical acumen if anachronisms are to be avoided. Also, for the later periods, the evidence flows unevenly, with perhaps the middle of the second millennium BC the least well-documented and hence least-known age.

As for the difficulties raised by differences in the ways of thinking between modern man and the ancients, they are of the kind that one always meets in trying to understand something unfamiliar and strange. A contemporary inquirer must keep his accustomed values and modes of thought in suspension and seek rather the inner coherence and structure of the data with which he deals, in order to enter sympathetically into the world out of which they came, just as one does, for example, in entering the sometimes intensely private world of a poem, or, on a slightly different level, in learning the new, unexpected meanings and overtones of the words and phrases of a foreign language.

SUMERIAN LITERATURE

Mesopotamian literature originated with the Sumerians, whose earliest known written records are from the middle of the fourth millennium BC. It constitutes the oldest known literature in the world. Moreover, inner criteria indicate that a long oral-literary tradition preceded, and probably coexisted with, the setting down of its songs and stories in writing. It may be assumed, further, that this oral literature developed the genres of the core literature. The handbook genres, however, in spite of occasional inclusions of oral formula—e.g., legal or medical—may generally be assumed to have been devised after writing had been invented, as a response to the remarkable possibilities that writing offered for amassing and organizing data.

The purpose underlying the core literature and its oral prototypes would seem to have been as much magical as aesthetic, or merely entertaining, in origin. In magic, words create and call into being what they state. The more vivid and expressive the words are, the more they are believed to be efficacious—so by its expressiveness literature forms a natural vehicle of such creativity. In ancient Mesopotamia its main purpose appears to have been the enhancement of what was seen as beneficial. With the sole exception of wisdom literature, the core genres are panegyric in nature (i.e., they praise something or someone), and the magical power and use of praise is to instill, call up, or activate the virtues presented in the praise.

That praise is of the essence of hymns, for instance, is shown by the fact that over and over again the encomiast, the official praiser, whose task it was to sing these hymns, closed with the standing phrase: "O [the name of a deity or human hero], thy praise is sweet." The same phrase is common also at the end of myths and epics, two further praise genres that also belonged in the repertoire of the encomiast. They praise not only in description but also in narrative, by recounting acts of valour done by the hero, thus sustaining and enhancing his power to do such deeds, according to the magical view.

In time, possibly quite early, the magical aspect of literature must have tended to fade from consciousness, yielding to more nearly aesthetic attitudes that viewed the praise hymns as expressions of allegiance and loyalty and accepted the narrative genres of myth and epic for the enjoyment of the story and the values expressed, poetic and otherwise.

Hymns, myths, and epics all were believed to sustain existing powers and virtues by means of praise, but laments were understood to praise blessings and powers lost, originally seeking to hold on to and recall them magically, through the power in the expression of intense longing for them and the vivid representation of them. The lamentation genre was the province of a separate professional, the elegist. It contained dirges for the dying gods of the fertility cults and laments for temples and cities that had been destroyed and desecrated. The laments for temples—which, as far as is known, go back no earlier than to the third dynasty of Ur—were used to recall the beauties of the lost temple as a kind of inducement to persuade the god and the owner of the temple to restore it.

Penitential psalms lament private illnesses and misfortunes and seek to evoke the pity of the deity addressed and thus to gain divine aid. The genre apparently is late in date, most likely Old Babylonian (c. 19th century BC), and in it the element of magic has, to all intents and purposes, disappeared.

The core genres of Mesopotamian literature were developed by the Sumerians apparently as oral compositions. Writing, which is first attested at the middle of the fourth millennium BC, was in its origins predominantly logographic (i.e., each word or morpheme was represented by a single graph or symbol) and long remained a highly imperfect means of rendering the spoken word. Even as late as the beginning of the early dynastic III period in southern Mesopotamia, in the early third millennium BC, the preserved written literary texts have the character of mnemonic (memory) aids only and seem to presuppose that the reader has prior knowledge of the text.

As writing developed more and more precision during the third millennium BC, more oral compositions seem to have been put into writing. With the third dynasty of Ur a considerable body of literature had come into being and was being added to by a generation of highly gifted authors. Fortunately for its survival, this literature became part of the curriculum in the Sumerian scribal schools. It was studied and copied by student after student so that an abundance of copies, reaching a peak in Old Babylonian times, duplicated and supplemented each other as witnesses to the text of the major works. Fifty or more copies or fragments of copies of a single composition may support a modern edition, and many thousands more copies probably lie unread, still buried in the earth.

Myths

The genre of myths in ancient Mesopotamian literature centres on praises that recount and celebrate great deeds. The doers of the deeds (creative or otherwise decisive acts), and thus the subjects of the praises, are the gods. In the oldest myths, the Sumerian, these acts tend to have particular rather than universal relevance, which is understandable since they deal with the power and acts of a particular god with a particular sphere of influence in the cosmos. An example of such myths is the myth of "Dumuzi's Death," which relates how Dumuzi (Producer of Sound Offspring; Sumerian: Tammuz), the power in the fertility of spring, dreamed of his own death at the hands of a group of deputies from the netherworld, and how he tried to hide himself but was betrayed by his friend after his sister had resisted all attempts to make her reveal where he was.

A similar, very complex myth, "Inanna's Descent," relates how the goddess Inanna (Lady of the Date Clusters) set her heart on ruling the netherworld and tried to depose her older sister, the queen of the netherworld, Ereshkigal (Lady of the Great Place). Her attempt failed, and she was killed and changed into a piece of rotting meat in the netherworld. It took all the ingenuity of Enki (Lord of Sweet Waters in the Earth) to bring Inanna back to life, and even then she was released only on condition that she furnish a substitute to take her place. On her return, finding her young husband Dumuzi feasting instead of mourning for her, Inanna was seized with jealousy and designated him that substitute. Dumuzi tried to flee the posse of

deputies who had accompanied Inanna, and with the help of the sun god Utu (Sun), who changed Dumuzi's shape, he managed to escape, was recaptured, escaped again, and so on, until he was finally taken to the netherworld. The fly told his little sister Geshtinanna where he was, and she went in search of him. The myth ends with Inanna rewarding the fly and decreeing that Dumuzi and his little sister could alternate as her substitute, each of them spending half a year in the netherworld, the other half above with the living.

A third myth built over the motif of journeying to the netherworld is the myth of "The Engendering of the Moongod and his Brothers," which tells how Enlil (Lord of the Air), when still a youngster, came upon young Ninlil (goddess of grain) as she—eager to be with child and disobeying her mother—was bathing in a canal where he would see her. He lay with her in spite of her pretending to protest and thus engendered the moon god Su-en (Sin). For this offense Enlil was banished from Nippur and took the road to the netherworld. Ninlil, carrying his child, followed him. On the way Enlil took the shape first of the Nippur gatekeeper, then of the man of the river of the netherworld, and lastly of the ferryman of the river of the netherworld. In each such disguise Enlil persuaded Ninlil to let him lie with her to engender a son who might take Su-en's place in the netherworld and leave him free for the world above. Thus three additional deities, all underworld figures, were engendered: Meslamtaea

(He Who Issues from Meslam), Ninazu (Water Sprinkler [?]), and Ennugi (the Lord Who Returns Not). The myth ends with a paean to Enlil as a source of abundance and to his divine word, which always comes true.

Most likely all of these myths have backgrounds in fertility cults and concern either the disappearance of nature's fertility with the onset of the dry season or the underground storage of food.

As Enlil is celebrated for engendering other gods that embody other powers in nature, so also was Enki in the myth of "Enki and Ninhursag," in which myth Enki lay with Ninhursag (Lady of the Stony Ground) on the island of Dilmun (modern Bahrain), which had been allotted to them. At that time all was new and fresh, inchoate, not yet set in its present mold. There Enki provided water for the future city of Dilmun, lay with Ninhursag, and left her. She gave birth to a daughter, Ninshar (Lady Herb), on whom Enki in turn engendered the spider Uttu, goddess of spinning and weaving. Ninhursag warned Uttu against Enki, but he, proffering marriage gifts, persuaded her to open the door to him. After Enki had abandoned Uttu, Ninhursag found her and removed Enki's semen from her body. From the semen seven plants sprouted forth. These plants Enki later saw and ate and so became pregnant from his own semen. Unable as a male to give birth, he fell fatally ill, until Ninhursag relented and—as birth goddess—placed him in her vulva and helped him to give birth to seven daughters, whom Enki then happily married off to various gods. The story is probably to be seen as a bit of broad humour.

Not only the birth of gods but also the birth, or creation, of the human race is treated in the myths. The myth of "Enki and Ninmah" relates how the gods originally had to toil for their food, dig irrigation canals, and perform other menial tasks until, in their distress, they complained to Enki's mother, Nammu, who took the complaints to Enki. Enki remembered the engendering clay of the Apsu (i.e., the fresh underground waters that fathered him), and from this clay, with the help of the womb goddesses and eight midwife goddesses led by Ninmah (another name for Ninhursag), he had his mother become pregnant with and give birth to man so that he could relieve the gods of their toil. At the celebration of the birth, however, Enki and Ninmah both drank too much beer and began to quarrel. Ninmah boasted that she could impair man's shape at will, and Enki countered that he could temper even the worst that she might do. So she made seven freaks, for each of which Enki found a place in society and a living. He then challenged her to alleviate the mischief he could do, but the creature he fashioned—a prematurely aborted fetus—was beyond help. The moral drawn by Enki was that both male and female contribute to the birth of a happy child. The aborted fetus lacked the contribution of the birth goddess in the womb.

Shamash, the sun god, rising in the morning from the eastern mountains between (left) *Ishtar (Sumerian: Inanna), the goddess of the morning star, and* (far left) *Ninurta, the god of thunder-storms, with his bow and lion, and* (right) *Ea (Sumerian: Enki), the god of fresh water, with* (far right) *his vizier, the two-faced Usmu.* Courtesy of the trustees of the British Museum

The ordering, rather than the creation, of the world is the subject of another myth about Enki, called "Enki and World Order." Beginning with long praises and self-praises of Enki, it tells how he blessed Nippur (Sumer), Ur, Meluhha (coastal region of the Indian Ocean), and Dilmun (Bahrain) and gave them their characteristics, after which he turned his attention to the Euphrates and Tigris rivers, to the marshes, the sea, and the rains, and then to instituting one facet after another of the economic life of Sumer: agriculture, housebuilding, herding, and so forth. The story ends with a complaint by Enki's granddaughter Inanna that she has not been given her due share of offices, at which he patiently pointed to various offices she had in fact been given and kindly added a few more.

Another myth about the world order but dealing with it from a very different point of view concerns Enlil's son, the rain god Ninurta, called from its opening word *Lugal-e* ("O King"). This myth begins with a description of the young king, Ninurta, sitting at home in Nippur when, through his general, reports reach him of a new power that has arisen in the mountains to challenge him—i.e., Azag, son of An (Sky) and Ki (Earth), who has been chosen king by the plants and is raiding the cities with his warriors, the stones. Ninurta sets out in his boat to give battle, and a fierce engagement ensues, in which Azag is killed. Afterward Ninurta reorganizes his newly won territory, builds a stone barrier, the near mountain ranges or foothills (the *hur-sag*), and gathers the waters that used to go up into the mountains and directs them

ERIDU GENESIS

This ancient Sumerian epic is primarily concerned with the creation of the world, the building of cities, and the Flood. According to the epic, after the universe was created out of the primeval sea and the gods were born, the deities fashioned humans from clay to cultivate the ground, care for flocks, and perpetuate the worship of the gods.

Cities were soon built and kingship was instituted on earth. For some reason, however, the gods determined to destroy humankind with a flood. Enki (Akkadian: Ea), who did not agree with the decree, revealed it to Ziusudra (Utnapishtim), a man well known for his humility and obedience. Ziusudra did as Enki commanded him and built a huge boat, in which he successfully rode out the Flood. Afterward, he prostrated himself before the gods An (Anu) and Enlil, and, as a reward for living a godly life, Ziusudra was given immortality.

into the Tigris to flood it and provide plentiful irrigation water from Sumer. The *hursag* he presents as a gift to his mother, who had come to visit him, naming her Ninhursag (Lady of the *Hursag*). Lastly he sits in judgment on the stones who had formed Azag's army. Some of them, who had shown special ill will toward him, he curses, and others he trusts and gives high office in his administration. These judgments give the stones their present characteristics so that, for example, the flint is condemned to break before the much softer horn, as it indeed does when the horn is pressed against it to flake it. Noteworthy also is the way in which order in the universe, the yearly flood and other seasonal events, is seen—consonantly with Ninurta's role as "king" and leader in war— under the pattern of a reorganization of conquered territories.

Other myths about Ninurta are *An-gim dím-ma* and a myth of his contest with Enki. The first of these tells how Ninurta, on returning from battle to Nippur, was met by Enlil's page Nusku, who ordered him to cease his warlike clamour and not scare Enlil and the other gods. After long speeches of self-praise by Ninurta, further addresses to him calmed him and made him enter his temple gently. The second tale relates how he conquered the Thunderbird Anzu with Enki's help but missed the powers it had stolen from him, and how, resentful at this, he plotted against Enki but was outsmarted and trapped. Another Sumerian myth, the "Eridu Genesis," tells of the creation of man and animals, of the building of the first cities, and of the Flood.

EPICS

The genre of epics appears generally to be younger in origin than that of myths and apparently was linked—in subject matter and values—to the emergence of monarchy at the middle of the early dynastic period. The works that have survived seem, however, all to be of later date. A single short Sumerian epic tale, "Gilgamesh and Agga of Kish," is told in the style of primary epic. It deals with Gilgamesh's successful rebellion against his overlord and former benefactor, Agga of Kish. More in the style of romantic epic are the stories of "Enmerkar and the Lord of Aratta," "Enmerkar and Ensuhkeshdanna," and the "Lugalbanda Epic," all of which have as heroes rulers of the first dynasty of Erech (c. 2500 BC) and deal with wars between that city and the fabulous city of Aratta in the eastern highlands.

Gilgamesh, also of that dynasty, figures as the hero of a variety of short tales. Some, such as "Gilgamesh and Huwawa" and "Gilgamesh and the Bull of Heaven," are in romantic epic style, and others, such as "The Death of Gilgamesh" and "Gilgamesh, Enkidu, and the Netherworld," concern the inescapable fact of death and the character of afterlife.

Cylinder seals (left) and their impressions showing scenes from the life of the mythological Sumerian character Gilgamesh. As the subject of many short tales in the epic style, Gilgamesh is a common subject for a variety of seals. Frank Scherschel/Time & Life Pictures/Getty Images

AKKADIAN LITERATURE

The first centuries of the second millennium BC witnessed the demise of Sumerian as a spoken language and its replacement by Akkadian. However, Sumerian (much as Latin in the Middle Ages) continued to be taught and spoken in the scribal schools throughout the second and first millennia BC because of its role as bearer of Sumerian culture, as the language of religion, literature, and many arts. New compositions were even composed in Sumerian. As time passed these grew more and more corrupt in grammar.

Akkadian, when it supplanted Sumerian as the spoken language of Mesopotamia, was not without its own literary tradition. Writing, to judge from Akkadian orthographic peculiarities, was very early borrowed from the Sumerians. By Old Babylonian times (c. 19th century BC), the literature in Akkadian, partly under the influence of Sumerian models and Sumerian literary themes, had developed myths and epics of its own, among them the superb Old Babylonian Gilgamesh epic (dealing with the problem of death) as well as hymns, disputation texts (evaluations of elements of the cosmos and society), penitential psalms, and not a few independent new handbook genres—e.g., omens, rituals, laws and legal phrasebooks (often translated from Sumerian), mathematical texts, and grammatical texts. There was a significant amount of translation from Sumerian; translations include incantation series such as the *Utukki lemnuti* ("The Evil Spirits"), laments for destroyed temples, penitential psalms, and others. The prestige of Sumerian as a literary language, however, is indicated by the fact that translations were rarely, if ever, allowed to supersede the original Sumerian text. The Sumerian text was kept with an interlinear translation to form a bilingual work.

The continued study and copying of literature in the schools, both Sumerian and Akkadian, by the middle of the second millennium led to a remarkable effort of standardizing, or canonizing. Texts of the same genre were collected, often under royal auspices and with royal support, and were then sifted and finally edited in series that henceforth were recognized as the canonical form. Authoritative texts were established for incantations, laments, omens, medical texts, lexical texts, and others. In myths and epics, such major and lengthy compositions as the Akkadian creation story *Enuma elish*, the Erra myth, the myth of Nergal and Ereshkigal, the Etana legend, the Gilgamesh epic, and the Tukulti-Ninurta epic were reworked or re-created.

Of special interest are philosophical compositions, such as the Akkadian *Ludlul bēl nēmeqi*, "Let Me Praise the Lord of Wisdom," and theodicies (justification of divine ways) that deal with the problem of the just sufferer, similar to the biblical Job. They constitute a high point in the genre of wisdom literature. From the first millennium BC the rise of factual historical chronicles and a spate of political and religious polemical writings reflecting the rivalry between Assyria and Babylonia deserve mention. Very late in the millennium, the first astronomical texts appeared.

MYTHS

The Akkadian myths are in many ways dependent on Sumerian materials, but

An imprint from a cylinder seal (left) depicting the rain god Adad, who plays a central part in the Akkadian creation story, the Myth of Atrahasis. Erich Lessing/Art Resource, NY

they show an originality and a broader scope in their treatment of the earlier Sumerian concepts and forms; they address themselves more often to existence as a whole. Fairly close to Sumerian prototypes is an Akkadian version of the myth of "Inanna's Descent." An Old Babylonian myth about the Thunderbird Anzu, who stole the tablets of fates and was conquered by Ninurta, who was guided by Enki's counsel, is probably closely related to the Sumerian story of Ninurta's contest with Enki.

Also important is an Old Babylonian "Myth of Atrahasis," which, in motif, shows a relationship with the account of the creation of man to relieve the gods of toil in the "Enki and Ninmah" myth, and with a Sumerian account of the Flood in the "Eridu Genesis." The Atrahasis myth, however, treats these themes with noticeable originality and remarkable depth. It relates, first, how the gods originally had to toil for a living, how they rebelled and went on strike, how Enki suggested that one of their number—the god We, apparently the ringleader who "had the idea"—be killed and humankind created from clay mixed with his flesh and blood, so that the toil of the gods could be laid on humankind and the gods left to go free. But after Enki and the birth goddess Nintur (another name for Ninmah) had created humans, they multiplied at such a rate that the din they made kept Enlil sleepless.

At first Enlil had Namtar, the god of death, cause a plague to diminish human numbers, but the wise Atrahasis, at the advice of Enki, had humans concentrate all worship and offerings on Namtar. Namtar, embarrassed at hurting people who showed such love and affection for him, stayed his hand. Next Enlil had Adad, the god of rains, hold back the rains and thus cause a famine, but, because of the same stratagem, Adad was embarrassed and released the rains. After this, Enlil planned a famine by divine group action that would not be vulnerable as the earlier actions by individual gods had been. Anu and Adad were to guard the heavens, Enlil himself earth, and Enki the waters underground and the sea so that no gift of nature could come through to the human race.

The ensuing famine was terrible. By the seventh year one house consumed the other and people began eating their own children. At that point Enki—accidentally he maintained—let through a wealth of fish from the sea and so the humans were saved. With this, however, Enlil's patience was at an end and he thought of the Flood as a means to get rid

of humanity once and for all. Enki, however, warned Atrahasis and had him build a boat in which he saved himself, his family, and all animals. After the Flood had abated and the ship was grounded, Atrahasis sacrificed, and the hungry gods, much chastened, gathered around the offering. Only Enlil was unrelenting until Enki upbraided him for killing innocent and guilty alike and—there is a gap in the text—suggested other means to keep human numbers down. In consultation with the birth goddess Nintur, Enki then developed a scheme of birth control by inventing the barren woman, the demon Pashittu who kills children at birth, and the various classes of priestesses to whom giving birth was taboo.

The myth uses the motif of the protest of the gods against their hard toil and the creation of humans to relieve it, which was depicted earlier in the Sumerian myth of "Enki and Ninmah," and also the motif of the Flood, which occurred in the "Eridu Genesis." The import of these motifs here is, however, new: they bring out the basic precariousness of human existence; humanity's usefulness to the gods will not protect them unless they take care not to annoy the gods, however innocently. They must stay within bounds; there are limits set for self-expression.

A far more trustful and committed attitude toward the powers that rule existence finds expression in the seemingly slightly later Babylonian creation story, *Enuma elish*, which may be dated to the later part of the first dynasty of Babylon

(c. 1894–c. 1595 BC). Babylon's archenemy at that time was the Sealand, which controlled Nippur and the country south of it—the ancestral country of Sumerian civilization. This lends political point to the battle of Marduk (thunder and rain deity), the god of Babylon, with the Sea, Tiamat; it also accounts for the odd, almost complete silence about Enlil of Nippur in the tale.

The myth tells how in the beginning there was nothing but Apsu, the sweet waters underground, and Tiamat, the sea, mingling their waters together. In these waters the first gods came into being, and generation followed generation. The gods represented energy and activity and thus differed markedly from Apsu and Tiamat, who stood for rest and inertia. True to their nature the gods gathered to dance, and in so doing, surging back and forth, they disturbed the insides of Tiamat. Finally, Apsu's patience was at an end, and he thought of doing away with the gods, but Tiamat, as a true mother, demurred at destroying her own offspring. Apsu, however, did not swerve from his decision, and he was encouraged in this by his page Mummu, "the original (watery) form." When the youngest of the gods, the clever Ea (Sumerian: Enki), heard about the planned attack he forestalled it by means of a powerful spell with which he poured slumber on Apsu, killed him, and built his temple over him. He seized Mummu and held him captive by a nose rope.

In the temple thus built the hero of the myth, Marduk, was born. From the first he was the darling of his grandfather, the god of heaven, Anu, who engendered the four winds for him to play with. As they blew and churned up waves, the disturbing of Tiamat—and of a faction of the gods who shared her desire for rest—became more and more unbearable. At last these gods succeeded in rousing her to resistance, and she created a mighty army with a spearhead of monsters to destroy the gods. She placed her consort Kingu ("Task[?]") at the head of it and gave him absolute powers.

When news of these developments reached the gods there was consternation. Ea was sent to make Tiamat desist, and then Anu, but to no avail. Finally Anshar, god of the horizon and king of the gods, thought of young Marduk. Marduk proved willing to fight Tiamat but demanded absolute authority. Accordingly, a messenger was sent to the oldest of the gods, Lahmu and Lahamu ("Silt[?]"), to call the gods to assembly. In the assembly the gods conferred absolute authority on Marduk, tested it by seeing whether his word of command alone could destroy a constellation and then again make it whole, hailed him king, and set him on the road of "security and obedience," a formula of allegiance that based his power and authority on the pressing need for protection of the moment.

In the ensuing encounter with Tiamat's forces Kingu and his army lost heart when they saw Marduk. Only Tiamat stood her ground, seeking first to throw him off his guard by flattery about his quick rise to leadership, but Marduk angrily denounced her and the older generation: "The sons [had to] withdraw [for] the fathers were acting treacherously, and [now] you, who gave birth to them, bear malice to the offspring." At this Tiamat, furious, attacked, but Marduk loosed the winds against her, pierced her heart with an arrow, and killed her. Kingu and the gods who had sided with her he took captive.

Having thus won a lasting victory for his suzerain, King Anshar, Marduk gave thought to what he might do further. Cleaving the carcass of Tiamat, he raised half of her to form heaven, ordered the constellations, the calendar, the movements of Sun and Moon, and, keeping control of atmospheric phenomena for himself, made the Earth out of the other half of her, arranging its mountains and rivers. Having organized the various administrative tasks, he put their supervision in Ea's hands; to Anu he gave the tablets of fate he had taken from Kingu. His prisoners he paraded in triumphal procession before his fathers, and as a monument to his victory he set up images of Tiamat's monsters at the gate of his parental home. The gods were overjoyed to see him; Anshar rushed toward him and Marduk formally announced to him the state of security he had achieved. He then bathed, dressed, and seated himself on his throne, with the spear Security and Obedience, named from his mandate, at his side. By now, however, the situation had subtly altered. The old fear and

urgent need for protection was gone, but in its stead had come a promise held out by Marduk's organizational powers; so when the gods reaffirmed their allegiance to him as king they used a new formula: "benefits and obedience." From then on Marduk would take care of their sanctuaries and they, in turn, would obey him.

Marduk then announced his intention of building a city for himself, Babylon, with room for the gods when they come there for assembly. His fathers suggested that they move to Babylon themselves to be with him and help in the administration of the world he had created. Next, he pardoned the gods who had sided with Tiamat and had been captured, charging them with the building tasks. Grateful for their lives, they prostrated themselves before him, hailed him as king, and promised to do the building.

Pleased with their willingness, Marduk magnanimously wanted to relieve them even from this chore and planned to create humans to do the toil for them. At the advice of his father, Ea, he then had them indict Kingu as instigator of the rebellion. Kingu was duly sentenced and executed, and from his blood Ea created humankind. Then Marduk divided the gods into a celestial and a terrestrial group, assigned them their tasks in the cosmos, and allotted them their stipends.

Thus freed from all burdens, the gods wanted to show their gratitude to Marduk, and as a token they took, of their own free will, for one last time, spade in hand to build Babylon and Marduk's temple, Esagila. In the new temple the gods then assembled and distributed the celestial and terrestrial offices. The "great gods" went into session and permanently appointed the "seven gods of destinies," or better "of the decrees," who would formulate in final form the decrees enacted by the assembly. Marduk then presented his weapons, and An (Anu) adopted the bow as his daughter and gave it a seat among the gods. Lastly, Marduk was enthroned, and after the gods had prostrated themselves before him they bound themselves by oath—touching their throats with oil and water—and formally gave him kingship, appointing him permanently lord of the gods of heaven and earth. After this they solemnly listed his 50 names expressive of his power and achievements.

The myth ends with a plea that it be handed on from father to son and told to future rulers, that they may heed Marduk. It is the song of Marduk who bound Tiamat and assumed the kingship.

The motifs from which this myth is built are in large measure known from elsewhere. The initial generation of the gods is a variant form of the genealogy of An (Anu) in the great god list *An: Anum*. The threat to annihilate the disturbers of sleep are known from the Atrahasis and the Sumerian Flood traditions. The battle of Marduk with Tiamat seems to stem from western myths of a battle between the thunder god and the sea. The organization of the universe after victory recalls the organization of conquered territory in *Lugal-e*. The killing of a rebel god to create the human race to take over the gods' toil is found in the Atrahasis myth and—without the rebel aspect—in a bilingual creation myth found in Ashur. New and original, however, is the way in which they have all been grouped and made dependent on the figure of the young king. The political form of the monarchy is seen as embracing the universe; it was the prowess of a young king that overcame the forces of inertia; it was his organizational genius that created and organized all; and it is he who—like his counterpart on earth, the human king—grants benefits in return for obedience.

The high value set on the monarchy as a guarantor of security and order in the *Enuma elish* can hardly have seemed obvious in Babylonia in the first troubled years of Assyrian rule. From this period (c. 700 BC) comes a myth usually called the *Erra Epic*, which reads almost like a polemic against *Enuma elish*. It tells how the god of affray and indiscriminate slaughter, Erra, persuaded Marduk to turn over the rule of the world to him while Marduk was having his royal insignia cleaned, and how Erra, true to his nature, used his powers to institute indiscriminate rioting and slaughter. Royal power here stands no longer for security and order but for the opposite: license to kill and destroy.

Two other Akkadian myths may be mentioned—both probably dating from the middle of the second millennium BC—the myth of the "Dynasty of Dunnum" and the myth of "Nergal and Ereshkigal." The first of these tells of succeeding divine generations ruling in Dunnum, the son usually killing his father and marrying, sometimes his mother, sometimes his sister, until—according to a reconstruction of the broken text—more acceptable mores came into vogue with the last generation of gods, Enlil and Ninurta. This myth underlies the Greek poet Hesiod's *Theogony*. The myth of Nergal and Ereshkigal relates the unorthodox way in which the god Nergal became the husband of Ereshkigal and king of the netherworld.

EPICS

The quick rise of Sargon, the founder of the dynasty of Akkad (*c.* 2334–*c.* 2154 BC), from obscurity to fame and his victory over Lugalzagesi of Erech (Uruk) form the theme of several epic tales. The sudden eclipse of the Akkadian empire long after Naram-Sin, which was wrongly attributed to that ruler's presumed pride and the gods' retaliation, is the theme of "The Fall of Akkad."

Akkadian epic tradition continues and gives focus to the Sumerian tales of Gilgamesh. The *Epic of Gilgamesh*, which relates he odyssey of Gilgamesh, the king of the Mesopotamian city-state Erech (Uruk), seems to have been composed in Old Babylonian times but was reworked by a certain Sin-leqe-unnini later in the first millennium BC. The fullest extant text of the Gilgamesh epic is on 12 incomplete Akkadian-language tablets found in the mid-19th century by the Turkish Assyriologist Hormuzd Rassam at Nineveh in the library of the Assyrian king Ashurbanipal (reigned 668–627 BC). The gaps that occur in the tablets have been partly filled by various fragments found elsewhere in Mesopotamia and Anatolia.

The Ninevite version of the epic begins with a prologue in praise of Gilgamesh, part divine and part human, the great builder and warrior, knower of all things on land and sea. In order to curb Gilgamesh's seemingly harsh rule, the god Anu causes the creation of Enkidu, a wild man who at first lives among animals. Soon, however, Enkidu is initiated into the ways of city life and travels to Erech, where Gilgamesh awaits him. Tablet II describes a trial of strength between the two men in which Gilgamesh is the victor; thereafter, Enkidu is the friend and companion (in Sumerian texts, the servant) of Gilgamesh. In Tablets III–V the two men set out together against Huwawa (Humbaba), the divinely appointed guardian of a remote cedar forest, but the rest of the engagement is not recorded in the surviving fragments.

In Tablet VI Gilgamesh, who has returned to Erech, rejects the marriage proposal of Ishtar, the goddess of love, and then, with Enkidu's aid, kills the divine bull that she sends to destroy him.

The Flood Tablet, 11th cuneiform tablet in a series relating the Gilgamesh epic, from Nineveh, 7th century BC; in the British Museum, London. © Photos.com/Jupiterimages

Tablet VII begins with Enkidu's account of a dream in which the gods Anu, Ea, and Shamash decide that Enkidu must die for slaying the bull. Enkidu then falls ill and dreams of the "house of dust" that awaits him. Gilgamesh's lament for his friend and the state funeral of Enkidu are narrated in Tablet VIII. Afterward, Gilgamesh makes a dangerous journey (Tablets IX and X) in search of

Utnapishtim, the survivor of the Babylonian Flood, in order to learn from him how to escape death. When he finally reaches Utnapishtim, Gilgamesh is told the story of the Flood and is shown where to find a plant that can renew youth (Tablet XI). But after Gilgamesh obtains the plant, it is seized and eaten by a serpent, and Gilgamesh returns, still mortal, to Erech.

An appendage to the epic, Tablet XII, relates the loss of objects called *pukku* and *mikku* (perhaps "drum" and "drumstick") given to Gilgamesh by Ishtar. The epic ends with the return of the spirit of Enkidu, who promises to recover the objects and then gives a grim report on the underworld.

Other Akkadian epics that deserve to be mentioned are the *Etana Epic*, which tells how Etana, the first king, was carried up to heaven on the back of an eagle to obtain the plant of birth so that his son could be born. Also important are the epic tales about Sargon of Akkad, one of which, the birth legend, tells of his abandonment in a casket on the river by his mother—much as the Bible tells that Moses was abandoned—and his discovery by an orchardman, who raised him as his son. Another Sargon tale is "The King of Battle," which tells about conquests in Asia Minor to protect foreign trade. Naram-Sin is the central figure in another tale dealing with that king's pride and also relating the destructive invasions by barbarous foes. A late flowering of primary epic is the Assyrian *Epic of Tukulti-Ninurta* (reigned 1243–07 BC), which deals with that king's wars with Babylonia.

THE MESOPOTAMIAN WORLDVIEW AS EXPRESSED IN MYTH

The more completely a given culture is embraced, the more natural will its basic tenets seem to the people involved. The most fundamental of its presuppositions are not even likely to rise into awareness and be consciously held but are tacitly taken for granted. It takes a degree of cultural decline, of the loosening of the culture's grip on thought and action, before its most basic structural lines can be recognized and, if need be, challenged. Since culture, the total pattern within which man lives and acts, is thus not likely to be conceived of consciously and as a whole until it begins to lose its obvious and natural character, it is understandable that those myths of a culture that may be termed existential—in the sense that they articulate human existence as a whole in terms of the culture and show its basic structure—are rarely encountered until comparatively late in the history of a culture. Before that occurs, it is, rather, the particular aspects and facets of existence that are apt to claim attention.

In ancient Mesopotamia the oldest known materials, the Sumerian myths, have relatively little to say about creation; scholars must, for the most part, turn to the introductions of tales and disputations to infer how things were believed to be in the beginning. Thus, a story about the hero Gilgamesh refers in its introductory lines to the times "after heaven had been moved away from earth, after earth had been separated from heaven." The same notion that heaven and earth were once close together occurs also in a bilingual Sumero-Akkadian text from Ashur about the creation of man. The actual act of separating them is credited to the storm god Enlil of Nippur in the introduction to a third tale that deals with the creation of the first hoe. From similar passing remarks scholars have inferred that the gods, before man came into being, had to labour hard at the heavy works of irrigation for agriculture and dug out the beds of the Tigris and the Euphrates.

COSMOGONY AND COSMOLOGY

Though the "Eridu Genesis" may have come close to treating existence as a whole, a true cosmogonic and cosmological myth that deals centrally with the origins, structuring, and functional principles of the cosmos does not actually appear until Old Babylonian times, when Mesopotamian culture was entering a period of doubt about the moral character of world government and even of divine power itself. Yet, the statement is a positive one, almost to the point of defiance. *Enuma elish* tells of a beginning when all was a watery chaos and only the sea, Tiamat, and the sweet waters underground, Apsu, mingled their waters together. Mummu, the personified original watery form, served as Apsu's page. In their midst the gods were born. The first pair, Lahmu and Lahamu, represented the powers in silt; the next, Anshar and Kishar, those in the horizon. They engendered the god of heaven, An (Anu), and he in turn the god of the flowing sweet waters, Enki (Ea).

This tradition is known in a more complete form from an ancient list of gods called *An: Anum*. There, after a different beginning, Lahmu and Lahamu give rise to Duri and Dari, "the time-cycle"; and these in turn give rise to Enshar and Ninshar, Lord and Lady Circle. Enshar and Ninshar engender the concrete circle of the horizon, in the persons of Anshar and Kishar, probably conceived as silt deposited along the edge of the universe. Next was the horizon of the greater heaven and earth, and then—omitting an intrusive line—heaven and earth, probably conceived as two juxtaposed flat disks formed from silt deposited inward from the horizons.

Enuma elish truncates these materials and violates their inner logic considerably. Though they are clearly cosmogonic and assume that the cosmic elements and the powers informing them come into being together, *Enuma elish* seeks to utilize them for a pure theogony (account of the origin of the gods). The creation of the actual cosmos is dealt with much later. Also, the introduction of Mummu, the personified "original form," which in the circumstances can only be that of water, may have led to the omission of Ki, Earth, who—as nonwatery—did not fit in.

The gods, who in *Enuma elish* come into being within Apsu and Tiamat, are viewed as dynamic creatures, who contrast strikingly with the older generation. Apsu and Tiamat stand for inertia and rest. This contrast leads to a series of conflicts in which first Apsu is killed by Ea; then Tiamat, who was roused later to attack the gods, is killed by Ea's son Marduk. It is Marduk, the hero of the story, who creates the extant universe out of the body of Tiamat. He cuts her, like a dried fish, in two, making one-half of her into heaven—appointing there Sun, Moon, and stars to execute their prescribed motions—and the other half into the Earth. He pierces her eyes to let the Tigris and Euphrates flow forth, and then, heaping mountains on her body in the east, he makes the various tributaries of the Tigris flow out from her breasts. The remainder of the story deals with Marduk's organization of the cosmos, his creation of man, and his assigning to the gods their various cosmic offices and tasks. The cosmos is viewed as structured as, and functioning as, a benevolent absolute monarchy.

THE GODS AND DEMONS

The gods were, as mentioned previously, organized in a polity of a primitive democratic cast. They constituted, as it were, a landed nobility, each god owning and working an estate—his temple and its lands—and controlling the city in which it was located. On the national level they attended the general assembly of the gods, which was the highest authority in the cosmos, to vote on matters of national import such as election or deposition of kings. The major gods also served on the national level as officers having charge of cosmic offices. Thus, for example, Utu (Akkadian: Shamash), the sun god, was the judge of the gods, in charge of justice and righteousness generally.

Highest in the pantheon—and presiding in the divine assembly—ranked An (Akkadian: Anu), god of heaven, who was responsible for the calendar and the seasons as they were indicated by their appropriate stars. Next came Enlil of Nippur, god of winds and of agriculture, creator of the hoe. Enlil executed the verdicts of the divine assembly. Equal in rank to An and Enlil was the goddess Ninhursag (also known as Nintur and Ninmah), goddess of stony ground: the near mountain ranges in the east and the stony desert in the west with its wildlife—wild asses, gazelles, wild goats, etc. She was also the goddess of birth. With these was joined—seemingly secondarily—Enki (Ea), god of the sweet waters of rivers and marshes; he was the cleverest of the gods and a great troubleshooter, often appealed to by both gods and men. Enlil's sons were the moon god Nanna (Sin); the god of thunderstorms, floods, and the plough, Ninurta; and the underworld figures Meslamtaea, Ninazu, and Ennugi. Sin's sons were the sun god and judge of the gods, Utu; the rain god Ishkur (Akkadian: Adad); and his daughter, the goddess of war, love, and morning

An Assyrian governor (right) standing before the deities Adad (centre) and Ishtar (left), *lime-stone relief from Babylon, 8th century BC; in the Museum of Oriental Antiquities, Istanbul.* Weidenfeld & Nicolson Ltd.

and evening star, Inanna (Akkadian: Ishtar). Inanna's ill-fated young husband was the herder god Dumuzi (Akkadian: Tammuz). The dread netherworld was ruled by the goddess Ereshkigal and her husband Nergal, a figure closely related to Meslamtaea and Ninurta. Earlier tradition mentions Ninazu as her husband.

Demons played little or no role in the myths or lists of the Mesopotamian pantheon. Their domain was that of incantations. Mostly, they were depicted as outlaws; the female demon Lamashtu, for instance, was hurled from heaven by her father An because of her wickedness. The demons attacked man by causing all kinds of diseases and were, as a rule, viewed as wind and storm beings. Consonant with the classical view of the universe as a cosmic state, it was possible for a person to go to the law courts against the demons—i.e., to seek recourse before Utu and obtain judgments against them. Various rituals for such procedures are known.

HUMAN ORIGINS, NATURE, AND DESTINY

Two different notions about human origin seem to have been current in ancient Mesopotamian religions. Brief mentions in Sumerian texts indicate that the first human beings grew from the earth in the manner of grass and herbs. One of these texts, the "Myth of the Creation of the Hoe," adds a few details: Enlil removed heaven from earth in order to make room for seeds to come up, and after he had created the hoe he used it to break the hard crust of earth in Uzumua ("the flesh-grower"), a place in the Temple of Inanna in Nippur. Here, out of the hole made by Enlil's hoe, people grew forth.

The other notion presented the view that humankind was created from select "ingredients" by Enki, or by Enki and his mother Nammu, or by Enki and the birth goddess called variously Ninhursag, Nintur, and Ninmah. In the myth of "Enki and Ninmah" recounted above, Enki had humans sired by the "engendering clay of the Apsu"—i.e., of the waters underground—and borne by Nammu. The Akkadian tradition, as represented by the "Myth of Atrahasis," had Enki advise that a god—presumably a rebel—be killed and that the birth goddess Nintur mix his flesh and blood with clay. This was done,

after which 14 womb goddesses gestated the mixture and gave birth to 7 human pairs. A similar—probably derived—form of this motif is found in *Enuma elish*, in which Enki (Ea) alone fashioned man out of the blood of the slain rebel leader Kingu. The creation of man from the blood shed by two slain gods is yet another version of the motif that appears in a bilingual myth from Ashur.

Human nature, then, is part clay (earthly) and part god (divine). The divine aspect, however, is not that of a living god, but rather that of a slain, powerless divinity. The Atrahasis story relates that the *etemmu* (ghost) of the slain god was left in human flesh and thus became part of human beings. It is this originally divine part of man, his *etemmu*, that was believed to survive at his death and to give him a shadowy afterlife in the netherworld. No other trace of a notion of divine essence in humankind is discernible; in fact, human beings were viewed as being utterly powerless to act effectively or to succeed in anything. For anything they might wish to do or achieve, they needed the help of a personal god or goddess, some deity in the pantheon who for one reason or other had taken an interest in them and helped and protected them, for "Without his personal god a man eats not."

About human destiny all sources agree. However they may have come into being, human beings were meant to toil in order to provide food, clothing, housing, and service for the gods, so that they, relieved of all manual labour, could live the life of a governing upper class, a landed nobility. In the scheme of existence humanity was thus never an end, always just a means.

INSTITUTIONS AND PRACTICES

A number of institutions and practices typify ancient Mesopotamian culture, from the structure of the community to the sacred calendar that organized human life.

CITY-STATE AND NATIONAL STATE

In early dynastic times, probably as far back as historians can trace its history, Mesopotamia was divided into small units, the so-called city-states, consisting of a major city with its surrounding lands. The ruler of the city—usually entitled *ensi*—was also in charge of the temple of the city god. The spouse of the *ensi* had charge of the temple of the city goddess, and the children of the *ensi* administered the temples of the deities who were regarded as children of the city god and the city goddesses. After the foundation of larger political units, such as leagues or empires, contributions were made to a central temple of the political unit, such as the temple of Enlil at Nippur in the Nippur league. On the other hand, however, the king or other central ruler might also contribute to the shrines of local cults. When, in the second and first

millennia BC, Babylonia and Assyria emerged as national states, their kings had responsibility for the national cult, and each monarch supervised the administration of all temples in his domain.

CULT

In the cultic practices, humans fulfilled their destiny: to take care of the gods' material needs. They therefore provided the gods with houses (the temples) that were richly supplied with lands, which people cultivated for them. In the temple the god was present in—but not bounded by—a statue made of precious wood overlaid with gold. For this statue the temple kitchen staff prepared daily meals from victuals grown or raised on the temple's fields, in its orchards, in its sheepfolds, cattle pens, and game preserves, brought in by its fishermen, or delivered by farmers owing it as a temple tax. The statue was also clad in costly raiment, bathed, and escorted to bed in the bedchamber of the god, often on top of the temple tower, or ziggurat. To see to all of this the god had a corps of house servants—i.e., priests trained as cooks, bakers, waiters, and bathers, or as encomiasts (singers of praise) and musicians to make the god's meals festive, or as elegists to soothe him in times of stress and grief. Diversions from the daily routine were the great monthly festivals and also a number of special occasions. Such special occasions might be a sudden need to go through the elaborate ritual for purifying the king when he was threatened by the evils implied in an eclipse of the Moon, or in extreme cases there might be a call for the ritual installation of a substitute king to take upon himself the dangers threatening, and various other nonperiodic rituals.

Partly regular, partly impromptu, were the occasions for audiences with the god in which the king or other worshipers presented their petitions and prayers accompanied by appropriate offerings. These were mostly edibles, but not infrequently the costly containers in which they were presented, stone vases, golden boat-shaped vessels, etc., testified to the ardour of the givers. Appropriate gifts other than edibles were also acceptable—among them cylinder seals for the god's use, superhuman in size, and weapons for him, such as maceheads, also outsize.

To the cult, but as private rather than as part of the temple cult, may be counted also the burial ritual, concerning which, unfortunately, little is known. In outgoing early dynastic times in Girsu two modes of burial were current. One was ordinary burial in a cemetery; the nature of the other, called laying the body "in the reeds of Enki," is not understood. It may have denoted the floating of the body down the river into the canebrakes. Elegists and other funerary personnel were in attendance and conducted the laments seeking to give full expression to the grief of the bereaved and propitiate the spirit of the dead. In later times burial in a family vault under the dwelling house was frequent.

SACRED TIMES

During most of the second millennium BC each major city had its own calendar. The months were named from local religious festivals celebrated in the month in question. Only by the second millennium BC did the Nippur calendar attain general acceptance. The nature of the festivals in these various sacred calendars sometimes reflected the cycle of agricultural activities, such as celebrating the ritual hitching up of the plows and, later in the year, their unhitching, or rites of sowing, harvesting, and other activities. The sacred calendar of Girsu at the end of the early dynastic period is rich in its accounting of festivals. During some of these festival periods the queen traveled through her domain to present funerary offerings of barley, malt, and other agricultural products to the gods and to the spirits of deceased charismatic human administrators.

The cycles of festivals celebrating the marriage and early death of Dumuzi and similar fertility figures in spring were structured according to the backgrounds of the various communities of farmers, herders, or date growers. The sacred wedding—sometimes a fertility rite, sometimes a harvest festival with overtones of thanksgiving—was performed as a drama: the ruler and a high priestess took on the identity of the two deities and so ensured that their highly desirable union actually took place. In many communities the lament for the dead god took the form of a procession out into the desert to find the slain god in his gutted fold, a pilgrimage to the accompaniment of harps and heart-rending laments for the god.

Of major importance in later times was the New Year Festival, or Akitu, celebrated in a special temple out in the fields. Originally an agricultural festival connected with sowing and harvest, it became the proper occasion for the crowning and investiture of a new king. In Babylon it came to celebrate the sun god Marduk's victory over Tiamat, the goddess of the watery deep. Besides the yearly festivals there were also monthly festivals at new moon, the seventh, the 15th, and the 28th of the month. The last—when the moon was invisible and thought to be dead—had a distinctly funereal character.

ADMINISTRATION

Supreme responsibility for the correct carrying out of the cult, on which the welfare of the country depended, was entrusted to the city ruler, or, when the country was united, the king. The city ruler and the king were, however, far more than administrators; they also were charismatic figures imparting their individual magic into their rule, thus creating welfare and fertility. In certain periods the king was deified; throughout the third millennium BC, he became, in ritual action, the god Dumuzi in the rite of the sacred marriage and thus ensured

fertility for his land. All the rulers of the third dynasty of Ur (c. 2112–c. 2004 BC) and most of the rulers of the dynasty of Isin (c. 2020–c. 1800 BC) were treated as embodiments of the dying god Damu and invoked in the ritual laments for him. As a vessel of sacred power the king was surrounded by strict ritual to protect that power, and he had to undergo elaborate rituals of purification if the power became threatened.

The individual temples were usually administered by officials called *sangas* ("bishops"), who headed staffs of accountants, overseers of agricultural and industrial works on the temple estate, and *gudus* (priests), who looked after the god as house servants. Among the priestesses the highest-ranking was termed *en* (Akkadian: *entu*). They were usually princesses of royal blood and were considered the human spouses of the gods they served, participating as brides in the rites of the sacred marriage. Other ranks of priestesses are known, most of them to be considered orders of nuns. The best-known are the votaries of the sun god, who lived in a cloister (*gagûm*) in Sippar. Whether, besides nuns, there were also priestesses devoted to sacred prostitution is a moot question. What is clear is that prostitutes were under the special protection of the goddess Inanna (Ishtar).

SACRED PLACES

Mesopotamian worshipers might worship in open-air sanctuaries, chapels in private houses, or small separate chapels located in the residential quarters of town, but the sacred place par excellence was the temple. Archaeology has traced the temple back to the earliest periods of settlement, and though the very early temple plans still pose many unsolved problems, it is clear that from the early dynastic period onward the temple was what the Sumerian (e) and Akkadian (*bītum*) terms for it indicate; i.e., the temple was the god's house or dwelling.

In its more elaborate form, such a temple would be built on a series of irregular artificial platforms, one on top of the other. By the third dynasty of Ur, near the end of the third millennium BC, these became squared off to form a ziggurat. On the lowest of these platforms a heavy wall—first oval, later rectangular—enclosed storerooms, the temple kitchen, workshops, and other such rooms. On the highest level, approached by a stairway, were the god's living quarters centred in the cella, a rectangular room with an entrance door in the long wall near one corner. The god's place was on a podium in a niche at the short wall farthest from the entrance; benches with statues of worshipers ran along both long walls, and a hearth in the middle of the floor served for heating. Low pillars in front of the god's seat seem to have served as supports for a hanging that shielded the god from profane eyes. Here, or in a connecting room, would be the god's table, bed, and bathtub.

At a later time in Babylonia the cella with its adjoining rooms were greatly enlarged so that it became an open court surrounded by rooms. Only the section separated by the hanging remained roofed and became a new cella, entered from the middle of its long side and with the god in his niche in the wall directly opposite. The development in Assyria took a slightly different course. There, the original door in the long side moved around the corner to the short side opposite the god, creating a rectangular cella entered from the end wall.

The function of the temple, as of all of the other sacred places in ancient Mesopotamia, was primarily to ensure the god's presence and to provide a place where he could be approached. The providing of housing, food, and service for the god achieved the first of these purposes. His presence was also assured by a suitable embodiment—the cult statue, and, for certain rites, the body of the ruler. To achieve the second purpose, greeting gifts, praise hymns as introduction to petitions, and other actions were used to induce the god to receive the petitioner and to listen to, and accept, his prayers.

In view of the magnitude of the establishment provided for the gods and the extent of lands belonging to them and cultivated for them—partly by temple personnel, partly by members of the community holding temple land in some form of tenure—it was unavoidable that temples should vie in economic importance with similar large private estates or with estates belonging to the crown. This importance, one may surmise, would lie largely in the element of stability that an efficiently run major estate provided for the community. With its capacity for producing large storable surpluses that could be used to offset bad years and with its facilities for production—such as its weaveries—the temple estates could absorb and utilize elements of the population, such as widows, waifs, captives, and others, who otherwise would have perished or become a menace to the community in one way or other. The economic importance of the temple primarily was local. The amount of foreign trade carried on by temples apparently was small. The power behind foreign trade seems rather to have been the king.

THE MAGICAL ARTS

In the ancient Mesopotamian view, gods and humans shared one world. The gods lived among men on their great estates (the temples), ruled, upheld law and order for humans, and fought their wars. In general, knowing and carrying out the will of the gods was not a matter for doubt. They wanted the practice of their cult performed faultlessly and work on their estates done willingly and well, and they disapproved, in greater or lesser degree, of breaches of the moral and legal order. On occasion, however, humans might well be uncertain. Did a god want his temple rebuilt or did he not? In all such cases and others like them, the Mesopotamians sought direct answers from the gods through divination, or, conversely, the gods might take the initiative and convey specific wishes through dreams, signs, or portents.

There were many forms of divination. Of interest to students of biblical prophecy is recent evidence that prophets and prophetesses were active at the court of Mari on the Euphrates in Old Babylonian times (c. 1800–c. 1600 BC). In Mesopotamia as a whole, however, the forms of divination most frequently used seem to have been incubation (sleeping in the temple in the hope that the god would send an enlightening dream) and hepatoscopy (examining the entrails, particularly the liver, of a lamb or kid sacrificed for a divinatory purpose, to read what the god had "written" there by interpreting variations in form and shape). In the second and first millennia BC, large and detailed handbooks in hepatoscopy were composed for consultation by the diviners.

Though divination in historical times was regularly presented in terms of ascertaining the divine will, there are internal indications in the materials suggesting that it was originally less theologically elaborated. Apparently it was a mere attempt to read the future from "symptoms" in the present, much as a physician recognizes the onset of a disease. This is particularly evident in that branch of divination that deals with unusual happenings believed to be ominous. Thus, if a desert plant sprouted in a city—indicating that desert essence was about to take over—it was considered an indication that the city would be laid waste.

Related to the observation of unusual happenings in society or nature, but far more systematized, was astrology. The movements and appearance of the Sun, the Moon, and the planets were believed to yield information about future events affecting the nation or, in some cases, the fate of individuals. Horoscopes, predicting the character and fate of a person on the basis of the constellation of the stars at his birth, are known to have been constructed in the late first millennium BC, but the art may conceivably be older.

Witchcraft was apparently at all times considered a crime punishable by death. Frequently, however, it probably was difficult to identify the witch in individual cases, or even to be sure that a given evil was the result of witchcraft rather than of other causes. In such cases, the expert in white magic, the *āšipu* or *mašmašu*, was able to help both in diagnosing the cause of the evil and in performing the appropriate rituals and incantation to fight it off. In earlier times the activities of the magicians seem generally to have been directed against the lawless demons who attacked humans and caused all kinds of diseases. In the later half of the second, and all through the first millennium BC, however, the fear of man-made evils grew, and witchcraft vied with the demons as the chief source of all ills.

RELIGIOUS ART AND ICONOGRAPHY

The earliest periods in Mesopotamia have yielded figurines of clay or stone, some of which may represent gods or demons.

Certainty of interpretation in regard to these figurines is, however, difficult to attain. With the advent of the Protoliterate period toward the end of the fourth millennium BC, the cylinder seal came into use. In the designs on these seals—often, it would seem, copies from monumental wall paintings now lost—ritual scenes and divine figures, recognizable from what is known about them in historical times, make their first appearance.

To this period also belongs the magnificent Uruk Vase, with its representation of the sacred marriage rite. Until the early centuries of the second millennium BC the cylinder seal remains one of the most prolific sources of religious motifs and representations of divine figures, but larger reliefs, wall paintings, and sculpture in the round greatly add to modern historians' understanding of who and what is rendered. In the second and first millennia BC, the humble categories of clay plaques and clay figurines often contained representations of deities, and the numerous sculptured boundary stones (*kudurrus*) furnish representations of symbols and emblems of gods, at times identified by labels in cuneiform. To the first millennium BC belong also the magnificent colossal statues of protective genies (spirits) in the shape of lions or human-headed bulls that guarded the entrances to Assyrian palaces, and also, on the gates of Nebuchadrezzar's (d. 562 BC) Babylon, the reliefs in glazed tile of lions and dragons that served the same purpose.

APPENDIX A: MESOPOTAMIAN GODS AND GODDESSES

ADAD

The weather god of the Babylonian and Assyrian pantheon was Adad. His name may have been brought into Mesopotamia toward the end of the third millennium BC by Western (Amorite) Semites. His Sumerian equivalent was Ishkur and the West Semitic was Hadad.

Adad had a twofold aspect, being both the giver and the destroyer of life. His rains caused the land to bear grain and other food for his friends; hence his title Lord of Abundance. His storms and hurricanes, evidences of his anger against his foes, brought darkness, want, and death. Adad's father was the heaven god An, but he is also designated as the son of Bel, Lord of All Lands and god of the atmosphere. His consort was Shalash, which may be a Hurrian name. The symbol of Adad was the cypress, and six was his sacred number. The bull and the lion were sacred to him. In Babylonia, Assyria, and Aleppo in Syria, he was also the god of oracles and divination. Unlike the greater gods, Adad quite possibly had no cult centre peculiar to himself, although he was worshiped in many of the important cities and towns of Mesopotamia, including Babylon and Ashur, the capital of Assyria.

AN

The sky god An (known to the Akkadians as Anu) was a member of the triad of deities completed by Enlil and Enki. Like most sky gods, An, although theoretically the highest god, played only a small role in the mythology, hymns, and cults of Mesopotamia. He was the father not only of all the gods but also of evil spirits and demons, most prominently the female demon Lamashtu, who preyed on infants. An was also the god of kings and of the yearly calendar. He was typically depicted in a headdress with horns, a sign of strength.

An dates from the oldest Sumerian period, at least 3000 BC. Originally he seems to have been envisaged as a great bull, a form later disassociated from the god as a separate mythological entity, the Bull of Heaven, which was owned by An. His holy city was Erech (Uruk), in the southern herding region, and the bovine imagery suggests that he belonged originally to the herders' pantheon. In Akkadian myth, where the god was called Anu, he was assigned a consort, Antum (Antu), but she seems often to have been confused with Inanna, or Ishtar, the celebrated goddess of love.

ASHUR

Ashur was the city god of Ashur and national god of Assyria. In the beginning he was perhaps only a local deity of the city that shared his name. From roughly 1800 BC onward, however, there appear to have been strong tendencies to identify him with the Sumerian Enlil, while under the Assyrian king Sargon II (reigned 721–705 BC), there were tendencies to identify Ashur with Anshar, the father of An in the creation myth.

Under Sargon's successor Sennacherib, deliberate and thorough attempts were made to transfer to Ashur the primeval achievements of Marduk, as well as the whole ritual of the New Year Festival of Babylon—attempts that clearly have their background in the political struggle going on at that time between Babylonia and Assyria. As a consequence, the image of Ashur seems to lack all real distinctiveness and contains little that is not implied in his position as the city god of a vigorous and warlike city that became the capital of an empire. The Assyrians believed that he granted rule over Assyria and supported Assyrian arms against enemies; detailed written reports from the Assyrian kings about their campaigns were even submitted to him. He appears a mere personification of the interests of Assyria as a political entity, otherwise having little character of his own.

ENKI

The god of water, Enki (called by the Akkadians Ea), was a member of the triad of deities completed by An and Enlil. From a local deity worshiped in the city of Eridu, Enki evolved into a major god, Lord of Apsu (also spelled Abzu), the fresh waters beneath the earth (although Enki means literally "lord of the earth"). In the Sumerian myth "Enki and the World Order," Enki is said to have fixed national boundaries and assigned gods their roles. According to another Sumerian myth Enki is the creator, having devised men as slaves to the gods. In his original form, as Enki, he was associated with semen and amniotic fluid, and therefore with fertility. He was commonly represented as a half-goat, half-fish creature, from which the modern astrological figure for Capricorn is derived.

Ea, the Akkadian counterpart of Enki, was the god of ritual purification: ritual cleansing waters were called "Ea's water." Ea governed the arts of sorcery and incantation. In some stories he was also the form-giving god, and thus the patron of craftsmen and artists; he was known as the bearer of culture. In his role as adviser to the king, Ea was a wise god although not a forceful one. In Akkadian myth, as Ea's character evolves, he appears frequently as a clever mediator who could be devious and cunning. He is also significant in Akkadian mythology as the father of Marduk, the national god of Babylonia.

ENLIL

Enlil was the god of the atmosphere and a member of the triad of gods completed by An and Enki. Enlil meant Lord Wind: both the hurricane and the gentle winds of spring were thought of as the breath issuing from his mouth and eventually as his word or command. He was sometimes called Lord of the Air.

Although An was the highest god in the Sumerian pantheon, Enlil had a more important role as the embodiment of energy and force and authority. Enlil's cult centre was Nippur. Enlil was also the god of agriculture. The Myth of the Creation of the Hoe describes how he separated heaven and earth to make room for seeds to grow. He then invented the hoe and broke the hard crust of earth; men sprang forth from the opening. Another myth relates Enlil's rape of his consort Ninlil, a grain goddess, and his subsequent banishment to the underworld. This myth reflects the agricultural cycle of fertilization, ripening, and winter inactivity.

Enlil was eventually replaced by Marduk as the executive of the Babylonian pantheon. He continued to be extolled, however, as high god of Nippur until the end of the second millennium BC. He remained an important deity there well into the next millennium.

ERESHKIGAL

The goddess Ereshkigal was Lady of the Great Place (i.e., the abode of the dead). In texts of the third millennium BC, she was the wife of the god Ninazu (elsewhere accounted her son); in later texts she was the wife of Nergal. Ereshkigal's sister was Inanna (Akkadian: Ishtar), and between the two there was great enmity. In the rendezvous of the dead, Ereshkigal reigned in her palace, on the watch for lawbreakers and on guard over the fount of life lest any of her subjects take of it and so escape her rule. Her offspring and servant was Namtar, the evil demon, Death. Her power extended to earth where, in magical ceremony, she liberated the sick possessed of evil spirits.

Ereshkigal's cult extended to Asia Minor, Egypt, and southern Arabia. In Mesopotamia the chief temple known to be dedicated to her was at Cuthah.

INANNA

Inanna, also known as Ishtar, was the goddess of war and sexual love. She is the Akkadian counterpart of the West Semitic goddess Astarte. Inanna, an important goddess in the Sumerian pantheon, came to be identified with Ishtar, but it is uncertain whether Inanna is also of Semitic origin or whether, as is more likely, her similarity to Ishtar caused the two to be identified. In the figure of Inanna several traditions seem to have been combined. She is sometimes the daughter of the sky god An, sometimes his wife. In other myths she is the daughter of Nanna, god of the moon, or of the wind god, Enlil. In her earliest manifestations she was associated with the storehouse and thus personified as the goddess of dates, wool, meat, and grain; the storehouse gates were her emblem. She was also the goddess of rain and thunderstorms—leading to her association with An, the sky god— and was often pictured with the lion, whose roar resembled thunder. The power attributed to her in war may have arisen from her connection with storms.

Inanna was also a fertility figure, and, as goddess of the storehouse and the bride of the god Dumuzi-Amaushumgalana, who represented the growth and fecundity of the date palm, she was characterized as young, beautiful, and impulsive—never as helpmate or mother. She is sometimes referred to as the Lady of the Date Clusters.

Inanna's primary legacy from the Sumerian tradition is the role of fertility figure; she evolved, however, into a more complex character, surrounded in myth by death and disaster, a goddess of contradictory connotations and forces—fire and fire-quenching, rejoicing and tears, fair play and enmity. The Akkadian Ishtar is also, to a greater extent, an astral deity, associated with the planet Venus. With Utu (Shamash), the sun god, and Nanna (Sin), the moon god, she forms a secondary astral triad. In this manifestation her symbol is a star with 6, 8, or 16 rays within a circle. As goddess of Venus, delighting in bodily love, Ishtar was the protectress of prostitutes and the patroness of the alehouse. Part of her cult worship probably included temple prostitution. Her popularity was universal in the ancient Middle East, and in many centres of worship she probably subsumed numerous local goddesses. In later myth she was known as Queen of the Universe, taking on the powers of An, Enlil, and Enki.

NANNA

Nanna was the god of the moon and father of the sun god, Utu (Shamash), and, in some myths, of Inanna (Ishtar), goddess of war and sexual love, and with them formed an astral triad of deities.

Nanna, who was also known as Sin, may have originally meant only the full moon, whereas Su-en, later contracted to Sin, designated the crescent moon. At any rate, Nanna was intimately connected with the cattle herds that were the livelihood of the people in the marshes of the lower Euphrates River, where the cult developed. (The city of Ur, of the same region, was the chief centre of the worship of Nanna.) The crescent, Nanna's emblem, was sometimes represented by the horns of a great bull. Nanna bestowed fertility and prosperity on the cowherds, governing the rise of the waters, the growth of reeds, the increase of the herd, and therefore the quantity of dairy products produced. His consort, Ningal, was a reed goddess. Each spring, Nanna's worshipers reenacted his mythological visit to his father, Enlil, at Nippur with a ritual journey, carrying with them the first dairy products of the year. Gradually Nanna became more human: from being depicted as a bull or boat, because of his crescent emblem, he came to be represented as a cowherd or boatman.

Sin was represented as an old man with a flowing beard—a wise and unfathomable god—wearing a headdress of four horns surmounted by a crescent moon. The last king of Babylon, Nabonidus (reigned *c.* 556–539 BC), attempted to elevate Sin to a supreme position within the pantheon.

NINLIL

Ninlil was the consort of the god Enlil and a deity of destiny. She was worshiped especially at Nippur and Shuruppak and was the mother of the moon god, Nanna, or Sin. In Assyrian documents, where she is called Belit, she is sometimes identified with Inanna (Ishtar) of Nineveh and sometimes made the wife of either Ashur, the national god of Assyria, or of Enlil, god of the atmosphere.

The Sumerian Ninlil was a grain goddess, known as the Varicoloured Ear (of barley). She was the daughter of Haia, god of the stores, and Ninshebargunu (or Nidaba). The myth recounting the rape of Ninlil by her consort, the wind god Enlil, reflects the life cycle of grain: Enlil, who saw Ninlil bathing in a canal, raped and impregnated her. For his crime he was banished to the underworld, but Ninlil followed. In the course of their journey Enlil assumed three different guises, and in each incident he ravished and impregnated Ninlil. The myth seems to represent the process of wind pollination, ripening, and the eventual withering of the crops and their subsequent return to the earth (corresponding to Ninlil's sojourn in the underworld).

TAMMUZ

Tammuz, or Dumuzi, was the god of fertility, embodying the powers for new life in nature in the spring. The name Tammuz seems to have been derived from the Akkadian form Tammuzi, based on early Sumerian Damu-zid, The Flawless Young. The later standard Sumerian form, Dumu-zid, in turn became Dumuzi in Akkadian. The earliest known mention of Tammuz is in texts dating to the early part of the early dynastic III period (*c.* 2600–*c.* 2334 BC), but his cult probably was much older. Although the cult is attested for most of the major cities of Sumer in the third and second millennia BC, it centred in the cities around the central steppe area (the *edin*), for example, at Bad-tibira (modern Madīnah) where Tammuz was the city god.

As shown by his most common epithet Sipad (Shepherd), Tammuz was essentially a pastoral deity. His father Enki is rarely mentioned, and his mother, the goddess Duttur, was a personification of the ewe. His own name, Dumu-zid, and two variant designations for him, Ama-ga (Mother Milk) and U-lu-lu

(Multiplier of Pasture), suggest that he actually was the power for everything that a shepherd might wish for: grass to come up in the desert, healthy lambs to be born, and milk to be plentiful in the mother animals.

When the cult of Tammuz spread to Assyria in the second and first millennia BC, the character of the god seems to have changed from that of a pastoral to that of an agricultural deity. The texts suggest that, in Assyria (and later among the Sabaeans), Tammuz was basically viewed as the power in the grain, dying when the grain was milled.

The cult of Tammuz centred around two yearly festivals, one celebrating his marriage to the goddess Inanna, the other lamenting his death at the hands of demons from the netherworld. During the third dynasty of Ur (c. 2112–c. 2004 BC) in the city of Umma (modern Tell Jokha), the marriage of the god was dramatically celebrated in February–March, Umma's Month of the Festival of Tammuz. During the Isin–Larsa period (c. 2004–c. 1792 BC), the texts relate that in the marriage rite the king actually took on the identity of the god and thus, by consummating the marriage with a priestess incarnating the goddess, magically fertilized and fecundated all of nature for the year.

The celebrations in March–April that marked the death of the god also seem to have been dramatically performed. Many of the laments for the occasion have as a setting a procession out into the desert to the fold of the slain god. In Assyria, however, in the seventh century BC, the ritual took place in June–July. In the major cities of the realm, a couch was set up for the god upon which he lay in state. His body appears to have been symbolized by an assemblage of vegetable matter, honey, and a variety of other foods.

Among the texts dealing with the god is "Dumuzi's Dream," a myth telling how Tammuz had a dream presaging his death and how the dream came true in spite of all his efforts to escape. A closely similar tale forms the second half of the Sumerian myth "The Descent of Inanna," in which Inanna (Ishtar) sends Tammuz as her substitute to the netherworld. His sister, Geshtinanna, eventually finds him, and the myth ends with Inanna decreeing that Tammuz and his sister may alternate in the netherworld, each spending half of the year among the living.

Tammuz's courtship and wedding were a popular theme for love songs and anecdotal verse compositions that seem to have been used primarily for entertainment. A number of true cult texts, however, follow the rite step by step as if told by a close observer, and many laments were probably performed in the actual rites.

Eventually a variety of originally independent fertility gods seem to have become identified with Tammuz. Tammuz of the cattle herders, whose main distinction from Tammuz the Shepherd was that his mother was the goddess Ninsun, Lady Wild Cow, and that he himself was imagined as a cattle herder, may have been an original aspect of the god. The agricultural form of Tammuz in the north, where he was identified with the grain, may also have been an originally independent development of the god from his role as the power in the vegetation of spring. A clear fusion, though very early, was the merger of Tammuz in Erech (Uruk) with Amaushumgalana, the One Great Source of the Date Clusters; i.e., the power of fertility in the date palm.

A later important fusion was the merger of Tammuz and Damu, a fertility god who probably represented the power in the sap of rising in trees and plants in spring. The relation of still other figures to Tammuz, such as Dumuzi-Apzu—a goddess who appears to have been the power in the waters underground (the Apzu) to bring new life to vegetation—is not entirely clear.

UTU

Utu (also called Shamash) was the god of the sun, who, with the moon god, Nanna (or Sin), and Inanna (Ishtar), the goddess of Venus, was part of an astral triad of divinities. Utu was the son of Nanna.

As the solar deity, Utu exercised the power of light over darkness and evil. In this capacity he became known as the god of justice and equity and was the judge of both gods and men. (According to legend, the Babylonian king Hammurabi received his code of laws from Shamash.) At night, Utu became judge of the underworld.

Shamash was not only the god of justice but also governor of the whole universe; in this aspect he was pictured seated on a throne, holding in his hand the symbols of justice and righteousness, a staff and a ring. Also associated with Shamash is the notched dagger. The god is often pictured with a disk that symbolized the Sun.

The sun god was considered to be the heroic conqueror of night and death who swept across the heavens on horseback or, in some representations, in a boat or chariot. He bestowed light and life. Because he was of a heroic and wholly ethical character, he only rarely figured in mythology, where the gods behaved all too often like mortals. The chief centres of his cult were at Larsa in Sumer and at Sippar in Akkad. Shamash's consort was Aya, who was later absorbed by Inanna.

APPENDIX B: MESOPOTAMIAN CITIES

ASHUR

The ancient religious capital of Assyria, Ashur (Assur) is located on the west bank of the Tigris River in what is now northern Iraq. The first scientific excavations there were conducted by a German expedition (1903–13) led by Walter Andrae. Ashur was a name applied to the city, to the country, and to the principal god of the ancient Assyrians.

The site was originally occupied about 2500 BC by a tribe that probably had reached the Tigris River either from Syria or from the south. Strategically, Ashur was smaller and less well-situated than Nimrūd (Kalakh) or Nineveh, the other principal cities of Assyria; but the religious sanctity of Ashur ensured its continuous upkeep until 614 BC, when it was destroyed by the Babylonians. A part of the city was later revived about the time of the Parthian conquest of Mesopotamia in the middle of the second century BC.

The inner city was protected by encircling walls nearly 2.5 miles (4 km) long. On the eastern side Ashur was washed by the Tigris, along which massive quays were first erected by Adad-nirari I (reigned c. 1295–c. 1264). On the north side an arm of the river and a high escarpment afforded natural defenses, which were augmented by a system of buttressed walls and by a powerful sally port called the *mushlalu*—a semicircular tower of rusticated stone masonry, built by Sennacherib and probably the earliest known example of this type of architecture. The southern and western sides were protected by a strong fortification system.

A catalog of Ashur's buildings inscribed during the reign of Sennacherib (704–681) lists 34 temples, although fewer than one-third of them have been found, including those of Ashur-Enlil, An-Adad, Sin-Shamash, and Ishtar and Nabu. Historically the most interesting temples are those devoted to the cult of the goddess Ishtar, or Inanna, as she was known to the Sumerians.

In addition to the temples, three palaces were identified. The oldest of these was ascribed to Shamshi-Adad I (c. 1813–c. 1781) and was later used as a burial ground. Many of the private houses found in the northwestern quarter of the site were spaciously laid out and had family vaults beneath their floors, where dozens of archives and libraries were uncovered in the course of the German excavations. The irregular planning of the town indicates a strict respect for property rights and land tenure. Other aspects of Assyrian law, particularly those relating to women, are known from a series of tablets compiled between 1450 and 1250.

Ashur was made a World Heritage site in 2003.

BORSIPPA

The ancient Babylonian city of Borsippa is situated southwest of Babylon in what is now central Iraq. Its patron god was Nabu, and the city's proximity to the capital, Babylon, helped it to become an important religious centre. Hammurabi (reigned 1792–50 BC) built or rebuilt the Ezida temple at Borsippa, dedicating it to Marduk (the national god of Babylonia); subsequent kings recognized Nabu as the deity of Ezida and made him the son of Marduk, his temple becoming second only to that of Marduk in Babylon.

During Nebuchadrezzar II's reign (605–562 BC), Borsippa reached its greatest prosperity. An incomplete and now ruined ziggurat built by Nebuchadrezzar was excavated in 1902 by the German archaeologist Robert Koldewey. The ziggurat appears to have been destroyed by an extremely hot fire, probably caused by the spontaneous combustion of reed matting and bitumen originally placed in the core of the structure for internal support. Borsippa was destroyed by the Achaemenian king Xerxes I in the early fifth century and never fully recovered.

ERECH

The ancient city of Erech (Sumerian: Uruk; modern Tall al-Warkā') is located northwest of Ur (modern Tall al-Muqayyar) in what is now southeastern Iraq. The site has been excavated from 1928 onward by the German Oriental Society and the German Archeological Institute. Erech was one of the greatest cities of Sumer and was enclosed by brickwork walls about 6 miles (10 km) in circumference, which according to legend were built by the mythical hero Gilgamesh. Within the walls, excavations traced successive cities that date from the prehistoric Ubaid period, perhaps before 5000 BC, down to Parthian times (126 BC–AD 224). Urban life in what is known as the Erech–Jamdat Nasr period (c. 3500–c. 2900 BC) is more fully illustrated at Erech than at any other Mesopotamian city.

The two principal Sumerian divinities worshiped in ancient Erech appear to have been An (Anu), a sky god, and the goddess Inanna (Queen of the Universe). One of the chief landmarks of the city is the An ziggurat crowned by the "White Temple" of the Jamdat Nasr period, which was one of great prosperity—gold, silver, and copper were skillfully worked, and seals and amulets reflected a brilliant miniature craftsmanship.

The temenos (sacred enclosure) of Eanna, another ziggurat, bore witness to the attention of many powerful kings, including Ur-Nammu (reigned 2112–2095 BC), first king of the third dynasty of Ur. Ur-Nammu also did much for the layout of the city, which then benefited from a neo-Sumerian revival. Various architectural developments were associated with the Isin-Larsa period (c. 2017–c. 1763) and with the Kassite period (*c.* 1595–*c.* 1157). Later rulers, including Cyrus the Great and Darius the Great, also built in the district of Eanna.

The city continued to prosper in Parthian times, when the last of an ancient school of learned scribes was still editing documents (*c.* 70 BC) in the cuneiform script.

ERIDU

An ancient Sumerian city south of Ur (modern Tall al-Muqayyar), Eridu was revered as the oldest city in Sumer according to the king lists. Its patron god was Enki, "lord of the sweet waters that flow under the earth." The site, located at a mound called Abū Shahrayn, was excavated principally between 1946 and 1949 by the Iraq Antiquities Department; it proved to be one of the most important of the prehistoric urban centres in southern Babylonia. Founded on sand dunes probably in the fifth millennium BC, it fully illustrated the sequence of the preliterate Ubaid civilization, with its long succession of superimposed temples portraying the growth and development of an elaborate mud-brick architecture.

The city continued to be occupied to about 600 BC, but was less important in historic periods.

ESHNUNNA

The ancient city of Eshnunna (modern Tall al-Asmar) is located in the Diyālā River valley lying about 20 miles (32 km) northeast of Baghdad in what is now east-central Iraq. The excavations carried out by the Oriental Institute of the University of Chicago revealed that the site was occupied sometime before 3000 BC. The city expanded throughout the early dynastic period, and during the third dynasty of Ur the city was the seat of an *ensi* (governor). After the collapse of Ur, Eshnunna became independent but was later conquered by Hammurabi, king of Babylonia. During the next century the city fell into decline and may have been abandoned.

The "Laws of Eshnunna" are inscribed on two broken tablets found in Tall Abū Harmal, near Baghdad. The two tablets are not duplicates but separate copies of an older source. The laws are believed to be about two generations older than the Code of Hammurabi; the differences between the two codes help illuminate the development of ancient law.

KISH

The ancient city-state of Kish (modern Tall al-Uhaimer) is located east of Babylon in what is now south-central Iraq. According to ancient Sumerian sources it was the seat of the first post-diluvian dynasty; most scholars believe that the dynasty was at least partly historical. A king of Kish, Mesilim, is known to have been the author of the earliest extant royal inscription, in which he recorded his arbitration of a boundary dispute between the south

Babylonian cities of Lagash and Umma. The dynasty ended when its last king, Agga, was defeated about 2660 by Gilgamesh, king of the first dynasty of Erech (Uruk). Although Kish continued to be important throughout most of ancient Mesopotamian history, it was never able to regain its earlier prominence.

LAGASH

One of the most important capital cities in ancient Sumer, Lagash (modern Telloh) is located midway between the Tigris and Euphrates rivers in what is now southeastern Iraq. The ancient name of the mound of Telloh was actually Girsu, while Lagash originally denoted a site southeast of Girsu, later becoming the name of the whole district and also of Girsu itself. The French excavated at Telloh between 1877 and 1933 and uncovered at least 50,000 cuneiform texts that have proved one of the major sources for knowledge of Sumer in the third millennium BC. Dedicatory inscriptions on stone and on bricks also have provided invaluable evidence for assessing the chronological development of Sumerian art.

The city was founded in the prehistoric Ubaid period (*c.* 5200–*c.* 3500 BC) and was still occupied as late as the Parthian era (247 BC–AD 224). In the early dynastic period the rulers of Lagash called themselves "king" (*lugal*), though the city itself never was included within the official Sumerian canon of kingship. Among the most famous Lagash monuments of that period is the Stele of the Vultures, erected to celebrate the victory of King Eannatum over the neighbouring state of Umma. Another is the engraved silver vase of King Entemena, a successor of Eannatum. Control of Lagash finally fell to Sargon of Akkad (reigned *c.* 2334–2279 BC), but about 150 years later Lagash enjoyed a revival. It prospered most brilliantly under Gudea, who was probably a governor rather than an independent king and was nominally subject to the Guti, a warlike people who controlled much of Babylonia from about 2230 to about 2130.

Lagash was endowed with many temples, including the Eninnu, "House of the Fifty," a seat of the high god Enlil. Architecturally the most remarkable structure was a weir and regulator, once doubtless possessing sluice gates, which conserved the area's water supply in reservoirs.

MARI

The ancient city of Mari (modern Tall al-Ḥarīrī) is situated on the right bank of the Euphrates River in what is now Syria. Excavations, initially directed by André Parrot and begun in 1933, uncovered remains extending from about 3100 BC to the seventh century AD.

The most remarkable of the discoveries was the great palace of Zimrilim, a local king whose exceptionally prosperous rule of almost 30 years was ended when Hammurabi of Babylon captured and destroyed the city in the 18th century BC.

The palace contained nearly 300 rooms, within which were concentrated all of the most important administrative offices. Numerous wall murals and hundreds of small objects were uncovered; nothing, however, equaled the thousands of archives discovered in various scribal chambers. They consisted of diplomatic correspondence and reports sent in from all parts of the country as well as historical archives and letters exchanged between King Shamshi-Adad I of Assyria and his two sons shortly before 1800 BC. Economic and legal texts were also abundant. Altogether the texts have extended the knowledge of Assyrian geography and history and have given a graphic picture of life of the period.

NINEVEH

Nineveh, the oldest and most populous city of the ancient Assyrian Empire, is situated on the east bank of the Tigris opposite what is now the city of Mosul, Iraq. Nineveh was located at the intersection of important north-south and east-west trade routes, and its proximity to a tributary of the Tigris, the Khawṣar River, added to the value of the fertile agricultural and pastoral lands in the district.

The first person to survey and map Nineveh was the archaeologist Claudius J. Rich in 1820, a work later completed by Felix Jones and published by him in 1854. Excavations have been undertaken intermittently since that period by many persons. A.H. (later Sir Henry) Layard during 1845–51 discovered the palace of Sennacherib and took back to England an unrivalled collection of stone bas-reliefs together with thousands of tablets inscribed in cuneiform from the great library of Ashurbanipal. Hormuzd Rassam continued the work in 1852. During 1929–32 R. Campbell Thompson excavated the temple of Nabu (Nebo) on behalf of the British Museum and discovered the site of the palace of Ashurnasirpal II. In 1931–32, together with M.E.L. (later Sir Max) Mallowan, Thompson for the first time dug a shaft from the top of the Quyunjik (Acropolis), 90 feet (30 metres) above the level of the plain, down through strata of accumulated debris of earlier cultures to virgin soil. It was then proved that more than four-fifths of this great accumulation is prehistoric.

The first settlement, a small Neolithic (New Stone Age) hamlet, was probably founded not later than the seventh millennium BC. Hassuna-Sāmarrā' and Tall Ḥalaf painted pottery of the subsequent Early Chalcolithic phases, characteristic of the north, was succeeded by gray wares such as occur westward in the Jabal Sinjār. Farmers during the fourth millennium used clay sickles of a type found in the Ubaid period, and these imply contact with the south.

One of the most remarkable discoveries that Mallowan and Thompson made in the prehistoric strata consisted of roughly made, beveled bowls, overturned in the soil and filled with vegetable matter. These may have been intended as magical offerings to expel evil spirits from houses. Their typology conforms exactly with that of Erech (Uruk) pottery, widespread throughout the Tigris–Euphrates Valley in the late fourth millennium. In these levels also large metal vases occur, again characteristic of southern Babylonia, and technologically this district of the Tigris had much in common with the cities of the lower Euphrates Valley at this period. This similarity is of particular interest because it indicates that some time before 3000 BC a period of economic prosperity had united the commercial interests of north and south; later these two civilizations diverged widely.

A little before and after 3000 BC, unpainted Ninevite pottery was similar to that used at Sumerian sites; to approximately the same period belongs a series of attractively painted and incised ware known as Ninevite V, which is a home product distinct from that of the south. Beads found in these strata may be dated c. 2900 BC.

The most remarkable object of the third millennium BC is a realistic bronze head—life-size, cast, and chased—of a bearded monarch. This, the finest piece of metal sculpture ever recovered from Mesopotamia, may represent the famous king Sargon of Akkad (c. 2334–c. 2279 BC). This bronze head, however, because of its brilliant technique and elaborately modeled features, is thought by some authorities to belong to a rather later stage of the Akkadian period (c. 2334–c. 2154 BC); if so, the head might represent King Naram-Sin (c. 2254–c. 2218 BC). The hypothesis for the earlier period seems preferable, for metal work advanced more rapidly in style in Mesopotamia at that period than did stone sculpture, and it is known from inscriptions that Sargon's second son, Manishtusu, had built the temple of E-mashmash at Nineveh by virtue of being the "son of Sargon"; thus a model of the founder of the dynasty would have been appropriately placed there.

Surprisingly, there is no large body of evidence to show that Assyrian monarchs built at all extensively in Nineveh during the second millennium BC. Later monarchs whose inscriptions have appeared on the Acropolis include Shalmaneser I and Tiglath-pileser I, both of whom were active builders in Ashur; the former had founded Calah (Nimrūd). Nineveh had to wait for the neo-Assyrians, particularly from the time of Ashurnasirpal II (ruled 883–859 BC) onward, for a considerable architectural expansion. Thereafter successive monarchs kept in repair and founded new palaces, temples to Sin, Nergal, Nanna, Shamash, Ishtar, and Nabu (Nebo). Unfortunately, severe depredations have left few remains of these edifices.

It was Sennacherib who made Nineveh a truly magnificent city (c. 700 BC). He laid out fresh streets and squares and built within it the famous "palace without a rival," the plan of which has been mostly recovered and has overall dimensions of about 600 by 630 feet (180 by 190 metres). It comprised at least 80 rooms, of which many were lined with sculpture. A large part of the famous "K" collection of tablets was found there; some of the principal doorways were flanked by human-headed bulls. At this time the total area of Nineveh comprised about 1,800 acres (700 hectares), and 15 great gates penetrated its walls. An elaborate system of 18 canals brought water from the hills to Nineveh, and several sections of a magnificently constructed aqueduct erected by the same monarch were discovered at Jerwan, about 25 miles (40 km) distant.

His successor Esarhaddon built an arsenal in the Nabī Yūnus mound, south of Quyunjik, and either he or his successor set up statues of the pharaoh Taharqa (Tarku) at its entrance as trophies to celebrate the conquest of Egypt. These were discovered by Fuad Safar and Muḥammad ʿAlī Muṣṭafā on behalf of the Iraqi Department of Antiquities in 1954.

Ashurbanipal later in the seventh century BC constructed a new palace at the northwest end of the Acropolis. He also founded the great library and ordered his scribes to collect and copy ancient texts throughout the country. The "K" collection included more than 20,000 tablets or fragments of tablets and incorporated the ancient lore of Mesopotamia. The subjects are literary, religious, and administrative, and a great many tablets are in the form of letters. Branches of learning

represented include mathematics, botany, chemistry, and lexicology. The library contains a mass of information about the ancient world and will exercise scholars for generations to come.

Fourteen years after the death of Ashurbanipal, however, Nineveh suffered a defeat from which it never recovered. Extensive traces of ash, representing the sack of the city by Babylonians, Scythians, and Medes in 612 BC, have been found in many parts of the Acropolis. After 612 BC the city ceased to be important, although there are some Seleucid and Greek remains. Xenophon in the *Anabasis* recorded the name of the city as Mespila. In the 13th century AD the city seems to have enjoyed some prosperity under the atabegs of Mosul. Subsequently, houses continued to be inhabited at least as late as the 16th century AD. In these later levels imitations of Chinese wares have been found.

From the ruins it has been established that the perimeter of the great Assyrian city wall was about 7.5 miles (12 km) long and in places up to 148 feet (45 metres) wide; there was also a great unfinished outer rampart, protected by a moat, and the Khawṣar River flowed through the centre of the city to join the Tigris on the western side of it.

The 15 great gates that intersected the Acropolis walls were built partly of mud brick and partly of stone. The long eastern sector, about 3 miles (5 km), contained six gates; the southern sector, 2,624 feet (800 metres), contained only one, the Ashur Gate; the western sector, about 2.5 miles (4 km), had five gates; the northern sector, about 1.2 miles (1.9 km), three gates, Adad, Nergal, and Sin. Several of these entrances are known to have been faced with stone colossi (lamassu). In the Nergal Gate two winged stone bulls, attributable to Sennacherib, have been reinstalled: a site museum has been erected adjacent to it by the Iraqi Department of Antiquities. The Adad Gate contained many inscribed tiles, and what may prove to be the Sin Gate contained a corridor that led through an arched doorway into a ramp or stairwell giving access to the battlements.

Most impressive was the Shamash Gate, which has been thoroughly excavated by Tariq Madhloum on behalf of the Iraqi Department of Antiquities. It was found to have been approached across two moats and a watercourse by a series of bridges in which the arches were cut out of the natural conglomerate. The wall was faced with limestone and surmounted by a crenellated parapet, behind which ran a defense causeway. The structure was constructed of mud as well as burnt bricks, which bore the stamp of Sennacherib. There was an entrance 14.8 feet (4.5 metres) wide in the centre of a long, projecting bastion, which was further strengthened by six towers. Crudely incised stone slabs on the inner side of the gateway depicted the burning of a tower; it is possible that these carvings represented the fall of Nineveh and are post-Assyrian. The internal plan of the gate includes six great chambers lined with uncarved orthostats (upright slabs), which were discovered by Layard and Rassam.

Archaeologists also have been active within the Quyunjik (Acropolis). Since 1966 restoration has proceeded on the throne room of Sennacherib's palace and some of the adjoining chambers. All the entrances to the two main chambers were found flanked by winged bull colossi, and a series of orthostats not recorded by any of the 19th-century excavators has been recovered. One such slab illustrates a foreign city, heavily defended by towers, surrendering to the Assyrian army. Adjoining the throne room is a stone-paved bathroom, and the great antehall contained no fewer than 40 carved orthostats. The subjects represented include Sennacherib's campaigns against mountain-dwelling peoples, besieged cities, and units of the Assyrian army.

NIPPUR

The ancient city of Nippur (modern Niffer, or Nuffar) is located in what is now southeastern Iraq. It lies northeast of the town of Al-Dīwānīyah. Although never a political capital, Nippur played a dominant role in the religious life of Mesopotamia.

In Sumerian mythology Nippur was the home of Enlil, the storm god and representation of force and the god who carried out the decrees of the assembly of gods that met at Nippur. Enlil, according to one account, created man at Nippur. Although a king's armies might subjugate the country, the transference to that king of Enlil's divine power to rule had to be sought and sanctioned. The necessity of this confirmation made the city and Enlil's sanctuary there especially sacred, regardless of which dynasty ruled Mesopotamia.

The first American archaeological expedition to Mesopotamia excavated at Nippur from 1889 to 1900; the work was resumed in 1948. The eastern section of the city has been called the scribal quarter because of the many thousands of Sumerian tablets found there; in fact, the excavations at Nippur have been the primary source of the literary writing of Sumer. Excavation in 1990 uncovered an Akkadian tomb and a large temple to Bau (Gula), the Mesopotamian goddess of healing.

Little is known about the prehistoric town, but by 2500 BC the city probably reached the extent of the present ruins and was fortified. Later, Ur-Nammu (reigned 2112–2095 BC), first king of the third dynasty of Ur, laid out Enlil's sanctuary, the E-kur, in its present form. A ziggurat and a temple were built in an open courtyard surrounded by walls.

Parthian construction later buried Enlil's sanctuary and its enclosure walls, and in the third century AD the city fell into decay. It was finally abandoned in the 12th or 13th century.

TALL AL-'UBAYD

The ancient site of Tall al-'Ubayd (Tell el-'Ubayd) is located near the ruins of ancient Ur in what is now southeastern Iraq. Its name was assigned to the prehistoric cultural period now known as the Ubaid period. Excavations have uncovered Ubaidian remains throughout southern Mesopotamia. The hallmark of the period was a painted pottery decorated with geometric and sometimes floral and animal designs in dark paint on a buff or drab clay. Many vessels seem to have been made on a slow wheel, and they had loop handles and spouts (the first historical occurrence of these).

In the south the Ubaid period is dated from about 5200 to c. 3500 BC, but in the north Ubaidian characteristics do not seem to appear until c. 4300. Some scholars believe the characteristics of the northern Ubaid period may have been outgrowths of the preceding Halaf period rather than the result of cultural influences received directly from the south, but the overall picture is one of great homogeneity throughout the entire area from the Persian Gulf to the Mediterranean Sea.

UR

The ancient city of Ur (modern Tall al-Muqayyar, or Tell el-Muqayyar) is situated about 140 miles (225 km) southeast of the site of Babylon and about 10 miles (16 km) west of the present bed of the Euphrates River. In antiquity the river ran much closer to the city; the change in its course has left the ruins in a desert that once was irrigated and fertile land.

The first serious excavations at Ur were made after World War I by H.R. Hall of the British Museum, and as a result a joint expedition was formed by the British Museum and the University of Pennsylvania that carried on the excavations under Leonard Woolley's directorship from 1922 until 1934. Almost every period of the city's lifetime has been illustrated by the discoveries, and knowledge of Mesopotamian history has been greatly enlarged.

At some time in the fourth millennium BC, the city was founded by settlers thought to have been from northern Mesopotamia, farmers still in the Chalcolithic phase of culture. There is evidence that their occupation was ended by a flood, formerly thought to be the one described in Genesis. From the succeeding "Jamdat Nasr" (Late Protoliterate) phase a large cemetery produced valuable remains allied to more sensational discoveries made at Erech.

In the next (early dynastic) period Ur became the capital of the whole of southern Mesopotamia under the Sumerian kings of the first dynasty of Ur (25th century BC). Excavation of a vast cemetery from the period preceding that dynasty (26th century) produced royal tombs containing almost incredible treasures in gold, silver, bronze, and semiprecious stones, showing not only the wealth of the people of Ur but also their highly developed civilization and art. Not the least remarkable discovery was that of the custom whereby kings were buried along with a whole retinue of their court officials, servants, and women, privileged to continue their service in the next world. Musical instruments from the royal tombs, golden weapons, engraved shell plaques and mosaic pictures, statuary and carved cylinder seals, all are a collection of unique importance, illustrating a civilization previously unknown to the historian. A further development of it, or perhaps a different aspect, was shown by the excavation at al-'Ubayd, a suburb of Ur, of a small temple also of a type previously unsuspected, richly decorated with statuary, mosaics, and metal reliefs and having columns sheathed with coloured mosaic or polished copper. The inscribed foundation tablet of the temple, stating that it was the work of a king of the first dynasty of Ur, dated the building and proved the historical character of a dynasty that had been mentioned by ancient Sumerian historians but that modern scholars had previously dismissed as fictitious.

A few personal inscriptions confirmed the real existence of the almost legendary ruler Sargon I, king of Akkad, who reigned in the 24th century BC, and a cemetery illustrated the material culture of his time.

To the next period, that of the third dynasty of Ur, when Ur was again the capital of an empire, belong some of the most important architectural monuments preserved on the site. Foremost among these is the ziggurat, a three-storied solid mass of mud brick faced with burnt bricks set in bitumen, rather like a stepped pyramid; on its summit was a small shrine, the bedchamber of the moon god Nanna (Sin), the patron deity and divine king of Ur. The lowest stage measures at its foot some 210 by 150 feet (64 by 46 metres), and its height was about 40 feet. On three sides the walls, relieved by shallow buttresses, rose sheer. On the northeast face were three great staircases, each of 100 steps, one projecting at right angles from the centre of the building, two leaning against its wall, and all three converging in a gateway between the first and the second terrace. From this a single flight of steps led upward to the top terrace and to the door of the god's little shrine. The lower part of the ziggurat, built by Ur-Nammu, the founder of the dynasty, was astonishingly well preserved; enough of the upper part survived to make the restoration certain.

The excavations showed that by the third millennium BC Sumerian architects were acquainted with the column, the arch, the vault, and the dome—i.e., with all the basic forms of architecture. The ziggurat exhibited its refinements. The walls all sloped inward, and their angle, together with the carefully calculated heights of the successive stages, leads the eye inward and upward; the sharper slope of the stairways accentuates that effect and fixes attention on the shrine, the religious focus of the whole huge structure. Surprisingly, there is not a single straight line in the structure. Each wall, from base to top and horizontally from corner to corner, is a convex curve, a curve so slight as not to be apparent but giving to the eye of the observer an

illusion of strength where a straight line might have seemed to sag under the weight of the superstructure. The architect thus employed the principle of entasis, which was to be rediscovered by the builders of the Parthenon at Athens.

The great brick mausoleums of the third-dynasty kings and the temples they built were sacked and destroyed by the Elamites, but the temples at least were restored by the kings of the succeeding dynasties of Isin and Larsa; and Ur, though it ceased to be the capital, retained its religious and its commercial importance. Having access by river and canal to the Persian Gulf, it was the natural headquarters of foreign trade. As early as the reign of Sargon of Akkad it had been in touch with India, at least indirectly. Personal seals of the Indus Valley type from the third dynasty and the Larsa period have been found at Ur, while many hundreds of clay tablets show how the foreign trade was organized. The "sea kings" of Ur carried goods for export to the entrepôt at Dilmun (Bahrain) and there picked up the copper and ivory that came from the east.

The clay tablets were found in the residential quarter of the city, of which a considerable area was excavated. The houses of private citizens in the Larsa period and under Hammurabi of Babylon (c. 18th century BC, in which period Abraham is supposed to have lived at Ur) were comfortable and well built two-story houses with ample accommodation for the family, for servants, and for guests, of a type that ensured privacy and was suited to the climate. In some houses was a kind of chapel in which the family god was worshipped and under the pavement of which the members of the family were buried. Many large state temples were excavated as were also some small wayside shrines dedicated by private persons to minor deities, the latter throwing a new light upon Babylonian religious practices; but the domestic chapels with their provision for the worship of the nameless family gods are yet more interesting and have a possible relation to the religion of the Hebrew patriarchs.

After a long period of relative neglect, Ur experienced a revival in the neo-Babylonian period, under Nebuchadrezzar II (605–562 BC), who practically rebuilt the city. Scarcely less active was Nabonidus, the last king of Babylon (556–539 BC), whose great work was the remodelling of the ziggurat, increasing its height to seven stages.

The last king to build at Ur was the Achaemenian Cyrus the Great, whose inscription on bricks is similar to the "edict" quoted by the scribe Ezra regarding the restoration of the Temple of Jerusalem. The conqueror was clearly anxious to placate his new subjects by honouring their gods, whatever those gods might be. But Ur was now thoroughly decadent; it survived into the reign of Artaxerxes II, but only a single tablet (of Philip Arrhidaeus, 317 BC) carries on the story. It was perhaps at this time that the Euphrates changed its course; and with the breakdown of the whole irrigation system, Ur, its fields reduced to desert, was finally abandoned.

Discoveries made on other sites have supplemented the unusually full record obtained from the Ur excavations. Knowledge of the city's history and of the manner of life of its inhabitants, of their business, and of their art is now fairly complete and remarkably detailed.

GLOSSARY

anthropomorphic Attribution of human motivation, characteristics, or behavior to inanimate objects, animals, or natural phenomena.

biliophylax An official who managed official archives in ancient Mesopotamia.

canoness A member of a religious community of women living under a common rule, but not bound by vows.

city-state A political system consisting of an independent city having sovereignty over contiguous territory and serving as a centre and leader of political, economic, and cultural life.

corvée Unpaid labour owed the state, either in addition to or in lieu of taxes.

cuneiform The most widespread and historically significant writing system in the ancient Middle East.

cylinder seal A small stone cylinder engraved in intaglio on its surface to leave impressions when rolled on wet clay.

ensi Sacred king.

hegemony The social, cultural, ideological, or economic influence exerted by a dominant group.

henotheism A belief in the worship of one god, though the existence of other gods is granted.

hepatoscopy Examining the entrails, particularly the liver, of a lamb or kid sacrificed for a divinatory purpose, to read what the god had "written" there by interpreting variations in form and shape.

incubation Sleeping in the temple in the hopes that the god would send an enlightening dream.

kudurru A type of boundary stone used by the Kassites of ancient Mesopotamia that served as a record of a grant of land made by the king to a favoured person.

lacuna An empty space or missing part; a gap.

pantheon All the gods of a people considered as a group.

plinth The usually projecting stone coursing that forms a platform, or base, for a building.

polytheism The worship of or belief in more than one god.

relief sculpture Any work in which the figures project from a supporting background, usually a plane surface.

satrapy A province within an empire that is decreed by the king or the empire's ruler.

Semitic Of, relating to, or constituting a subgroup of Afro-Asiatic cultures whose language group includes Arabic, Hebrew, Amharic, and Aramaic.

soothsaying The art or practice of foretelling events.

stela A standing stone slab used in the ancient world primarily as a grave marker, but also for dedication, commemoration, and demarcation.

usurpation The act of seizing and holding (as office, place, or powers) in possession by force or without right.

wardum A person in bondage who could be bought and sold; a slave.

ziggurat A pyramidal, stepped temple tower that is an architectural and religious structure characteristic of the major cities of Mesopotamia.

BIBLIOGRAPHY

GENERAL WORKS

The Cambridge Ancient History contains much relevant information, especially vol. 1–2, 3rd ed. (1971–75), vol. 3–4, 2nd ed. (1982–88), and vol. 6 (1994); they include lengthy and richly documented chapters covering Mesopotamian prehistory to the time of Alexander the Great's conquest of the region. Chapters on Mesopotamia under the Seleucids, Parthians, and Sāsānians are included in *The Cambridge History of Iran*, vol. 3 (1983). Robert McC. Adams, *The Land Behind Baghdad: A History of Settlement on the Diyala Plains* (1965); Nicholas Postgate, *The First Empires* (1977); Georges Roux, *Ancient Iraq*, 2nd ed. (1980); Richard N. Frye, *The History of Ancient Iran* (1984); Seton Lloyd, *The Archaeology of Mesopotamia: From the Old Stone Age to the Persian Conquest*, rev. ed (1984); and Michael Roaf, *Cultural Atlas of Mesopotamia and the Ancient Near East* (1990), also provide broad coverage. I. M. Diakonov (ed.), *Ancient Mesopotamia: Socio-Economic History*, trans. from Russian (1969, reissued 1981), collects representative articles by Diakonov and others on Mesopotamian history, with emphasis on social and economic aspects. A. Leo Oppenheim, *Ancient Mesopotamia: Portrait of a Dead Civilization*, rev. ed. completed by Erica Reiner (1977), includes some controversial views.

PREHISTORY TO THE OLD BABYLONIAN PERIOD

A balanced picture of political, social, and economic history may be found in Jean Bottéro, Elena Cassin, and Jean Vercoutter (eds.), *The Near East: The Early Civilizations* (1968; originally published in German, 3 vol., 1965–67), with contributions on prehistory and protohistory, Akkad, early dynastic history, the third dynasty of Ur, and the Old Babylonian period. Adam Falkenstein, *The Sumerian Temple City*, trans. from French (1974), is a very short work describing the Sumerian temple economy and its political implications. Dietz Otto Edzard, *Die zweite Zwischenzeit Babyloniens* (1957), offers details on the history of the Old Babylonian period from the third dynasty of Ur to the end of Hammurabi. Mogen Trolle Larsen, *The Old Assyrian City-State and Its Colonies* (1976), is a standard work on the Old Assyrian trade colonies in Anatolia. Gernot Wilhelm, *The Hurrians* (1989; originally published in German, 1982), is the best book on the third cultural element in early Mesopotamian history. Fiorella Imparati, *I Hurriti* (1964), offers a short synopsis. Hans J. Nissen, *Mesopotamia Before 5000 Years* (1987), includes a comprehensive bibliography for the early periods.

MESOPOTAMIA TO THE END OF THE ACHAEMENIAN PERIOD

Histories of Assyria and Babylonia include Wolfram Von Soden, *Einführung in die Altorientalistik* (1985); J. A. Brinkman, *Prelude to Empire: Babylonian Society and Politics, 747–626 BC* (1984); Stefan Zawadzki, *The Fall of Assyria and Median-Babylonian Relations* (1988); and H. W. F. Saggs, *The Might That Was Assyria* (1984, reprinted 1990), and *The Greatness That Was Babylon: A Survey of the Ancient Civilization of the Tigris-Euphrates Valley* (1988). Joan Oates, *Babylon*, rev. ed. (1986), deals with history and civilization. Wolfram Von Soden, *Herrscher im alten Orient* (1954), examines Assyrian and Babylonian politics. Standard works, now partly out-of-date, include A. T. Olmstead, *History of Assyria* (1923, reprinted 1975); and Bruno Meissner, *Babylonien und Assyrien*, 2 vol. (1920–25). J. A. Brinkman, *A Political History of Post-Kassite Babylonia, 1158–722 BC* (1968), is an extensive special study, with complete documentation. Muhammad A. Dandamaev, *Slavery in Babylonia: From Nabopolassar to Alexander the Great (626–331 BC)*, rev. ed. (1984; originally published in Russian, 1974), includes an extensive bibliography. Jacob Neusner, *A History of the Jews in Babylonia*, 5 vol. (1965–70), studies in detail the history of the Jews in Mesopotamia.

MESOPOTAMIA FROM *c.* 320 BC TO *c.* AD 620

Getzel M. Cohen, *The Seleucid Colonies: Studies in Founding, Administration, and Organization* (1978), discusses the relationship of the central government with provinces and client states. Details of Seleucid rule may be found in Maurice Meuleau, "Mesopotamia Under the Seleucids," in Pierre Grimal (ed.), *Hellenism and the Rise of Rome* (1968; originally published in German, 1965), pp. 266–289; and in the essays in Amélie Kuhrt and Susan Sherwin-White (eds.), *Hellenism in the East: Interaction of Greek and Non-Greek Civilizations after Alexander's Conquest* (1987). Neilson C. Debevoise, *A Political History of Parthia* (1938, reissued 1968), is a standard political history of the Arsacid dynasty. Louis Dillemann, *Haute Mésopotamie orientale et pays adjacents* (1962), offers a historical geography of northern Mesopotamia with many details. J. M. Fie, *Assyrie chrétienne*, 3 vol. (1965–68), provides a historical geography of the Christian communities of northern Mesopotamia from Syriac sources.

INDEX